From Vodou to Zouk

RECENT AND FORTHCOMING TITLES IN THE BLACK MUSIC REFERENCE SERIES

From Vodou to Zouk: A Bibliographic Guide to Music of the French-speaking Caribbean and its Diaspora

Jamaican Popular Music, From Mento to Dancehall Reggae: A Bibliographic Guide

Afro-Cuban Music: A Bibliographic Guide

Baila!: A Bibliographic Guide to Afro-Latin Dance Musics, From Mambo to Salsa

Afro-Brazilian Music: A Bibliographic Guide

Carnival, Calypso and Steel Pan: A Bibliographic Guide to Popular Music of the English-Speaking Caribbean and Its Diaspora

Music of the African Diaspora: An International Bibliography and Resource Guide. Vol. 1. Latin America, the Caribbean, Europe, Asia and Australia

Music of Sub-Saharan Africa: An Annotated Bibliography and Resource Guide

From Free Jazz to Free Improv: A Bibliography of the Jazz Avant-Garde, 1959-Present (in progress)

FROM VODOU TO ZOUK

A Bibliographic Guide to Music
of the French-speaking
Caribbean and its Diaspora

John Gray

Foreword by Julian Gerstin

Black Music Reference Series, Volume 1

AFRICAN DIASPORA PRESS
Nyack, New York

Publisher's Cataloging-in-Publication Data
Gray, John, 1962–
    From vodou to zouk : a bibliographic guide to music of the French-speaking Caribbean and its diaspora / John Gray ; foreword by Julian Gerstin.
        p. cm. — (Black music reference series; v. 1)
    Includes indexes.
    ISBN: 978-0-9844134-0-9 (cloth : alk. paper)
    1. Folk music—West Indies, French—Bibliography. 2. Popular music—West Indies, French—Bibliography. 3. Musicians, Black—West Indies, French—Bibliography. 4. Folk music—Haiti—Bibliography. 5. Popular music—Haiti—Bibliography. 6. Folk music—Guadeloupe—Bibliography. 7. Popular music—Guadeloupe—Bibliography. 8. Folk music—Martinique—Bibliography. 9. Popular music—Martinique—Bibliography. 10. Folk music—French Guiana—Bibliography. 11. Popular music—French Guiana—Bibliography. 12. Zouk (Music)—West Indies, French—History and criticism—Bibliography. 13. Voodoo music—Bibliography. 14. Carnival—West Indies, French—Bibliography. 15. West Indies, French—Social life and customs—Bibliography. I. Title. II. Series.
    ML120.W47 G7 2010
    016.78

First published in 2010

African Diaspora Press
30 Marion St., Nyack, NY 10960
www.african-diaspora-press.com

Contents

Foreword

Until recently, Caribbean music scholarship has left French-speaking islands on the margins. While English-speaking writers have focused on English-speaking islands, Spanish-speaking writers on Spanish-speaking islands, and so on, Guadeloupe, Martinique, and French Guiana (Guyane) have been left largely to the French.

Thankfully, the paths of scholarship have begun to cross. This remarkable bibliography is a testament to that fact. Over 1,200 entries cover the Caribbean's French- and Creole-speaking communities from eastern Cuba to St. Lucia to mainland French Guiana, as well as their diasporas in France, the United States, and Canada. Entries are in French and English but also Spanish and German. They cover popular music, religious music (Catholic, Protestant, and African-based traditions), and secular folk music of all kinds, along with biographical and critical material on hundreds of important musicians, past and present. Materials range from books and scholarly articles to fanzines, newspaper articles, films, and archival field recordings, along with information on where they may be found.

Below I offer an overview of the Creolophone and Francophone Caribbean musical world and the scholarship that has emerged to describe it.

The Music

From a distance, the sphere of French cultural influence in the Caribbean appears smaller than that of England, Spain, or the United States. It encompasses Haiti; the three overseas French départements of Guadeloupe, Martinique, and French Guiana; the nominally Anglophone islands of Dominica and St. Lucia, where Creole is in common use; and the diasporas of these islands in Cuba, the Dominican Republic, France, the United States, and Canada.

The modern map exaggerates Spanish and British dominance. French slave trading was as intense as Portuguese, British, or Dutch. Martinique and Haiti were for many years the richest colonies in the Caribbean. Creole remains a major regional language. A few islands not covered in this book, such as Trinidad and Tobago, were Creole-speaking until recently and retain many cultural connections to their Creole-speaking neighbors.

Today these islands contain hundreds of musical genres and thousands upon thousands of noteworthy musicians. To begin describing them you need to use some sort of system, even if, as is frequently the case, the artists and their creativity subvert whatever categories you try to place them in. Historically, one of the main methods for grouping musics has been by race—black music, white music, and so forth. Another has been to organize it geographically, e.g., the music of Haiti, Guadeloupe, etc. Here I wish to focus on regional themes that cross national boundaries. Thus I'll fall back on another set of categories: popular, Carnival, religious, traditional/folkloric. These are not really satisfactory either, as musicians are constantly crossing aesthetic borders. However they do help to point out some cultural continuities.

Popular Music

Caribbean tastes are cosmopolitan. Audiences enjoy a wide range of musics, both local and foreign. At family parties in Fort-de-France in the early 1990s, people played successive sets of *zouk, konpa, salsa, biguine, kadans, ragga,* and *soukous.* Some of these styles were nominally associated with certain generations (*biguine* for the grandparents, *ragga* for the kids), but everyone danced to them all. At downtown discos it was the same story. Moreover, American and European hip-hop was very popular, and jazz, blues, classical music, choral music, and gospel all had significant followings. In nearby St. Lucia, U.S. country music was widespread, along with soca and steel band music from Trinidad. What people listen to most is a combination of local and global styles. There are some language barriers (steel bands are not widespread in Martinique) as well as racial ones (hip hop but not rock), yet tastes are broad.

Popular styles everywhere tend to change with local economic and political conditions, with influences from abroad, and with the passing of generations. The end of slavery (1804 in Haiti, 1834 in Dominica and St. Lucia, 1848 in the French colonies), urbanization, and the availability of European instruments (saxophones, trumpets, accordion, violin, piano, bass) through military bands and the Church, led to 19th century urbanized styles. Some of these were adaptations of European music, e.g., *valse creole* (from waltz) and *mazouk* (from mazurka) in Guadeloupe and

Martinique. Other styles were more strikingly autocthonous—*meringue* in Haiti, *biguine* in Guadeloupe and Martinique. This process was similar to the foundation of jazz—ex-slaves left the plantations, moved to the cities, picked up European instruments and song forms, and played them in their own way. Early recordings of *biguine* from the 1920s and '30s are uncannily parallel to New Orleans and Chicago-style jazz (164).

19th century popular styles continued to mutate throughout the 20th century, sometimes persisting, sometimes disappearing, sometimes re-emerging in surprising ways. They followed generational waves as well. Haitian *meringue* adopted a youthful punch and became *mini-jazz* in the 1950s, then *konpa direk* in the '60s. By the 1970s, musicians in Dominica had turned the latter into *kadans.* In Guadeloupe and Martinique, *biguine* expanded to a big-band format in the 1940s and '50s, then found itself eclipsed by the more modern-sounding *konpa* and *kadans.* In the late 1970s, *zouk* emerged to resuscitate the careers of Guadeloupean and Martinican musicians. But it is easy to hear *zouk* as an updating of *biguine* and a slight indigenization of *konpa* and *kadans* (156). *Zouk's* dominance proved to be short-lived. By the 1990s young audiences, steeped in U.S. hip-hop and Jamaican dancehall, began producing a local version in Creole, raggamuffin (ragga).

Politics has long played a role in Haitian music, perhaps more directly than on the smaller islands. *Meringue,* caught up in nationalist fervor, was considered Haiti's national dance from the late 19th century until well into the 20th (534). *Mini-jazz,* and to some extent *konpa,* was taken up by successive dictatorships and expected to serve their ends. The political crises of the 1980s and '90s spawned musical resistance in the form of *mizik rasin* ("roots music"), a popular style drawing on the transgressive spirit of Carnival music and the populism of Haiti's indigenous religion, Vodou (421). *Mizik rasin,* along with *zouk,* has proved cosmopolitan enough to have success abroad, both in dance clubs in Paris and New York City, and on the "world music" circuit. These two styles seem to appeal to First World audiences despite the language barrier (most of the songs are in Creole).

This sketch of a few popular styles that have spread regionally or internationally omits many others that have remained local, such as *aleke* in French Guiana or *jing ping* in Dominica. It doesn't take into account musicians who have blended and extended genres, or mixed popular styles with local idioms, with United States jazz, r&b, funk, or hip-hop, with Cuban son and African soukous, or innumerable other influences.

Carnival

Closely related to popular styles on many islands is the music of Carnival. Since the 19th century both Carnival and popular music have continued to influence one another. For example, in the late 1800s Carnival musicians began incorporating brass band instruments, and nowadays amplified guitars and sound systems are common. *Zouk* often draws on Carnival rhythms to evoke the *défoulement* (letting-go, craziness) of that celebration, while, as noted above, Haitian *mizik rasin* calls on Carnival transgressiveness for its rebellious fervor.

In general, Carnival bands are large and democratic—many musicians playing percussion and horns, or garbage cans and car horns when orthodox instruments are unavailable, or anything else loud and portable. The goal is to draw a crowd and get them dancing and singing, so most songs are either traditional or quickly learned. Lyrics are often topical or sexual satires, or both. In Martinique, for example, almost everyone knows *Bo fè-a, bo fè-a, Lilité pa jandam ankô* (Kiss the sword, Lilité is no longer a gendarme). This song dates from 1925 and refers to an abusive police chief forced to leave office, who sanctimoniously kissed his sword as he gave it up. The words easily become *Bo fè-a, bo fè-a, yo pété bonda Lilité* (Kiss the sword, they fucked Lilité in the ass). Numerous other variations come and go.

Religious Music

Catholicism is the dominant European faith on the French islands, with Evangelical Protestant sects increasing in importance everywhere in the Caribbean (bringing U.S.-influenced Christian rock and black gospel with them). Church music and choirs have been important on every island for centuries, particularly in the education of Caribbean musicians. Unfortunately, this music has been little studied, particularly from an ethnomusicological perspective.

African-based religions, on the other hand, have been a magnet for scholars. We tend to take this for granted now, but for many decades these traditions were treated with condescension and horror. It was only in the 1930s that the generation of Caribbean intellectuals influenced by *négritude* (Jean Price-Mars and the writers of Haiti's Bureau d'Ethnologie) and anthropologists trained by Franz Boas or Boas' students in the U.S.— Herskovits, Hurston, Dunham, Courlander, Kolinski, Simpson—began to validate African-based religions in any serious way. While some of the essentialism in the writing of those years now seems dated, it was a necessary step.

These "danced faiths" (Thompson 1966) took root in many places where the slave economy was strong, e.g. Haiti, Cuba, Brazil, Trinidad, with the prevalent influence being from the Yoruba of SW Nigeria and Kongo/Bantu from the Congo River basin. These traditions mixed with one another, and with Catholicism, Protestantism, spiritism, and other influences. Vodou in Haiti, Santeria and Palo Mayombe in Cuba, Candomble and Umbanda in Brazil, Shango in Trinidad, are all products of this history. Vodou adds important influences from the Fon and Arara peoples, whose culture is fairly close to the Yoruba, from the area known during colonialism as Dahomey (now Benin).

In Vodou, as in related religions, each deity (*loa, lwa*) controls specific aspects of the human, natural, and supernatural worlds and each has his or her own allies and enemies, stories, foods, costumes, and ritual objects. Each deity also has his or her own songs, dances, and drum rhythms, so that in Vodou as a whole there are thousands of songs and many dozens of drum rhythms. The language of the songs are largely remnants of African languages which are only partly understood by many people, in the way Latin used to be the language of the Catholic Mass. Drumming tends to be highly polyrhythmic, played on a battery of three drums, iron bell, and shaker. The smaller instruments hold ostinati while the largest drum leads the ensemble and calls the *lwa.*

Outside of Haiti, African-based religion has barely survived in the Creolophone world. There is Voodoo in Louisiana, of course, but that was brought by Haitians. In French Guiana, the Maroons (descendants of escaped slaves), known as the Aluku and Boni, maintain African-based beliefs. In St. Lucia there is Kèlè, a Yoruba-based religion. In Guadeloupe and Martinique, slave populations apparently were too small to withstand Catholicism and the repression of African worship.

Music for semi-religious or secular ceremonies also exists. Funeral wakes, for example, are an important part of Caribbean culture, and specific music is performed for them. In Guadeloupe, men sing rowdy *bouladjèl* ("mouth drumming") outside the house while women sing the more pious *kantikamò* inside. In Martinique, *chanté noël* is a fairly recent tradition performed during the Christmas season. Haitian Rara music played on bamboo trumpets (*vaccines*), attends the Easter season and overlaps with Carnival music in both musical style and rebelliousness.

Secular Folklore

For centuries, secular music accompanied everyday events in the Antilles—work of all sorts, play of many kinds. Much of this music has died off or become restricted to small pockets of traditional families. It survives where it has proved adaptable to modern life—in tourist shows, as an inspiration for popular music, or in revivals.

Music for work included agricultural labor, which was made easier and more enjoyable when done in groups, e.g., *lasoté* music for hoeing and planting in Martinique. There were plenty of very specialized styles—in St. Lucia, songs for sawing wood (*chanté siay*), for house-raising, and for pulling boats; in Martinique, *lavwa bèf* songs encouraging oxen to work. *Chouval bwa,* on both Guadeloupe and Martinique, was a specific orchestra (accordion, bamboo flute, and drums adapted from Carnival) that accompanied hand-pushed merry-go-rounds.

Africans also enjoyed martial arts such as wrestling, both as sport and as training for young warriors, and often performed them to music. Several New World examples survive. Brazilian *capoeira* and Trinidadian *kalenda* stick-fighting are the best-known, but in Guadeloupe one finds *mayolé,* and in Martinique *danmyé* (a.k.a. *ladja*), which is undergoing a major revival.

Specific forms of music for play included children's game songs. Adults, too, used music for danced forms of play. In Martinican villages, on moonlit nights people used to gather for *lalin klé* ("full moon") events featuring participatory, often flirtatious dances. At *lalin klé* one also heard *kont kwéyol,* a traditional body of stories, which were enjoyed by adults as well as children. These stories contained their own call-and-response singing, led by the storyteller.

Lalin klé brings us, finally, to what will seem most familiar to North Americans—music for secular dancing. This includes, of course, all the popular styles discussed above (*konpa, biguine, zouk,* and so forth), as well as plenty of styles that remain "folkloric," i.e., that have never made a transition to modern electric instruments, or become known outside their own island. Dominican *jing ping* is an example.

A distinction such as this, between popular and folkloric, is in many cases problematic since the styles have interpenetrated throughout their history. On Guadeloupe and Martinique, for instance, rural and urban *biguine* traditions have coexisted for a hundred years. Rural bands used to tend towards accordions, fiddles, bamboo flutes, and light percussion, while urban bands used sax, clarinet, trombone, piano, and drumset. But the dancing was the same, and the same songs flipped from one context to the other. Today rural bands often incorporate more modern instruments (electric guitar, drumset, a horn or two) alongside traditional ones, and they play not only *biguine* but other urban styles such as *konpa* and *soukous.* They may be seen at town fêtes and local parties—the indigenous garage bands of Martinique.

Some styles are almost impossible to peg as modern or traditional, global or local. When *biguine* went out of fashion in the 1960s, so did *mazouk,* and when *zouk* resuscitated *biguine* in the 1980s, *zouk* bands invented an updated version of *mazouk* as well. *Zouk* bands almost never play their updated *mazouk* abroad—how would American or European audiences dance to it? However, these songs are still popular in Martinique.

The deeper history of many entertainment dances goes back to colonial antecedents. Both African slaves and European colonials had entertainment dances, and the Antilles today presents a dizzying array of dances that remain close to either African or European models, or blend them in various ways. African dances tended to use either circles of dancers moving counterclockwise, or successive soloists or couples inside a circle of participant/onlookers. The popular European choreographies of the early colonial era featured soloists (jigs, hornpipes) or lines (minuet, bransles, etc.). In the late 1600s a new form of line dancing emerged— contradance, derived both from French *contredanse* (with lines of men contra lines of women) and English country dance. Lively and flirtatious, contradance became the rage in Europe and soon reached the colonies. By the second half of the 1700s contradances had developed hundreds of variations, notably quadrilles (squares), which became the next big dance craze. Contradances and quadrilles were often performed in "sets," that is, several dances done in a sequence, with different music for each. The mark of a good dancer was being able to perform the entire set, aided by a dance caller or *kommandyé* (Fr.: commandeur).

Caribbean slaves maintained the African circle choreography, along with the orchestra of multiple drums and call-and-response singing. At the same time they observed, imitated, satirized, and improved upon white dances. By the waning years of slavery or shortly thereafter, i.e., the 1820s–1850s, they consolidated their own distinct contradance and quadrille styles. They utilized European instruments (fiddle, accordion, bamboo or cane flutes, triangle, snare drum) or added their own (drums, shakers, rasps, banjo—itself derived from African lutes). Generally, French Antilleans call these styles *kwadril.*

In some cases neo-African circle dances and creolized European *kwadril* styles remained separate, but in many cases they mixed together. The results run the gamut from those appearing "more African," with low centers of gravity, much hip movement, call-and-response singing, and an emphasis on percussion, to "more European," with upright postures and European instrumentation. A partial list includes Haiti's *tanbou matinik* ("Martinican drum"), with an accordion, fiddle, or fife accompanying drums and *kommandyé;* French Guiana's *kaseko* or *mizik creole*, with multiple drums and call-and-response singing; Dominica's *lapo kabwit,* with a single drum and call-and-response singing; and St. Lucian *bele*, again with solo drum and call-and-response. *Tumba francesa* ("French drum") is a quadrille style brought to eastern Cuba by Haitians fleeing the unrest of the revolution, and maintained there ever since. In Guadeloupe one finds both accordion-led *kwadril,* and the drum-dance *gwoka*, with multiple drums, call-and-response singing, and the African choreography of successive soloists or couples in a dance ring. (*Gwoka* is comparable to *rumba* in Cuba, *bomba* in Puerto Rico.) Martinique has five separate genres—*bele du nord* (quadrille choreography, African-esque movement, one drum, call-and-response singing); *lalin klé* (circles as well as lines, one drum, call-and-response); *kalenda* (successive soloists)—these first three from the northern part of the island; *bele du sud* from the south (couple choreography, two or three drums playing heterophonically rather than polyrhythmically, call-and-response); and *haute taille* from the mid-Atlantic coast (quadrille choreography, upright movement style, accordion and light percussion, *kommandyé*). Remember that most of the genres I've listed include several specific dances, each with its own songs and steps. The variety is enormous.

In the second half of the 19th century, another wave of dances appeared in Europe, the closed-couple dances--waltz, polka, and mazurka. Because of the couple's intimacy these were considered still more flirtatious than contradances and quadrilles. Antilleans adapted them into their own versions, e.g., *valse creole* and *mazouk.* They also invented their own couple dances, such as Haitian *meringue,* Guadeloupean/Martinican *biguine,* and Dominican *jing ping.* These latter were part of a larger trend in New World dance history. Throughout Latin America and the Caribbean, 19th century European couple dancing indigenized with a more-or-less Africanized "break-body" movement style became the preferred style for urbanized, post-slavery populations, both elite and proletarian. With the rise of independence movements during the same era, these dances were seized upon by nationalist sentiment, becoming known as "national dances"—*tango* in Argentina, *lundu* and *maxixe* in Brazil, *merengue* in the Dominican Republic, *habanera* and *danzón* in Cuba, *meringue* in Haiti (Chasteen 2004). These in turn became the basis of later popular styles. There is thus a skein of connections between secular dances of all types— neo-African drum dances, creolized *kwadril,* indigenized couple dances, and both older and contemporary popular genres. All coexist in a very tangled web.

Writings on Caribbean Music

Colonial Descriptions

The theme of race dominated early colonial descriptions of Caribbean music (216, 227, 332). Observers felt it natural to group dances as "black," "creole," or "white"—the three racial categories of the Caribbean world. (Antilleans recognize many gradations of each category, but these are the main ones.) In this type of description, white music was always privileged over black and creole, even when colonial observers were fascinated by exotic music.

These early accounts are mainly descriptive, depicting colorful customs and scenes of island life for people back home. There is little effort to be comprehensive, or even objective. This varies from author to author, of course, and some quite detailed descriptions do exist. A few writers even attempt to analyze the music—always with value judgments implied: What does this music lack? What makes it so bad? Or, at best: Why do we like it even though it lacks the aspects of music we value? There is no attempt to understand the music in its own aesthetic and cultural context.

1930s–1960s: Anthropologically Informed Work, Descriptive Surveys, and the Validation of Afro-Caribbean Culture

During the 1930s and '40s writings about French Caribbean music changed dramatically as a new generation of American (and to a lesser degree French) anthropologists, and Caribbean writers influenced by *négritude,* came on the scene. Examples of work by American anthropologists includes Herskovits and Herskovits (452), Parsons (161), Courlander (444–

445, 486–487), Simpson (508), and the ethnomusicologist Kolinski, who often collaborated with Herskovits and Courlander (452). All of these (excepting Parsons) focus on Haiti, which was then under U.S. occupation. Ethnographies of this era were typically generalist, with chapters devoted to subsistence, kinship, religion, and so on. Many also included a chapter on the arts, or a collection of songs or drum rhythms as an appendix. Most were written in response to Herskovits' notion of music and dance as an African/Diasporic "cultural focus."

In the 1940s Haiti's Bureau d'Ethnologie, organized by Jean Price-Mars, began publishing as well (15–17, 99, 106, 116, 455, 457, 554). Haitian composer Werner Jaegerhuber also authored several folklore collections of his own (423, 550, 580). The first general descriptions of Antillean music for a popular audience also began to appear (e.g., 157). Outside of Haiti, however, we find little in the way of serious descriptive surveys. Martinican music, for example, had to await the work of Romanian folklorist Anca Bertrand in the 1960s (236, 633, 634).

The mere fact that these works collected and described black music, fairly comprehensively and far more objectively than before, is significant. For the great work of this generation was to begin validating black culture. It surprises me that there is little overt polemic in the above works. Few authors spent time arguing the value of black culture; apparently, their aim was to promote understanding through objective scientific description.

Validating black music meant accepting the existence of the categories "black" and "white" while reversing their values—that is, celebrating blackness. Musically, this meant highlighting elements perceived as African—polyrhythms, drums, call-and-response singing, improvisation, ecstatic dancing, open eroticism. Later writers were to question whether this emphasis simply reiterated stereotypes. Are such characteristics really accurate for African or diasporic music? Are "black" and "white" elements separable in such densely layered performances?

The focus on black and white also meant that the mulatto/creole realm was ignored. "Creole" is a polysemous word in the Caribbean. First, it can refer to a race (considered separate from "black," though the boundaries are fluid). Second, it can refer to a cultural moment—the emergence of an indigenous, Antillean culture, neither African nor European. This began even before the end of slavery, with the growth of cities and a free urban population of ex-slaves and *affranchisées,* mainly laborers and craftspeople. As this population continued growing after abolition, its "creole culture" consolidated, cobbled together from both black and white roots, but indigenous. The Creole language is part of this culture, as are urban, popular, 19th century musical styles such as *meringue* and *biguine.* From the emergence of this culture through much of the 20th century, it was seen as fashionable and up-to-date. Now much of it seems quaint and folkloric—another shade of meaning for "creole." In addition, the urbanized creole population was better educated than the black proletariat, and came to fill many business, administrative and political positions as the islands moved towards their varying degrees of autonomy and independence. Tension arose between blacks and creoles, and persists today. So many authors who labored to validate "black" music ignored what they saw as "creole," e.g., the many quadrille-based styles.

Moreover, scholars of this era did not know what to do about popular music, and for the most part they avoided discussing it. Seen as neither "traditional folklore" nor "classical," it was lowbrow without having the romantic cachet of folklore. Furthermore, in the French Caribbean popular music was often seen as "foreign" (usually from the United States), or as imitative of foreign styles and destructive of local traditions (e.g., 208, 231, 234). With a few notable exceptions (e.g., 606), writings on popular music from this era appeared largely in the popular press rather than in scholarly literature (e.g., 532–533, 535, 537 for *meringue;* 151, 180, 185, 215, 238 for *biguine*).

1980s–Present: Analytical Ethnography and Emergent Ideas

By the 1970s both French- and English-language anthropology had begun turning away from general descriptive ethnography towards more focused, analytical work. In the 1980s anthropology became heavily influenced by postmodernist theory, a largely French invention (buttressed by its British counterpart, Cultural Studies). The chief thrust of postmodernist theory has been to unveil how power and culture intersect—that is, how political ideology and force affects, and is sometimes affected by, everyday life. Realms of meaning and symbol, and realms of power, are seen as interpenetrating. This implies that both culture and power are contingent, engaged with one another in a continual process of making and remaking. It implies that human agency, while greatly outgunned, still has the possibility of changing the world. It also suggests that many elements of identity—race, nation, gender, etc.—are flexible, constructed by cultures, power, and individuals.

Accordingly, ethnomusicologists since the 1980s have become both more focused in their research and more analytical in their approach. They have concerned themselves greatly with issues of politics, ideology and identity. While I have found just one early piece of writing here that addresses politics in folkloric music, 485 (Courlander 1941), it is hard to find anything in North American ethnomusicology post-1980 that does not discuss the subject.

In the Caribbean, the obvious categories of identity and music are ideologically powerful but are not complex or subtle enough to really explain things. People talk in terms of race, but musical choices cluster around parameters of education, class, degree of urbanization, gender, and generation as much as they do around race. Nationalism is strong, but musicians constantly cross national, regional, insular, and international boundaries. They also cross boundaries between folkloric, popular, jazz, and classical, and between genres within these. On the other hand, musicians and audiences constantly think in terms of race, nationality and genre in creating and interpreting music. The categories live; status and power still operate through them. Thus, the task of Caribbean ethnomusicologists over the past twenty years has become how to dissect how these categories of identity operate. How are they constructed? How do they work? How do people view their nation, or their race, or their gender through music?

Two influential monographs in this vein have been 156 (Guilbault 1993) and 421 (Averill 1997). It is significant that both of them concern popular music (*zouk* and *mizik rasin,* respectively). Guilbault deals with economics, cultural policy, gender, inter-island flows of music, and musical aesthetics. Averill tackles history, class, violence, ideology, cultural policy, and resistance. Both authors simply steamroll over the notion that popular music is not intellectually rewarding, either for its social or musical content.

Guilbault also addresses issues of Creole (the language) and *créolité* (creolism), a French Antillean philosophy of identity that has become a major theme in both scholarly and popular discourse over the past twenty-odd years. Creolism marks a decided turn from the previous era, when the validation of black styles was the driving motive and creole culture was often ignored. From the *créoliste* point of view, virtually all Caribbean music is creole: the "most African" styles (Haitian vodou) are not African, nor are the "whitest" (Caribbean classical composition) European. They are all indigenous. Creolism is a very inclusive philosophy, aiming to celebrate all registers of culture. Compared to the earlier perspective that focused on black culture exclusively, it is the product of a generation that has become more psychologically secure. People committed to the earlier perspective point out that such security marks the success of their efforts, but also criticize creolism as prematurely moving the focus away from black identity and black issues.

The *créoliste* point of view emerged in the 1980s, largely on Martinique, an island where economic dependency tempers the sense of autonomy, and ideas of identity are particularly subtle. Harbingers in musical writing were two surveys by local popular authors, 603 (Cally 1990) and 158 (Jallier and Lossen 1985). Both surveys tried to include everything, from *gwoka* and *bele,* to *biguine* and *zouk,* to *chanté noël* and choral music. They were closely followed by Desroches' more scholarly surveys (211–212, 608–609), which included discussion of Martinique's tiny East Indian population and examined musical creolization theoretically. In part, attention to musical creolization resulted from efforts by cultural activists and linguists to revitalize the Creole language, seen as being under siege by French. This effort brought together not only Martinique and Guadeloupe (373, 605) but also Dominica (339) and St. Lucia, through the work of its dynamic Folk Research Center (197).

Attention to creolism connects to another newly emerging trend—studies of quadrille. Antillean quadrille dancing is inescapably creole, blending European with African choreographies and instruments in a variety of ways. Analytic (as opposed to solely descriptive) studies of quadrille began in the 1980s in Guadeloupe (408) and St. Lucia (680), and have increased in the 2000s (170, 194, 209, 607). Also relevant are the increasing number of studies of Cuban *tumba francesa.*

Another postmodernist theme is folklorization, i.e., staged folklore. This is an important part of the musical life of many Caribbean performers, yet it raises uncomfortable issues of authenticity. Touristic performance tends towards the quaint—older popular styles such as *meringue* or *biguine;* traditional dances adapted for the stage, with fancy costumes, flashy dancing, and shortened performance times. Many tourist groups also perform stage shows for locals, and here the clash of expectations can be heightened. Martinican tourist troupes such as Les Ballets Folkloriques Martiniquais (627, 738) pleased tourists with highly sterotyped skits, but local audiences hated the stereotypes.

Few authors addressed staged folklore before the 1990s (e.g., 11, 738), although many observers who thought they were seeing "authentic" folklore were actually watching staged versions. The contemporary view tends to be that staged folklore is a negotiation of identity, as is all performance. Writings on the relationship of French Caribbean music to folklorization (515, 553, 591, 614, 683, 685, 1117) or tourism (462, 572) are still relatively rare. However, their role in other parts of the Caribbean, most notably Cuba (Daniel 1995, Hagedorn 2001), has received greater attention.

Another contemporary trend in the literature is found in studies of diaspora and transnationalism. Here the flexible elements of identity are nation and geography. Many Caribbean people live in locations outside the Caribbean, or in multiple locations. How do they experience this musically? This book contains entries on Antilleans in France (4–7, 345–352), Canada (1, 258–261), and the United States (456, 682–699). The U.S. entries all concern Haitians in New York City and Miami. A lone reference to the Dominican Republic (344) discusses Haitians there, and two pieces on transnationalism (438, 1107) are also about Haiti.

Writings about Carnival have also shifted from descriptive (in many cases touristic promotion) to analytical. In this case, authors are looking at political factors. Because Carnival celebrations are intense and potentially uncontrolled, authorities have sometimes repressed them, at other times attempted to co-opt them. Carnival groups themselves may express political criticism directly, e.g., the group Akiyo in Guadeloupe, or indirectly, as do many Haitian groups. Virtually everything written on Haitian Carnival over the past twenty-five years discusses its politics. There is a potential problem with this approach. Despite Bakhtin and Victor Turner-influenced theories of liminality, there is nothing inherently rebellious in Carnival. Carnival can be a general letting-go with little or no political content, as I found in Martinique in the 1990s (614).

Contemporary ideas about identity and power would not be what they are without feminism and gender studies. Yet there is remarkably little in the Caribbean musical literature reflecting these fields. I note items 152, 162, 175, 619 on Martinique and Guadeloupe, and 258, 497, 506, 713 on Haiti, but not all of these writings are feminist; some are simply populist descriptions of female singers. Only one writer, to my knowledge, has discussed homosexuality and Antillean music (Murray: 23, 130, 141–142).

Outside of ethnomusicology proper, literary critics have often treated music as a theme in images of identity (86, 125, 172, 178, 199, 618). Others focus on song lyrics, combing them for political or cultural relevance (152, 369, 619). Such approaches have usually been informed more by literary theory than by ethnographic fieldwork. For instance, many of the items I've just listed discuss *créolité,* but treat it as French literary theory rather than practical Caribbean reality. (See 406 for an exception). Contrast this to *créolité-*inspired but ethnographically oriented recent work on *kont kwéyol* story songs (225, 335, 488, 607) and on the Creole language per se (447, 605).

Modern analytical ethnomusicology, tightly focused on political and ideological concerns and with a flexible concept of identity, has been mainly a product of First World authors. For several of the contemporary themes I've discussed—folklorization, transnationalism, gender—almost all of the published writers are North American. In contrast, Caribbean scholars continue to deal with basic issues such as cultural preservation, for they are all too aware of local musical styles that are dying out and that they wish to see preserved. They continue to view popular genres as threatening traditions (e.g., 208, 231, 654, 663) or as encroaching external influences (217). And they continue to tackle the need for racial validation and consciousness-raising.

As a result, much writing by Caribbean authors (or French authors commissioned by Antillean cultural ministries) is still of the ethnographic survey type, or, to put it more judiciously, combines that approach with a contemporary analytical one. In these works a focus on folkloric music is still the norm. Examples include 13, 382, 387, 392 (Guadeloupe); 608–609 (Martinique); 40, 334, 341 (Dominica); and 357, 360–362 (French Guiana). Indeed, there is still a need for such work. However popular styles need documentation as well. For example only four entries here discuss *aleke* from French Guiana (356, 363) and Dominican *jing ping* (251, 341), two important popular music styles.

Cultural revivals are active in the French Antilles, often linked to nationalist sentiment or to the promotion of Creole. Revival movements are behind many efforts at documentation. I was struck, for instance, by a surprising number of percussion and dance instruction method books from Guadeloupe (370–2, 380, 384, 389, 391, 418) and Martinique (602, 617, 621, 623). All of these are the direct outgrowth of revitalization efforts. Cultural revivals in themselves, however, have not received much scholarly attention (614, 649).

Popular Sources

Popular literature, which is also included here, has its own set of strengths and weaknesses. Many publications on Carnival, for instance, are basically tourist brochures. Nonetheless this body of literature contains valuable material. For instance, *Paralleles,* a 1960s tourist magazine covering Martinique and Guadeloupe, was the forum for several important articles on folklore in those islands (78–79, 236, 633, 634). In addition, articles in music fanzines or local newspapers are often the only historical sources available on many lesser known artists, groups, and musical events.

Two examples deserving special mention are *Antilla* and *The Beat.* *Antilla,* published since the early 1980s, is a general interest magazine on Martinique and Guadeloupe. Its perspective is *créoliste,* that is, genteely anti-establishment, "the establishment" being both metropolitan France and the islands' own rather accommodationist governments. Given that perspective, you are not surprised to find, say, an article critiquing a government-funded festival for artistic complacency (20). However at the same time you learn surprising details about that festival, which ties into other useful articles about music production and government policy (8, 12, 14, 636–638, 641).

Fanzines are to some degree about consumerism, and *The Beat* is no exception. However, since it began publishing articles on French Antillean music scene in the late 1980s it has become a useful source of English-language reporting on contemporary developments from the region.

The Future

As noted above, gender, folklorization, tourism, cultural revival, and diaspora all need more attention. There is a shocking dearth of oral histories of musicians—just two for Martinique (625, 950) and one for Guadeloupe (797). There has been little scholarship on French Caribbean music as part of the larger "world music" phenomenon, or of the effect of the "world music" boom on French Caribbean music (421, 437). Music education is a highly important area, but only two pieces deal with it (422, 431), and one of these is from 1951. In addition many musical styles of Dominica, St. Lucia, and French Guiana remain understudied, as do the region's jazz and church music traditions.

During the 1930s and '40s, validating Caribbean music by showing its links to Africa was an important step. Unfortunately, vague pronouncements about African retentions soon grew predictable, yet given the sketchiness of many historical sources it was difficult to go further. With improved historical databases (such as Eltis 2000), the investigation of historical/ethnic connections is starting to make a comeback (209, 218, 461, 542, 556, 577, 612, 667). So are inter-island musical and dance analyses by scholars intimately familiar with multiple research sites (398, 465, 628).

These are just a few potential areas for future research. Your own work with this bibliography will guide you to many more.

References

Chasteen, John Charles. 2004. *National rhythms, African roots: the deep history of Latin American popular dance.* Albuquerque: University of New Mexico Press.

Daniel, Yvonne. 1995. *Rumba: dance and social change in contemporary Cuba.* Bloomington: Indiana University Press.

Eltis, David. 2000. *The rise of African slavery in the Americas.* Cambridge: Cambridge University Press.

Hagedorn, Katherine J. 2001. *Divine utterances: the performance of Afro-Cuban Santeria.* Washington, D.C.: Smithsonian Institution Press.

Thompson, Robert Farris. 1966. "An aesthetic of the cool: West African dance." *African Forum* 2 (2): 85–102.

Acknowledgments

Although all of the research for this project was done by myself, a number of people made contributions, both large and small, which helped to make its creation possible.

I am especially grateful for the financial assistance provided by a 2003–04 residency at the New York Public Library's Schomburg Center for Research in Black Culture. That award, as a Schomburg Center/Samuel I. Newhouse Fellow, was a pivotal factor in helping me to finish this book.

Thanks also go to Ken Bilby, Dominique Cyrille, Julian Gerstin, Gerard Lockel, and Elizabeth McAlister for their generous gifts of publications relating to music of the French-speaking Caribbean.

I'd also like to recognize a few of the librarians who were of particular help in this project. They include Genette McLaurin, Curator of the Schomburg Center's General Reference and Research Division, and Channan Willner of the New York Public Library for the Performing Arts's Music Division, for their willingness to field my never ending stream of acquisition suggestions. Betty Odabashian of the Schomburg Center and the ILL team of the New York Public Library's Humanities and Social Sciences Library processed my untold numbers of Inter-Library Loan requests with grace and good humor. Without their efforts this work would not be what it is. Thanks also go to the staff of the Nyack Library, in particular ILL librarian Tom Berman, for their generous assistance.

Bob McGrath of Eyeball Productions and Bernadette Zoss of Indiana University Press provided gracious, and much appreciated, advice on publishing issues.

A special mention goes to my one-time MoMA cohort Dan Nolting for his excellent design of the ADP website.

And finally, thanks go to my mother for her innumerable forms of aid and technical assistance during this project's very long genesis.

Introduction

Without a comprehensive bibliographic foundation for research into black music, we cannot hope to ever really know the music— its repertory, its composers and performers, its history and sociology, its reasons for being.

—Eileen Southern in *The Black Perspective in Music,* Spring 1984

When Eileen Southern made this statement bibliographies on black music were limited almost exclusively to John Szwed and Roger Abrahams' *Afro-American Folk Culture* (1978), a 2-volume work covering all forms of black folklore in the Americas, and Dominique-Rene de Lerma's 4 volume *Bibliography of Black Music* (1981–1984), an unannotated work whose citations extend only to the mid-1970s. When published both were pioneering efforts, valiant attempts at representing the breadth and depth of the known literature as well as touchstones for future scholarship. Unfortunately, neither work has ever been updated, nor has anything of their scope been attempted since.

Three decades later, much about black music studies has changed. Once the province of a relatively small body of dedicated researchers, it has now grown into a worldwide network of scholars, journalists and fans. This has resulted in a virtual flood of new research in the form of monographs, biographies, journal articles, websites, and DVDs, on topics ranging from reggae to rap and a host of other new idioms and artists only just emerging in the 1970s. Even the academy, which for generations ignored, dismissed or denied the existence of a black musical legacy, has joined in with contributions from fields as diverse as cultural anthropology, folklore, literature, ethnomusicology, history, ethnic and area studies, and more.

The field's research infrastructure has also been radically reshaped. The print-based library of the past with its card catalogs, indexes and bibliographies has given way to one dominated by the World Wide Web, Online Public Access Catalogs and an ever expanding array of electronic databases and digital resources.

Unlike more traditional disciplines though, the corpus of materials relevant to black music studies cuts across a wide range of geographic, linguistic and disciplinary boundaries making the task of identifying and locating materials both difficult and time-consuming. In addition, many of the electronic indexes available to researchers today offer only limited coverage of foreign language material or journals published before their inception in the 1980s. The number of subject bibliographies in the field has also remained relatively small, with virtually none available for developments from the Caribbean and Latin America. Until now.

Starting in 1993 I began a project to document the full breadth and scope of resources relating to music of the African diaspora, with particular focus on vernacular traditions. Meant to expand upon earlier works by De Lerma, Szwed/Abrahams, and others, and to complement my own publications—*Blacks in Classical Music* (1988), *African Music* (1991), and *Fire Music* (1991)—the intent was to gather as comprehensive an array of materials on black music and musicians born outside of the African sub-continent as possible. Aimed at students, scholars, writers and librarians the work would be multi-disciplinary and multi-lingual in scope and would encompass both scholarly and popular works of all types—print, electronic, and audio-visual. Sources consulted would include library catalogs, computer databases, the Internet, and a large body of general interest, humanities, folklore, social science, and music journals, many of them never before indexed. The ultimate goal—a selective, state-of-the-art reference guide to music and culture of the African diaspora covering its evolution from the 1500s to the present day.

Over the years that project has morphed into a database now equivalent to some four thousand manuscript pages. Because of its size, and the high costs of publishing such a behemoth, I've decided to release its contents first as a series of smaller, regionally-oriented titles focusing on Afro-diasporic musics from the French, Spanish and English-speaking Caribbean and Brazil. The present title, the first in the series, covers vernacular musics—sacred, folk and popular—from the French and Creole-speaking Caribbean and its diaspora in France, the United States and Canada.

Scope and Contents

Geographical coverage in *From Vodou to Zouk* is broad, encompassing not only the islands traditionally seen as part of the French-speaking Caribbean, i.e. Haiti, Martinique, Guadeloupe, and French Guiana, but also Dominica and St. Lucia, two neighboring islands with dual French and

English heritages, and three Spanish-speaking islands with important influences from Haiti—Cuba, the Dominican Republic, and Puerto Rico. Sites abroad with large Haitian and French West Indian communities, e.g. Montreal, Canada; New York, Boston and South Florida in the United States; and Paris, France, are also represented.

Core islands—Haiti, Martinique, Guadeloupe and French Guiana—are covered comprehensively while the Spanish-speaking islands and foreign sites are treated more selectively. In the latter case I have included only materials pertaining to French Antillean or Haitian-influenced genres and musicians. For example, on the eastern end of Cuba there exists a sizable population of Cubans of Haitian descent who were initially brought there by French planters fleeing the Haitian Revolution. There they developed a rich legacy of Haitian-influenced idioms ranging from the sacred music of Vodou to secular folk genres such as *changui,* the precursor to Cuban son, and *tumba francesa,* a local drum and dance idiom similar to Puerto Rican *bomba*. Here users will find a wealth of information on these traditions but little about the range of other Afro-Cuban musics found on the island. The same applies to St. Lucia and Dominica where I have focused on French/Creole traditions but not on English ones such as calypso and steel pan.

The majority of the book's citations refer to materials in English, French and Spanish, with a smattering in Creole, and range in date from 1698 to 2008. The bulk of these cover works published or recorded between the 1930s and 2008. Among its sources are books, book sections, theses, periodical and newspaper articles, media materials (films, videos and field recordings), archival materials, and even a select number of electronic resources. These range from academic studies, most from the humanities and social sciences, to popular reportage. Idioms discussed include all forms of music from the region—sacred (Vodou and church musics), folk (*kalenda, ladja, gwo ka, bele, kwadril, chouval bwa*) and popular (Carnival music, biguine, zouk, ragga, jazz, *meringue, compas direct, mizik rasin*). Among its subjects are: music's role as a marker of ethnic and national identity, both in the Caribbean and abroad; the nature of the immigrant experience in Antillean song; cultural policy and politics in the French West Indies; cultural tourism and development; representations of women and gender roles in the French Caribbean; the French Antillean music industry; the Creolite movement; music and literature, with specific reference to works by Jean Rhys, Patrick Chamoiseau, and Aime Cesaire; regional traditions of Carnival; the folklore movement in Haiti during the 1940s and '50s, and much more.

Biographical works cover not only the big names—Gordon Henderson and Exile One, Jacob Desvarieux, Jocelyne Beroard and Kassav', Boukman Eksperyans, Tabou Combo, Nemours Jean-Baptiste—but also a number of lesser known folk artists—A.M.4, Carnot, Velo, Frisner Augustin—and even the men behind the Antillean recording scene—producers Georges and Henri Debs, Fred Paul, and others. In addition, I have attempted to provide authoritative biographical data for each person included, i.e. birth and/or stage name, place of birth and/or current country of residence, and year of birth and/or death, through the end of 2008. A few individuals not of African descent, e.g. Georges Debs, Henri Debs, and Simon Jurad, have also been included in recognition of their extensive involvement with, and influence on, the region's black music scene. Their presence is noted here by a dagger (†) in front of their name.

The main criteria for a work's inclusion has been: (a) that the item was deemed to have some potential use for researchers, regardless of its provenance; (b) that its existence was verifiable either via physical examination or a bibliographic utility such as a library catalog; and (c) that it was held by an institution accessible to researchers. Works known only to reside in private collections, items for which no location could be located, and works cited as "forthcoming" as of December 2008 have not been included. Also excluded are brief book and record reviews, album liner notes and CD booklets. Items not physically examined—mainly foreign theses and domestic theses below the Ph.D. level, non-book materials such as films and videos, archival and field recording collections, and items held in foreign collections—are noted here by an asterisk (*). In most of these cases I have still been able to provide a description of the work and its contents, usually based on a cataloging record or finding aid. When items are held by institutions that don't contribute records to OCLC/Worldcat, the consortium library catalog for a majority of North American colleges and universities, I have included the name of the holding institution in brackets at the end of the citation, e.g. [Held by the Bibliotheque nationale de France].

Since I was able to view nearly 95 percent of all items included users will find detailed bibliographical information for each entry, including whether or not a discography is included in the work. Unfortunately, due to the project's long gestation and the time it would have taken to retrospectively update records, diacritics for foreign language works have been omitted.

The bibliographic style used follows a modified form of US MARC, the standard Machine Readable Cataloging format used to enter and display records in library catalogs. The choice of whether or not to provide an annotation, and the level of detail included in each, varies, based partly on whether or not I was able to view the item, how revealing the title of an item is, and the type of material in question. For example many articles included in the *Biographical and Critical Works* section are referred to simply as "interview" (an edited transcript of a Q&A conversation), "feature" (a work combining interview fragments with narrative sections about the featured individual's biography), or "profile" (a biographical portrait usually lacking any input from the subject). Since these works are filed under the individual they refer to I felt these descriptors were sufficient. However in the case of more general works, particularly English-language monographs and doctoral theses, I have tried to include detailed contents notes or abstracts, usually based on an author's summary, foreword or introduction. For foreign language items I have provided annotations based on my own translations. It is hoped that this added level of content will assist user's in determining whether or not an item is relevant for their work.

Methodology

To ensure the work's comprehensiveness I began my research with systematic queries of OCLC/Worldcat, the online consortium of more than 10,000 domestic and foreign libraries, for each country represented in the book as well as a number of the region's musical idioms, e.g. gwo ka. This process was then repeated in SUDOC, a consortium database of French library holdings, the catalog of the Bibliotheque nationale de France, the library catalog of the three campuses which make up the Universite des Antilles et de la Guyane, and the library catalog of the Universite de Montreal. These results were then supplemented by searches of two free online article databases, *ArticleFirst* and *IngentaConnect*, and three subscription databases, *MLA, RILM,* and *ProQuest Digital Dissertations.* I also scoured several non-electronic sources such as the "Americas" sections of all "Current Bibliography and Discography" sections published in *Ethnomusicology* (1958–2005) and the print volumes of *Dissertation Abstracts* (1990–2006). I then attempted to locate and examine all relevant results from these searches either in person or via numerous inter-library loan requests. The bibliographies in each of these works was also scoured for leads.

In addition to this I indexed full, or nearly full, runs of some 70 general interest, folklore, social science, arts and music journals, e.g. *Antilla* (1981–1993), *The Beat* (1988–2007), *Bohemia* (1925–2005), *Carteles* (1925–1960), *Conjonction* (1946–2006), *Ethnomusicology* (1958–2007), *Global Rhythm* (2002–2007), the majority of which have never been indexed. before. The cutoff date for this phase of the project was December 2007.

For users interested in a more complete list of titles indexed and other items used in the book's compilation please see my list of *Sources Consulted* (1144–1243).

Organization

The book is organized into four main sections followed by two reference sections, two appendices and two indexes. Section One, the book's shortest, covers works on the arts and cultural policy in the francophone Caribbean. Section Two includes works on regional festival and Carnival traditions, annual events in which music plays a central role. Section Three, the largest, offers an in-depth look at both general materials and regional studies relating to music of the French- and Creole-speaking Caribbean. The fourth section, *Biographical and Critical Studies,* includes material on nearly 350 artists, ensembles, and music industry figures, most not represented in any other biographical dictionary or reference source.

These main sections are followed by a list of *Sources Consulted* and a survey of important *Libraries and Archives* which includes information on each institution's location, website and holdings. The two appendices provide a list of individuals and ensembles organized by musical style and/or occupation and a list of individuals and ensembles organized by country. In the latter it is important to note that the country under which an individual is listed is not necessarily the country of their birth. For instance many artists were born in the Caribbean but moved as children to new homes in France, the U.S. or Canada where they were raised and continue to live. Or, they may have migrated from their birthplaces during their teens or even adulthood and made their name in places other than their home country. Thus they are listed under the country where their work has had the most impact. On occasion, an artist has had two parts to their career, one at home and one abroad. In these cases their name will be found under both countries.

Concluding the work are two separate indexes for Authors and Subjects, providing a key to the book's 1294 entries.

Numerous cross references are provided throughout in order to guide users to related topics and entries. In addition, when the volume of material in any given section is sufficiently large I have broken it down by type: books; book sections; dissertations and theses; journals; articles; and media materials. A brief glance at some of the book's opening sections should make this system clear.

In the *Biographical and Critical Works* section performers who are best known by their stage name, e.g. Carnot, Velo, etc., are filed under that name rather than their given name. In instances where there might be some confusion because an individual is referred to in the press by both their original and/or stage name I have included a *See Also* reference for the performer's birth name.

Availability of Works

The bulk of the research for this project was carried out at three of the New York Public Library's Research Divisions—Humanities and Social Sciences, the Library for the Performing Arts, and the Schomburg Center for Research in Black Culture—along with various libraries at Columbia University and New York University's Bobst Library. Thus, I can safely say that a large portion of the works included may be found in their collections. However additional locations for most works cited may be found in WorldCat (www.worldcat.org) and, if an item is not available locally, it is quite possible that it may be obtained via your library's Inter-Library Loan department.

Conclusion

Music permeates societies of the African diaspora in much the same way it does sub-Saharan Africa, whether the community is rural or urban, primarily oral or highly educated and literate. It is like a food stuff, a staple of everyday life that helps to energize a person's existence and give voice to their yearnings, pleasures, sorrows and joy. It is found at parties, wakes, weddings, worship ceremonies, cultural events, political rallies, and everywhere in between. It reflects on the social, political and economic realities of its audience and can function as a form of social commentary, as in the *chant pwen* of Haiti; an icon of cultural nationalism as in Martinique's *bele* movement or Haiti's *mizik rasin* (roots music); or a call to party, e.g. zouk, cadence-lypso or compas. In whatever form it takes music reveals elements of its creators, performers and consumers when they are most themselves, not only as individuals but also as members of families, communities and nations. It is, in essence, a window into the soul of a people.

Whether you are working on an undergraduate term paper or a doctoral dissertation, *From Vodou to Zouk* will assist you in identifying some of the wealth of materials now available on this rich legacy. I also hope that it will spur other researchers to build on its contents by pursuing some of the sources I have overlooked here such as the region's many local newspapers.

I

Cultural History and the Arts

CANADA

1. "Artistes africains du Quebec." *Africultures*, No. 16 (mars 1999). Special issue. Collection of features and profiles covering African and African Caribbean performing and visual artists based in Montreal, Quebec.

CUBA

2. Barrios Montes, Osvaldo. "De la insercion cultural haitiana en la Cuba del siglo XX." *Del Caribe*, No. 38 (2002): 11–24. On the influence of Haitian culture in Cuba.

3. Verges Martinez, Orlando. "La Haitianidad en el contexto de la cultura popular tradicional cubana." *Del Caribe*, No. 39 (2002): 43–45. Examination of Haitian contributions to Cuban culture.

FRANCE

4. Beriss, David. *Black skins, French voices: Caribbean ethnicity and activism in urban France*. Boulder, CO: Westview, 2004, pp. 73–88. Chapter on the role of the arts/performance in helping to define racial and cultural identity among French Antilleans living in France.

5. ———. "High folklore: challenges to the French cultural world order." *Social Analysis* (Adelaide), No. 33 (1993): 105–129. Discusses efforts by Martinicans and Guadeloupeans living in France to establish and assert a distinctly Antillean cultural identity.

6. "Black africains, antillais...cultures noires en France." *Autrement* (Paris), No. 49 (avril 1983). Special issue on African and Caribbean culture in France.

7. *Ethnicolor* / dirige par Njami Simon et Bruno Tilliette. Paris: Editions Autrement, 1987. 190 p.: ill. On African and Caribbean arts activity in France.

GUADELOUPE
See also **FRANCE**

8. "L'Action culturelle en Gwadloup." *Antilla*, No. 64 (juil. 28–aout 4 1983): 36–38; No. 66 (sept. 1–8 1983): 14–17. Two-part interview with Ernest Pepin, director of Guadeloupe's C.A.C.G. (Centre Guadeloupeen d'Action Culturelle).

9. *Bilan d'activites* / Ville de Basse-Terre, Office municipal de la culture. [Basse-Terre?]: OMC, [198?]–. Annual calendar of arts events in Guadeloupe.

10. *Culture et politique en Guadeloupe et Martinique* / J. Blaise ... [et al.]. Paris: Karthala: Alizes, 1981. 98 p.

11. Fortune, Roger. "Notre folklore." *Revue Guadeloupeenne*, No. 39 (jan–mars 1960): [3]–6. Commentary reflecting on the history of staged folklore performances in Guadeloupe from the 1930s to 1960.

12. Pepin, Ernest. "L'action culturelle en Guadeloupe." *Antilla*, No. 91 (fev. 24–mars 2 1984): 37–39. The ex-director of the C.A.C.G. discusses his organization's policies and the state of culture in the French Antilles.

13. Rey-Hulman, Diana. *Les voies du patrimoine: pour que vive notre culture Guadeloupe.* Paris: Editions caribeennes, 1990. 78 p. Ethnographic portrait of folk culture in Guadeloupe providing details about its oral literature, games, lewoz events (p. 28–30), and more.

14. Saintot, Guy. "Voyage a l'interieur des organismes culturels guadeloupeens: Michelle Montantin, directrice du C.A.C.G." *Antilla*, No. 97 (avril 6–13 1984): 25–27. Interview with the director of Guadeloupe's C.A.C.G.

HAITI
See also 2–3

15. Charlier-Doucet, Rachelle. "Anthropologie, politique et engagement social: l'experience du Bureau d'ethnologie d'Haiti." *Gradhiva*, nouv. ser., No. 1 (2005): 109–125. History of the Bureau's central role in researching and promoting Haitian folk culture starting in the mid-1940s.

16. Oriol, Jacques, et al. *Le mouvement folklorique en Haiti* / introduction de Lorimer Denis et Francois Duvalier. Port-au-Prince: Impr. de l'Etat, 1952. 116 p.: ill., music. (Haiti. Bureau d'ethnologie. Publication. Serie II, no. 9). Overview of the Haitian folklore movement of the 1940s and early '50s. Includes photos of Haitian dancers and musical instruments (p. 47–55).

17. Romain, J.B. *Africanismes haitiens*. Port-au-Prince: Impr. M. Rodriguez, 1978. 102 p.: ill. (Revue de la Faculte d'ethnologie, Universite d'Etat d'Haiti; no. 31). Covers topics such as social organization, religion, art, music (p. 20–26), folklore, language, and cultural identity.

18. Weber, Bruce. "Determined to preserve Haitian arts in Miami." *New York Times* (May 25 1999): E1–E2. Feature on writer and bookstore owner Jan Mapou, a leading advocate for Haitian arts in Miami, Florida.

MARTINIQUE
See also **FRANCE**

19. Bernabe, Joby. "Reflexions discontinues a propos du statut de l'artiste martiniquais." *Carbet* (Fort-de-France), No. 5 (1986): 65–75. A leading Martinican poet/performer reflects on the status of the artist in present-day Martinique.

20. Chamoiseau, Patrick. "Plaidoyer pour un nouveau festival." *Antilla*, No. 341 (juillet 10–16 1989): 24–29. Examines the history of Fort-de-France's annual Festival Culturel and the changes which have taken place in Martinican culture and cultural policy since its inception in 1971.

21. *Culture et politique en Guadeloupe et Martinique* / J. Blaise ... [et al.]. Paris: Karthala: Alizes, 1981. 98 p.

22. Murray, David A.B. "'Martiniquais': the construction and contestation of a cultural identity." Dissertation (Ph.D.)—

University of Virginia, 1995. v, 292 leaves. See in particular chapters two to five for a discussion of Martinican cultural policy and identity construction on the island.

23. ———. *Opacity: gender, sexuality, race, and the 'problem' of identity in Martinique*. New York: P. Lang, 2002, pp. 45–60. Essay on Martinican cultural policy and identity.

24. Zames, Georges. "Le concept culture a la Martinique: comment le concevoir?" *Antilla*, No. 424 (mars 8–14 1991): 37–38.

II

Festivals and Carnival

See also 165, 226

25. Berard, Stephanie. "Au carrefour du theatre antillais: litterature, tradition orale et rituels dans les dramaturgies contemporaines de Guadeloupe et de Martinique." Dissertation (Ph.D.)—University of Minnesota, 2005, pp. 333–376. Chapter on Carnival traditions in the French Antilles.

26. Bertrand, Anca. "Carnaval a la Martinique et a la Guadeloupe." *Paralleles*, No. 21 (1967): 4–15. Photo-feature.

27. Boussat, Michel, et al. "Vaval, le carnaval des Antilles et sa specificite." In *Le carnaval, la fete et la communication*. Ville de Nice: Serre, 1985, pp. 517–524. 1984 conference paper discussing Carnival traditions from the French Antilles—Martinique, Guadeloupe and French Guiana.

28. "Le carnaval aux Antilles et a travers le monde." *Antilla*, No. 230 (fev 26–mars 5 1987): 10–13. Short history of Carnival in the French West Indies.

29. Chanson, Philippe. "'Vaval, Dieu endiable': anthropologie et missiologie du carnaval des Antilles et de la Guyane." In *Anthropologie et missiologie XIXe–XXe siecles*, eds. Olivier Servais and Gerard van't Spijker. Paris: Karthala, 2004, pp. 387–417.

30. Corzani, Jack. "Carnaval." In *Dictionnaire encyclopedique Desormeaux,* ed. Jack Corzani. Fort-de-France: Ed. Desormeaux, 1992, v. 2, pp. 515–524. Historical survey of French Antillean Carnival traditions.

31. *Femmes: livre d'or de la femme creole.* Pointe-a-Pitre: Raphy Diffusion, 1988, v. 3, pp. 81–101. Partial contents: Les grandes figures du carnaval de la Martinique / Alexandre Cadet-Petit — Les femmes et le carnaval en Guadeloupe / Michelle Beylier-Rechal. Two essays on women's contributions to the Carnivals of Martinique and Guadeloupe.

32. Julien-Lung Fou, Marie-Therese. *Le carnaval aux Antilles.* Fort-de-France: Desormeaux, 1979. 109 p.: col. ill. Brief study of Carnival traditions in the West Indies, with an emphasis on the French Antilles (Martinique, Guadeloupe, Guyane, Haiti).

33. Nunley, John W. "Caribbean festival arts: each and every bit of difference." *African Arts*, Vol. 22, No. 3 (May 1989): 68–75. A curator of the exhibition "Caribbean festival arts" describes how the show was conceived, some of the fieldwork involved and the reasons behind some of the show's curatorial choices. *See also* 34.

34. ———, and Judith Bettelheim. *Caribbean festival arts: each and every bit of difference.* [Saint Louis]: Saint Louis Art Museum, etc., 1988. 218 p.: ill. Published in conjunction with an exhibition held at the Saint Louis Art Museum, Dec. 11, 1988–Feb. 19, 1989, and several other locations. Partial contents: Recapturing heaven's glamour: Afro-Caribbean festivalizing arts / Robert Farris Thompson — Caribbean festival arts: an introduction / Judith Bettelheim, et al. — Festivals in Cuba, Haiti, and New Orleans [Carnival; Rara; Mardi Gras Indians] / Judith Bettelheim, et al. — Implications for Caribbean development / Rex Nettleford.

CUBA

35. Guanche, Jesus, and Dennis Moreno. *Caidije.* Santiago de Cuba: Editorial Oriente, 1988, pp. 111–120. Chapter on the Rara festival traditions of Caidije in eastern Cuba, a legacy of Haitian slaves brought to the island at the beginning of the 19th century.

36. Martiatu, Ines Maria. "Costumbres y tradiciones: El banda Rada." *Cuba Internacional*, No. 277 (enero 1993): 69. On the Haitian-Cuban Rara traditions of Cuba's Oriente Province in which bands of masked revelers associated with Vodu societies take to the streets during the weeks leading up to Easter.

DOMINICA

37. Blondel, Ezra. *Carnival in Dominica: Bann Move masquerade.* London: Education Service Providers International, 2004. 47 p.: col.

ill. Illustrated portrait of a masquerade tradition from Colihaut, Dominica. Includes brief oral history accounts from longtime participants.

38. *Carnival Dominique ... souvenir programme.* [Roseau: Central Carnival Committee]. Description based on: 1972.

39. *Carnival souvenir programme 88.* [Dominica]: Carnival Organising Committee, [1988]. 60 p.: ill. Alt. title: Mas Domnik souvenir programme magazine 1988.

40. Honychurch, Lennox. *Our island culture.* [Roseau: Dominica Cultural Council, 1982]. Includes a short overview of Carnival and its history in Dominica (p. 39–42).

41. *Mas Domnik 1992 souvenir magazine.* [Roseau, Dominica: Apex Services, 1992]. 44 p.: col. ill. Alt. title: Mas Domnik: the Caribbean's most spontaneous carnival!

42. *Souvenir programme magazine celebrating 150th anniversary of Carnival in Dominica: Feb. 22–Mar. 6 1984.* [Dominica]: Carnival Organizing Committee, [1984]. 34 p.: ill.

Articles

43. Davis, Cynthia. "Jamette carnival and Afro-Caribbean influences on the work of Jean Rhys." *Anthurium* [e-journal], Vol. 3, No. 2 (Fall 2005). http://scholar.library.miami.edu/anthurium/volume_3/issue_2/davis-jamette.htm. Essay on representations of Dominican working class female Carnivalists in the fiction of Jean Rhys.

44. Frampton, H.M. "Carnival time in Dominica." *Canada–West Indies Magazine*, Vol. 47, No. 5 (May 1957): 9. Report on the 1957 Carnival season.

45. ———. "News notes of Dominica, B.W.I." *Canada–West Indies Magazine*, Vol. 48, No. 5 (May 1958): 17. Includes details on the 1958 Carnival in Dominica.

46. Pulvar, J.M. "Carnaval: Vide jump up a la Dominique." *Antilla*, No. 373 (mars 9–16 1990): 14–15. Report describing the 1990 Carnival in Dominica and its role in the government's efforts to increase tourism to the island.

DOMINICAN REPUBLIC

47. Hernandez, Ricardo, and Felipe Bautista Orozco. *Las fiestas de carnaval en la Provincia Sanchez Ramirez.* Santo Domingo, R.D.: Editora Manati, 2000. 107 p.: col. ill. Describes Carnival and Haitian-derived Gaga traditions from the towns of Cotui, Fantino, and Cevicos in the Sanchez Ramirez region of the Dominican Republic.

FRENCH GUIANA
See also 27, 29, 32

48. Belfort-Chanol, Aline. *Le bal pare-masque: un aspect du carnaval de la Guyane francaise.* Petit-Bourg, Guadeloupe: Ibis Rouge Editions, 2000. 110 p.: ill. Contents: Les festivals au temps de l'esclavage — L'emergence d'un rituel carnavalesque au debut du XXe siecle — Les evolutions contemporaines de 1946 a nos jours.

49. *Le carnaval a Cayenne au XXeme siecle: (d'apres temoignages).* Cayenne: [s.n.], 1987. 44 p.: ill. [Copy held by the Black Arts Research Center (1285)]

50. Cherubini, Bernard. *Interculturalite et creolisation en Guyane francaise.* Paris: L'Harmattan, etc., 2002, pp. 137–167. Ethnographic portrait of ethnic festival traditions in French Guiana.

51. Contout, Auxence. *Langues et cultures guyanaises.* Guyane: [s.n., 197–?], pp. 115–134. Section on Carnival in French Guiana.

52. ———. *Vaval: l'histoire du carnaval de la Guyane francaise.* Petit-Bourg, Guadeloupe: Ibis Rouge Editions, 2000. 127 p.: ill. Contents: Histoire de Prince Vaval — Vaval en Guyane — Vaval dans le monde — De choses et d'autres.

53. Hidair, Armand. *Carnaval en Guyane.* [Cayenne]: Editions G. Delabergerie, 1990. 157 p.: chiefly col. ill. Photo portrait of Carnival in Cayenne, the French Guianese capital, accompanied by brief explanatory texts.

54. Hidair, Isabelle. *Anthropologie du carnaval cayennais: une representation en reduction de la societe creole guyanaise.* Paris: Publibook, 2005. 105 p.: col. ill. Examines the changing face of Carnival in French Guiana.

55. Lavergne, Bernard. *Carnaval en Guyane: touloulous, diablesses, "vaval".* [Cayenne, Guyane]: La Realite, [1988]. 107 p.: chiefly col.

ill. Contents: Les origines du carnaval — Le carnaval en Guyane — Sa preparation et son deroulement — Son attrait touristique. Profusely illustrated introduction to the traditions and characters of French Guiana's Carnival.

56. Manguer-Quivar, Monique, and Maryse Sauphanor. *Carnaval traditionnel guyanais.* Cayenne: CDDP Guyane, 1998. 48 p.: ill. Pamphlet outlining the major characters and costumes of French Guiana's Carnival and the musical instruments used to accompany it.

57. Mauffret, Blodwenn. *Le carnaval de Cayenne: le jeu carnavalesque, une esthetique de proximite.* Matoury, Guyane: Ibis Rouge, 2005. 156 p. Contents: Le carnaval comme lieu de l'utopie et de la proximite — Apparition du carnaval guyanais au sein de la societe esclavagiste — Evolution du carnaval guyanais de l'abolition a nos jours — Soiree touloulou et soiree tololo: une esthetique du proximite.

*58. Montford, Thierry. *Couleur carnaval.* [Cayenne, French Guiana]: Plume Verte, 2003. 53 p.: col. ill. Copiously illustrated booklet on the Carnival of French Guiana.

59. Nicolas, Jerome. "Le carnaval: un imaginaire politique: etude anthropologique des carnavals de Cayenne, Saint-Gilles de Reunion et Chalon sur Saone." These de doctorat—Universite de Lyon II, 2006. 2 v. (628 leaves): ill. Also available online at: http://demeter.univ-lyon2.fr/sdx/theses/lyon2/2006/nicolas_j. Comparative study of Carnival in French Guiana, Reunion, and France.

*60. Sinai, Danielle. "Le carnaval de Cayenne a l'epreuve du droit." Memoire DEA—Universite de Paris II (Pantheon-Assas), 2005. 149 leaves: col. ill.

Journals

*61. *Touloulou Magazine.* Cayenne: Federation des Festivals et Carnaval de Guyane. Description based on: No. 3 (1997). Annual journal of the Cayenne Carnival in French Guiana.

Articles

62. Bouhier de L'Ecluse, Sophie. "A Cayenne, au temps du carnaval: la metamorphose des touloulous." *Danser* (Paris), No. 152 (fev. 1997): 22–25. Illustrated feature on the masked balls and dancers of French Guiana's Carnival.

*63. Geraud, Marie-Odile. "Figures imposees: l'ambiguite de la reference au Bresil dans le Carnaval de Cayenne." *Cahiers de l'Imaginaire* (Toulouse), No. 19 (2000): 27–38.

64. Jolivet, Marie-Jose. "Creolisation et integration dans le carnaval de Guyane." *Cahiers des Sciences Humaines*, Vol. 30, No. 3 (1994): 531–549.

65. ———. "Tenue de ville, vetements de fete, ou l'art creole du paraitre." *Autrepart* (Paris), n.s., No. 1 (1997): 113–128. Includes a discussion of costuming in French Guiana's Carnival (p. 119–123).

66. Migerel, Helene. "Chez Nana: un des aspects de l'emancipation feminine en Guyane." *Les Temps Modernes*, Vol. 41, No. 470 (sept. 1985): 476–845. On the female touloulou dancers of French Guiana's Carnival.

*67. Peaud, Carol. "Le carnaval guyanais, derriere les masques." *Equinoxe* (Cayenne), No. 23 (jan. 1987): 95–100.

68. Pedro Leal, Odile. "La geste de Fem'Touloulou dans le carnaval creole de la Guyane francaise: un theatre cache-montre." *L'Annuaire Theatral*, No. 28 (automne 2000): 35–43.

69. P.I., Alexandre. "Vaval ... sur commande." *Antilla*, No. 278 (mars 10–16 1988): 28–29. Report on the 1988 Carnival in Cayenne, French Guiana.

70. Smith, Robert. "Touloulou time: carnival in French Guiana." *The Beat*, Vol. 16, No. 2 (1997): 51. Brief report from a visitor to the 1997 Carnival in French Guiana.

GUADELOUPE

See also 25–32, 381, 411, 414

71. Mulot, Stephanie. "Les masques de l'identite: expressions culturelles et strategies identitaires dans le carnaval guadeloupeen." In *Tropiques metis*. Paris: Editions de la Reunion des Musees Nationaux, 1998, pp. 72–77. Also available online at: http://svrl.cg971.fr/lameca/dossiers/carnaval_mulot/mulot_masques_identite.pdf.

72. Pineau, Gisele. "La vie-carnaval." In *Guadeloupe: temps incertains*, eds. Marie Abraham and Daniel Maragnes. Paris: Autrement, 2001, pp. 149–157. (Autrement. Collection Monde; h.s. no 95). Descriptive account of Carnival in Guadeloupe during the late 1990s and early 2000s.

73. *Vie & mort de Vaval*. Pointe-a-Pitre, Guadeloupe: Association Chico-Rey, 1991. 1 v. (unpaged): ill. Contents: Carnaval, carnavals: le mouvement perpetuel / Eric Nabajoth — Transmission et reappropriation / Louis Collomb — Can'naval mi mass'es / Roger Fortune — Vie et mort de Vaval / Michele Montantin — Excerpt from Life and death of Vaval: scene II / translated by Richard Philcox. Consists of two essays on carnival in Guadeloupe along with an excerpt from a carnival drama by Michele Montantin.

Articles

74. Belair, Nadya. "Quand le carnaval devient 'l'affaire du GDCF.'" *Le Magazine Guadeloupeen*, No. 4 (fev.–mars 1982): 40, 42. Discusses the state of Carnival in Guadeloupe following its takeover by Guadeloupe's Federation Regionale du Carnaval.

75. "Carnaval 83 en Guadeloupe." *Amina*, No. 138 (decembre 1983): 24–25. Photos of the 1983 Carnival.

76. "Le carnaval basse-terrien a l'heure de la restruturation." *Grin Fos*, No. 2 (oct–nov 1987): 43–44. Conversation with Ernest Dahome of the Federation Regionale du Carnaval de la Basse-Terre.

77. Fissier, Jean B. "Carnaval." *Guadeloupe 2000 Magazine*, No. 76 (janv–fev 1982): 13–14. Traces the history of Carnival in Guadeloupe from the early 1900s to the 1940s.

78. Fortune, Roger. "Le carnaval a la Guadeloupe." *Paralleles*, No. 4 (1965): 13–15. Reprints excerpts from a piece first published in *Revue Guadeloupeenne* (mars–avril 1946). Offers a discussion of "L'Assassin et le Malheureux," a French contribution to Guadeloupe's Carnival from the 19th century.

79. ———. "Les masques Congos aux Antilles francaises." *Paralleles*, No. 5 (1965): 11–13, 17. Reprinted from: *Revue Guadeloupeenne* (mars–avril 1954). Looks at the African contribution to Guadeloupean Carnival known as 'les masques a Congo.' Describes the dances, music and songs associated with this masquerade.

80. "Guadeloupe Carnaval 1982." *Amina*, No. 121 (juillet 1982): 36–37. Short report on the 1982 Carnival.

81. Melidor, Jean-Pierre. "Le carnaval." *Guadeloupe 2000 Magazine*, No. 71 (mars 1981): 12–13. Brief sketch of Carnival's recent history in Guadeloupe focusing on the years 1973 to 1981.

82. Mulot, Stephanie. "Histoire d'une eclipse, eclipse de l'histoire: esclavage et identite culturelle dans le carnaval basse-terrien." *Derades*, No. 2 (juin 1998): 81–86. Also available online at: http://svrl.cg971.fr/lameca/dossiers/carnaval_mulot/mulot_histoire_eclipse.pdf.

83. ———. "Politiques identitaires et conscience historique dans le carnaval guadeloupeen: mises en scene et representations d'une dynamique creole." *Anthroepotes*, Vol. 3, No. 2 (1998): 2–14. Also available online at: http://svrl.cg971.fr/lameca/dossiers/carnaval_mulot/mulot_%20politiques_identitaires.pdf.

84. ———. "La trace des masques: identite guadeloupeenne entre pratiques et discours." *Ethnologie Francaise*, Vol. 33, No. 1 (jan–mars 2003): 111–122. Also available online at: http://svrl.cg971.fr/lameca/dossiers/carnaval_mulot/mulot_trace_masques.pdf. Ethnographic portrait of Voukoum, a leading Guadeloupean Carnival group.

GUYANE
See **FRENCH GUIANA**

HAITI
See also 32, 34–36, 444, 524–529

85. Cosentino, Donald. "'My heart don't stop': Haiti, the carnival state." In *Carnaval!*, ed. Barbara Mauldin. Seattle: University of Washington Press, 2004, pp. 269–297. Detailed, well-illustrated, essay on Haiti's Carnival traditions.

86. Danticat, Edwidge. *After the dance: a walk through Carnival in Jacmel, Haiti*. New York: Crown Journeys, 2002. 158 p. Personal narrative describing the author's 2001 visit to Jacmel. Includes only scattered references to Carnival.

87. Divers, Michelet. *Le carnaval jacmelien*. [Haiti: s.n., 1997?]. 150 p.: ill. Introduction to Carnival in Jacmel—its history, characters, artisans, masks and costumes, Carnival bands, and more.

*88. Dubuisson, Wilfrid. "Le Vodou dans le carnaval gonaivien." These de Licence—Faculte d'Ethnologie, Universite d'Etat d'Haiti, 1970. Study of Vodou's influence in the Carnival of Gonaives, Haiti.

89. Louis-Charles, Thony. "Le carnaval haitien a travers le temps." In *Le compas direct*. Port-au-Prince: Thony Louis-Charles, etc., 2003,

pp. 155–168. History of Carnival in Port-au-Prince, the Haitian capital.

90. McAlister, Elizabeth A. "The Jew in the Haitian imagination: a popular history of anti-Judaism and proto-racism." In *Race, nation, and religion in the Americas*, eds. Henry Goldschmidt and Elizabeth McAlister. Oxford: Oxford University Press, 2004, pp. 61–82. Explores 'how participants in Haiti's annual Rara festival—a Lenten carnival and public performance of Vodou—both inherit and transform the anti-Jewish sentiments of the clergy in colonial Saint Domingue.'

91. ———. "'Men moun yo': 'Here are the people': Rara festivals and transnational popular culture in Haiti and New York City." Dissertation (Ph.D.)—Yale University, 1995. 359 leaves. Published in revised form as 92.

92. ———. *Rara!: Vodou, power, and performance in Haiti and its diaspora*. Berkeley: University of California Press, 2002. xviii, 259 p.: ill. + 1 CD. Discography: p. 246–248. Excellent ethnographic study of Rara, the Haitian Lenten festival, based on fieldwork carried out between 1990 and 1995. Gives particular attention to the event's performance practices and meaning, historical background, religious aspects, and its music and dances. For additional photos, field recordings and videos see author's companion website at: http://rara.wesleyan.edu.

93. Mirville, Ernst. *Considerations ethno-psychanalytiques sur le carnaval haitien*. Port-au-Prince: [s.n.], 1978. xv, 91 p.: ill.

94. Paul, Emmanuel C. *Panorama du folklore haitien: presence africaine en Haiti*. Port-au-Prince: Impr. de l'Etat, 1962, pp. 125–203. Detailed study of the traditional Carnival in Haiti.

95. Romain, J.B. *Africanismes haitiens: compilations et notes*. Port-au-Prince: Impr. M. Rodriguez, 1978, pp. 63–65. (Revue de la Faculte d'Ethnologie, Universite d'Etat d'Haiti; no. 31). Discusses the Rara processions of rural Haiti.

96. Sainvill, Ed Rainer, and Katia Millien Sainvill. "Aux origines du carnaval haitien." In *Tambours frappes, Haitiens campes*. [New York]: Heritage, [2001], pp. 73–85.

*97. Stephen Niort, Kately. "Le carnaval en Haiti: aspects ethno-psychiatriques, role en matiere d'hygiene." Doctorat d'universite—Universite de Bordeaux 2 (France), 1983.

Articles

98. Alexis, Gerson. "Les danses Rara." *Bulletin du Bureau d'Ethnologie,* Ser. 3, No. 17–19 (dec. 1958–mars 59): 41–62. Detailed look at dances performed as part of Rara celebrations in rural Haiti.

99. ———. "Notes sur le Rara." *Bulletin du Bureau d'Ethnologie,* Ser. 3, No. 27 (avril 1961): 42–45. A follow-up to previous entry.

100. "Carnaval 90: Avril avec un chapeau de paille et 150 blesses." *Haiti Progres* (mars 7–13 1990): 3. Commentary on the heavy-handed attempts of junta leader Prosper Avril to stage-manage Haiti's 1990 Carnival.

101. "Le Carnaval dans nos moeurs." *Bulletin du Bureau National d'Ethnologie,* Numero special (1987–1992): 82–100, 104–105. Photos of Haitian costumes and other carnival-associated artifacts displayed at a 1993 exhibition presented by Haiti's Bureau National d'Ethnologie. Accompanied by brief explanatory texts.

102. Claude, Franck. "Rara." *Conjonction,* No. 44 (avril 1953): 40–42. Introduction to Rara, a Lenten carnival tradition from Haiti.

103. Cosentino, Donald. "Vodou carnival." *Aperture,* No. 126 (Winter 1992): 23–29. Describes the Port-au-Prince Carnival of February 1991.

104. Dalencour, Francois. "Le carnaval rural de la Semaine Sainte doit etre officiellement, legalement aboli." *La Sociologie Haitienne,* No. 5 (janvier–mars 1942): 25–31. Discusses a new ordinance barring Rara celebrations in Haiti during Easter week.

105. "Des festivites carnavalesques en Haiti pour 1997." *Kreyol Connection,* Vol. 3, No. 10 (1997): 3. Preview of the upcoming Port-au-Prince Carnival.

106. Douyon, Lamarck. "Carnaval & personnalite." *Revue de la Faculte d'Ethnologie et du Centre de Recherches en Sciences Humaines et Sociales d'Haiti,* No. 13 (1968): 25–27. A Haitian psychologist offers his perspective on Haitian Carnival and its meaning.

107. Duc, Gerard. "Les Raras." *Optique,* No. 27 (mai 1956): 59–62. Excerpt from the author's novel *Terre en Gesine* (Port-au-Prince, 1954?) describing Rara revels during Easter week in Haiti.

108. French, Howard W. "Despite agreement, Haitians express pessimism." *New York Times* (March 1 1992): 12. Reports on the

gloomy mood of Haitians heading into 1992's Carnival season, the first following the ouster of President Jean Bertrand Aristide.

109. ———. "For Haitians, the carnival must go on." *New York Times* (February 13 1994): 4. Report on the sense of anguish and discontent pervading the island as Haitians prepare for Carnival, their third under the military dictatorship of Raoul Cedras.

110. Harrison, John. "Carnival in Haiti." *Ballet* (London), Vol. 9, No. 2 (February 1950): 40–45. Describes a Carnival season in Port-au-Prince.

111. McAlister, Elizabeth. "New York, Lavalas, and the emergence of Rara." *Journal of Haitian Studies*, Vol. 2, No. 2 (Autumn 1996): 131–139. Explores Rara traditions in Haitian New York.

112. ———. "Rara demonstrations: traditional ritual turns political weapon." *International Forum at Yale* (Spring 1992): 10–13. On Haitian Rara processions in New York and their increasing use as a form of political commentary.

113. Marcelin, Milo. "Les fetes en Haiti." *Optique*, No. 16 (juin 1955): 33–45. Descriptive calendar of annual festivals, including Carnival, held in Haiti.

114. Maximilien, Louis. "Quelques apports indiens dans la vie haitienne." *Cahiers d'Haiti*, Vol. 1, No. 5 (December 1943): 42–47. Essay on Amerindian contributions to Haitian culture. Includes a section on Wild Indian characters in Haitian Carnival (p. 44–47) along with a portrait of two "Rois du Carnaval haitien" (p. 44).

115. Paul, Emmanuel C. "Carnaval, Rara, Vodou." *Optique*, No. 23 (janvier 1956): 57–65.

116. ———. "Le carnaval traditionnel." *Bulletin du Bureau d'Ethnologie*, Ser. 3, No. 28 (mars 1962): 5–35. Detailed ethnography of Haitian Carnival traditions with information on the types of groups involved, their organizational structure, costumes, performance practices, and more. Also includes a section on Rara groups (p. 32–35).

117. Rohter, Larry. "Carnival's theme: let Lent come, Haiti has hope." *New York Times* (March 1 1995): A4. Report on Haiti's first carnival celebration following Aristide's return.

118. Tejeda Ortiz, Dagoberto. "Carnaval y colonialismo en Dominicana y en Haiti." *Cariforum* (Santo Domingo), No. 4 (abril 2001): 20–24. French and English summaries.

119. Tselos, Susan Elizabeth. "Threads of reflection: costumes of Haitian Rara." *African Arts*, Vol. 29, No. 2 (Spring 1996): 58–65, 102. On the costumes worn by participants in Haiti's Lenten carnival, Rara.

120. Watrous, Peter. "At carnival, a homecoming for Haitians." *New York Times* (Feb. 13 1997): C19, C22. Report on the 1997 Carnival in Haiti, "the biggest since the end of the military dictatorship in 1991," and its large number of returning expatriates.

121. Yonker, Dolores M. "Rara: a Lenten festival." *Bulletin du Bureau National d'Ethnologie*, No. 2 (1985): 63–71. Discusses the origins and meanings of Rara, a raucous Lenten celebration from rural Haiti.

Media Materials

*122. Brooklyn Museum. *Ra-Ra [videorecording]: a Haitian festival & an interview with Gerard Valcin* / produced by Gail Pellett for the Brooklyn Museum. Brooklyn: The Museum, [1978?]. 1 videocassette (18 min.). Shot on location in Haiti. Includes an examination of musical instruments used to accompany Rara processions and the techniques for their construction.

123. *Divine Horsemen [videorecording]: the living gods of Haiti*. New York: Mystic Fire Video, [1986], c1985. 1 videocassette (52 min.). Maya Deren's pioneering documentary on Haitian rituals shot between 1947 and 1951 and edited posthumously by Teiji and Cherel Ito. Along with its footage of Vodou ceremonies the film also includes a lengthy section on the annual Lenten festival known as Rara.

*124. *Rara [videorecording]* / produced by Verna Gillis and Gail Pellett. Tivoli, NY: Original Music, Inc., [1995?]. 1 videocassette (15 min.). Brief documentary on the pre-Easter Rara celebrations of rural Haiti, a mixture of music, religious ritual, street parades, and dance. Includes footage of Rara revelers singing, drumming and performing on the bamboo trumpets known as vaccines.

MARTINIQUE

See also 25–32, 606, 614, 616, 655, 657, 664

125. Aching, Gerard. *Masking and power: carnival and popular culture in the Caribbean*. Minneapolis: University of Minnesota Press, 2002. vii, 180 p. Analysis of Caribbean masking and Carnival as seen through the fiction of Trinidad's Earl Lovelace (*The Dragon Can't Dance*), Cuba's Guillermo Cabrera Infante (*Tres Tristes Tigres*) and Martinique's Patrick Chamoiseau (*Solibo Magnifique*).

126. Bourgois, Jean Jacques. *Martinique et Guadeloupe, terres francaises de antilles*. Paris: Horizons de France, 1958, pp. 8–23. Chapter on Carnival in Fort-de-France, Martinique.

127. Dufougere, William. *Madinina, "Reine des Antilles": etudes de moeurs martiniquaises*. Paris: Berger-Levrault, 1929, pp. 143–150. Traveler's account of Carnival in Fort-de-France.

128. Hearn, Lafcadio. *Two years in the French West Indies*. New York: Harper & Brothers, 1890, pp. 202–216. Vivid description of the 1887 Carnival in Martinique's former capital, St. Pierre. Reprint of 140.

129. *Livre d'or des 20 ans de carnaval en Martinique* / Carnaval Foyal; [directeur de la publication, Simone Coppet]. [Martinique]: Editions l'Editeur, [1988]. 51 p.: col. ill. Booklet celebrating the history of modern Carnival in Martinique and the role of Association Carnaval Foyal in its evolution. Focuses on the years 1966 to 1988.

130. Murray, David A.B. *Opacity: gender, sexuality, race, and the 'problem' of identity in Martinique*. New York: P. Lang, 2002, pp. 135–148. Partial contents: Quel travesti! Spontaneity and ambivalence in Carnival performances.

*131. Rochais, Veronique, and Patrick Bruneteaux. *Le carnaval des travestis*. Case-pilote [Martinique]: Editions Lafontaine, 2006. 159 p.: ill.

Articles

132. "Antilla Dossier: L'energie carnaval." *Antilla*, No. 369 [i.e. 370] (fev. 15–21 1990): 19–26. Special section on Carnival in Martinique. Includes descriptions of Carnival characters, a personal narrative from the longtime organizer of Fort-de-France's Carnival, Solange Londas, and brief profiles of several Martinican Carnival bands—Tanbou bo kannal; Plastic System Band; Sasayesa; Ba Lan.

133. Beauregard, C. de. "Tourisme et developpement: pour un calendrier annuel de festivals a la Martinique." *Paralleles*, No. 31 (1969): 42–49. Looks at three festivals—Noel (Christmas), Carnival, and 14 juillet (French independence day), and their potential as tourist draws for the island.

134. Bertrand, Anca. "Images de carnaval a Fort-de-France." *Paralleles*, No. 4 (1965): 5, 7–11. Offers descriptions of Martinican Carnival spanning from the late 1880s to 1964.

135. ———, and Robert Rose-Rosette. "Carnaval et tourisme a la Martinique." *Horizons Caraibes*, annee 3, no. 17 (janvier 1955): 14–16.

136. "Carnaval an tan lontan: Loulou Boislaville raconte l'ambiance du passe inedit!" *Fouyaya*, No. 46 (fevrier 1986): 16–17. Conversation with Boislaville about the Martinican Carnival and its evolution from the 1930s to the 1980s.

137. Dels[h]am, Tony. "Exploiter l'energie Vaval." *Antilla*, No. 373 (mars 9–16 1990): 7–8. Reflections on the 1990 Carnival in Martinique.

138. Domi, Serge. "Carnaval et illusion rationaliste." *Antilla*, No. 319 (fevrier 6–12 1989): 25. Reflections on Martinican Carnival and its shortcomings.

139. ———. "Le carnaval: un phenomene sociologique." *Antilla*, No. 39 (fevrier 4 1983): 38–40. Feature on Carnival in Martinique.

140. Hearn, Lafcadio. "La Verette and the carnival in St Pierre, Martinique." *Harper's New Monthly Magazine*, Vol. 77, No. 461 (October 1888): 737–748. Detailed description of the 1887 Carnival season in St Pierre. Reprinted in 128.

141. Murray, David A.B. "Defiance or defilement? Undressing crossdressing in Martinique's Carnival." *Sexualities*, Vol. 1, No. 3 (August 1998): 343–354. Exploration of male cross-dressing in Martinican Carnival. Reprinted in 130.

142. ———. "Re-mapping carnival: gender, sexuality and power in a Martinican festival." *Social Analysis* (Adelaide), Vol. 44, No. 1 (April 2000): 103–112. Close analysis of two elements of the Martinican Carnival—the Queen of Carnival competition and male to female crossdressing in its street parades.

143. Rosemain, Jacqueline. "Rencontre avec ... Roger Robinel." *Antilla*, No. 277 (mars 3–9 1988): 8. Interview with a leading Martinican Carnival designer.

144. Watrous, Peter. "Catching carnival fever; Martinique's great drum groups signal five days of frenzied festivities—and a chance to hear some of the best bands in the Caribbean." *New York Times* (October 25 1998): Sec. 5, pp. 12, 30. Travel feature on Martinique and its Carnival, both urban and rural, with a focus on its music.

Media Materials

*145. *Carnivals of the Caribbean [videorecording]* / director, Sonia Fritz. San Juan, P.R.: Isla Films, 2004. 1 DVD (60 min.). Documentary on Carnival traditions in Trinidad, Puerto Rico, and Martinique. Explores the elements that unite them as well those make each one distinct.

ST. LUCIA

*146. *Carnival*. [Saint Lucia]: Voice Pub. Description based on: 2003. Saint Lucia Carnival program.

147. Crowley, Daniel J. "La Rose and La Marguerite Societies in St. Lucia." *Journal of American Folk-lore*, Vol. 71, No. 282 (Oct–Dec 1958): 541–552.

148. Dunstan, Raymond David. "St. Lucian carnival: a Caribbean art form." Dissertation (Ph.D.)—State University of New York at Stony Brook, 1978. xii, 361 leaves: ill. Based on field work conducted during the 1976–77 Carnival seasons.

*149. *Mas in May, 1980* / compiled by Augustus Justin. Castries, St. Lucia: Lithographic Press, [1980]. 59 p.: ill. [Held by the University of the West Indies, St. Augustine, Trinidad]

150. *Oral and folk traditions of Saint Lucia*, ed. Joyce Auguste. Saint Lucia, West Indies: Lithographic Press, 1986, pp. 5–6, 8 9. Brief discussion of St. Lucia's Carnival and flower festival traditions.

III

Music of the French-Speaking Caribbean and its Diaspora

General Works

See also 1158–1159, 1164–1165, 1168, 1170–1172, 1244–1245, 1269, 1286

151. Baysse, Geo. *En dansant la biguine: souvenir de l'Exposition coloniale.* [Senlis: Imprimeries Reunies], 1931. 105 p.: ill. Typewritten mss., "La Biguine (danse creole)" (3 leaves), inserted. Includes a portrait of bandleader Alexandre Stellio and his orchestra.

152. Berrian, Brenda F. *Awakening spaces: French Caribbean popular songs, music, and culture.* Chicago: University of Chicago Press, 2000. xiv, 287 p.: ill. Discography: p. [269]–271. Explores themes of 'childhood and exile, gender, cultural politics, Creole language, public performance, recontextualization, and the deferential space of the drum' in French Antillean songs and music created between 1970 and 1996. Artists and topics covered include Malavoi; Kassav; Antillean women's voices—Leona Gabriel, Jocelyne Beroard, Edith Lefel, Joelle Ursull, Lea Galva, Suzy Trebeau, and Tanya St. Val; angage singers Eugene Mona, Djo Dezormo, Kali, and Poglo; the music industry; recent artists and trends led by Marius Cultier, Mario Canonge, Celine Fleriag, the Bernard Brothers and Fal Frett, Franck Donatien and Taxikreol, Kwak, Palavire, and Volt Face; and the drum—gwo ka and bele—in music by Velo, Henri Guedon, Dede Saint Prix, Bago, Marce, Claude Vamur, Sully-Cally, and others.

153. Carbet, Marie Magdeleine. *Comptines et chansons antillaises.* [Montreal]: Lemeac, [1975]. 75 p.: ill. Collection of song texts for children's counting and game songs from the French Antilles.

*154. Desroches, Monique. *Stages de formation en ethnomusicologie dans 4 iles de la Caraibe.* Montreal: Centre de Recherches Caraibes, Universite de Montreal, 1983–1987. 1 v. (various pagings). Report on the state of ethnomusicology in Martinique, Guadeloupe, Dominica, and Saint Lucia. [Held by the University of Montreal Library]

*155. Fanfant, Jean Philippe. *Afro-Caribbean grooves for drumset = Les plus grands rythmes Caribeens.* Petaluma, CA: Sher Music Co., 2007. 47 p. of music: ill. + 1 CD. Method book. Includes CD with audio selections from each section of the book along with video demonstrations of selected songs.

156. Guilbault, Jocelyne. *Zouk: world music in the West Indies.* Chicago: University of Chicago Press, 1993. 279 p.: ill., music + 1 CD. Discography: p. 229–231. Contents: Zouk and the isles of the Caribees — "Zouk-la se sel medikaman nou ni" [Kassav, Compagnie Creole, Malavoi] — On zouk and family resemblance: biguine, compas direct, and cadence-lypso — Biguine: popular music of Guadeloupe, 1940–1960 / Edouard Benoit — "Toujou sou konpa": issues of change and interchange in Haitian popular dance music / Gage Averill — Cadence: the Dominican experience / Gregory Rabess — Three constructions of zouk — Zouk in the eighties — Zouk and the local music industries — Zouk as a world music in the lesser antilles. Groundbreaking study of popular music from the francophone Caribbean.

157. Hayet, Armand. *Chansons des iles.* Paris: Editions Denoel, 1937. 218 p.: ill., music. Popular discussion of folk songs from the French West Indies. Includes numerous song texts in French and Creole.

158. Jallier, Maurice, and Yollen Lossen. *Musique aux Antilles = Mizik bo kay.* Paris: Editions Caribeennes, 1985. 145 p.: ill. History of popular music in Guadeloupe, Martinique and French Guiana. Includes interviews with Al Lirvat (p. 43–49), Fernand Donatien (p. 50–52), Loulou Boislaville (p. 97–100), Gerard La Viny (p. 101–107), Ernest Leardee (p. 116–120), Gaston Lindor (p. 128–131), and Gratien Midonet (p. 132–136), each a pioneering figure in the music of the French-speaking Caribbean.

159. ———, and Vivette Jallier-Prudent. *Musique aux Antilles: Zouk a la Mazouk*. Paris: L'Harmattan, 1999. 180 p.: ill. Companion to the previous entry focusing on developments in Antillean folk and popular musics since the 1980s. Includes brief interviews with Gesip Legitimus, Georges Debs, Moune de Rivel, Jean-Pierre Meunier, Francky Vincent, and Claudy Siar, along with profiles of Kali, Eugene Mona, Paulo Rosine, Marius Cultier, Ti Emile, Lucien Fabien Montout, Malavoi, Kassav, and Zouk Machine.

160. Martinez, Pierre, et al. *Jeux et chansons dans la Caraibe*. Pointe-a-Pitre: CDDP Guadeloupe, 1987. 50 p. of music: ill. Collection of children's songs.

161. Parsons, Elsie Worthington Clews. *Folk-lore of the Antilles, French and English*. Millwood, NY: Kraus Reprint Co., 1969–1976. 3 v.: ill., music. (American Folk-lore Society. Memoirs; v. 26). Reprint. First published: New York: American Folk-lore Society, etc., 1933–1943. A major source of folk songs from around the Caribbean based on fieldwork conducted in 1924–25 and 1927.

162. Pierre-Charles, Livie. *Femmes et chansons*. Paris: L. Soulanges, 1975. 182 p.: ill., music. Chiefly song texts from the francophone Caribbean.

163. Rosemain, Jacqueline. *La danse aux Antilles: des rythmes sacres au zouk*. Paris: L'Harmattan, 1990. 90 p.: music. Contents: La musique — Danse sacree — Les rythmes — Les danses creoles nationales — Les danses antillaises contemporaines. Brief study of the rhythms and dances of the French-speaking Caribbean and Cuba.

164. ———. *Jazz et biguine: les musiques noires du Nouveau-Monde*. Paris: L'Harmattan, 1993. 154 p.: music. Contents: Les evangelisations — Les chants de l'esclavage — Les danse de l'esclavage — Les musiques noires de la liberte. Brief general study which attempts to delineate the different historical and stylistic developments of Afro-American and Afro-Antillean musical forms.

*165. *Se carnaval: chansons de carnaval: textes et partitions* / [recueil] realise par Michel Beroard. Terreville: CEDIM, [1996]. 40 p. of music. Collection of Carnival songs. [Copy held by the Bibliotheque nationale de France]

Book Sections

166. "Antillean jazz." In *The new Grove dictionary of jazz.* 2nd ed. New York, 2002, v. 1. Short entry on jazz influence in the French Antilles.

167. Berrian, Brenda F. "Se cho (it's hot): French Antillean musicians and audience reception." In *Caribe 2000: definiciones, identidades y culturas regionales y/o nacionales: Simposio III*, eds. Lowell Fiet and Janette Becerra. San Juan, PR: Caribe 2000, Facultad de Humanidades, Universidad de Puerto Rico, Recinto de Rio Piedras, 1999, pp. 117–126. Focuses on the work of two French Antillean groups, Malavoi and Kassav.

168. Bilby, Kenneth M. "The Caribbean as a musical region." In *Caribbean contours*, eds. Sidney W. Mintz and Sally Price. Baltimore: Johns Hopkins University Press, 1985, pp. 181–218. Wide-ranging regional survey covering the folk musics of St. Lucia, Haiti, Guadeloupe, French Guiana, and elsewhere; popular music styles of the region; musics of the Caribbean diaspora; and Caribbean influence on world music traditions, e.g. African pop.

169. *Caribbean and Latin America.* London: Continuum, 2005. (Continuum encyclopedia of popular music of the world; v. 3). Contents: Part I: Caribbean — Part II: Latin America (Mexico; Central America; South America). Landmark work offering the most up-to-date, comprehensive, and well-researched coverage yet of the Caribbean and Latin American region, including its francophone countries. Each entry is written by a leading ethnomusicologist in straight-forward language understandable by layman and specialist alike.

170. *Caribbean dance from abakua to zouk: how movement shapes identity* / edited by Susanna Sloat. Gainesville, FL: University Press of Florida, 2002. Partial contents: Haitian Vodou ritual dance and its secularization / Henry Frank — Spirit unbound: new approaches to the performance of Haitian folklore / Lois E. Wilcken — Sa ki ta nou (This belongs to us): Creole dances of the French Caribbean / Dominique Cyrille.

171. Conrath, Philippe. "Mizik Antiye." In *Antilles*, eds. Daniel Bastien and Maurice Lemoine. Paris: Autrement, 1996, pp. 223–226. (Autrement. Serie Monde; No. 41). Article on zouk, the French Antillean dance music idiom.

172. Crosta, Suzanne. "Toward a cross-cultural poetics of African drumming: recollection, reconnection, and imagination in French Caribbean fiction." In *Remembering Africa*, ed. Elisabeth Mudimbe-Boyi. Portsmouth, NH: Heinemann, 2002, pp. 206–233. On drums and drummers as motifs in fiction of the French-speaking Caribbean.

*173. Desroches, Monique. "La musique aux Antilles." In *La Grande encyclopedie de la Caraibe*, ed. Bruno Caredda. [Italy]: Sanoli, 1990, v. 10, pp. 178–193. Survey article.

174. Entiope, Gabriel. "Musique, danse dans le vecu de l'esclave caribeen (approche historique)." In *Social and festive space in the Caribbean*, eds. Masao Yamaguchi and Masao Naito. Tokyo, Japan: ILCAA, 1987, pp. 253–297. (Comparative studies on the plural societies in the Caribbean; v. 2)

175. *Femmes: livre d'or de la femme creole.* Pointe-a-Pitre: Raphy Diffusion, 1988, v. 6, pp. 19–102. Partial contents: Soubassement de toute expression: la musique traditionnelle / Lena Blou, et al. — L'image de la femme a travers la chanson Antan Lontan / Eliane Surena — Les rythmes ensorceles / Alexandre Cadet-Petit, et al. Three essays on women in Afro-Antillean music. The first deals with their role in folk idioms such as *gwo ka* and *bele* and the second with their image in songs. The third offers biographical sketches of a diverse range of female singers from the French-speaking Caribbean.

176. Gilbert, Will G. *Rumbamuziek: volksmuziek van de Midden-Amerikaansche Negers.* 's-Gravenhage: J.P. Kruseman, [1945]. 119 p.: ill., music. Contents: Wezen van de Amerikaansche negermuziek — Midden-Amerikaansche muziekvormen: ritueele muziek, danslied en lied — Muziekinstrumenten van den neger — Godsdienstige muziek — Het satirische danslied — Danslied en liefdeslied. Includes discussion of black music traditions from the French Antilles, Haiti, Martinique, and other islands of the Caribbean region.

177. Guilbault, Jocelyne. "On interpreting popular music: zouk in the West Indies." In *Caribbean popular culture*, ed. James A. Lent. Bowling Green, OH: Bowling Green State University Popular Press, 1990, pp. 79–97. Discussion of the French Antillean dance music known as zouk with a focus on its best known ensemble, Kassav. Covers developments in Martinique, Guadeloupe, St. Lucia, and Dominica.

178. *Heritage de la musique africaine dans les Ameriques et les Caraibes*, eds. Alpha Noel Malonga & Mukala Kadima Nzuji. Paris: L'Harmattan, etc., 2007. Partial contents: Grapa-Kongo en Guadeloupe, 'une nation culturelle' vivante / Auguste Miabeto — Presence musicale africaine dans l'oeuvre d'Aime Cesaire / Antoine Yila — Le tam-tam dans Texaco de Patrick Chamoiseau ou la musique africaine et les Caraibes / Alpha Noel Malonga. Collection of papers from the fifth Festival Panafricain de Musique held in Congo-Brazzaville in 2005.

179. Laferl, Christopher F. "'Ah! Gade chabine-la' und 'Neg ni move mannye': Genus- und Ethnizitatsmarkierungen in den Texten der fruhen Popularmusik der franzosischen Antillen." In *Wenn Rander Mitte werden*. Wien: WUV, 2001, pp. 402–411. Analysis of two French Antillean biguine lyrics, the first written by musician and bandleader, Alexandre Stellio.

180. Leaf, Earl. *Isles of rhythm*. New York: A.S. Barnes, 1948. Partial contents: Isles of rhythm — Haitian halftones — Beginning of the Beguine [Martinique] — Caribbean medley. Travelogue offering a snapshot of the folk and popular dance-music scenes of several Caribbean capitals during the mid- to late-1940s. Of particular value are the many photographs of dancers and musicians in performance. The precursor for later studies such as 182 and 170.

181. Ledesma, Charles de. "Zouk takeover: the music of the French Antilles." In *World music: the rough guide*, eds. Simon Broughton, et al. London: Rough Guides, 1994, pp. 514–520.

182. Lekis, Lisa. *Dancing gods*. New York: Scarecrow Press, 1960. Partial contents: Haiti — French West Indies. Survey of folkloric dance traditions from the Caribbean which includes reference to their accompanying musics.

183. Leymarie, Isabelle. *Du tango au reggae: musiques noires d'Amerique latine et des Caraibes*. Paris: Flammarion, 1996. Survey of black music traditions from around the Americas. Includes brief chapters on local traditions from the French Antilles, Haiti, Dominica/St. Lucia, the Guyanas, and beyond, along with sketches of the biguine, compas and zouk.

184. ———. *Musiques caraibes*. Arles: Cite de la Musique, etc., 1996. Contents: Introduction aux mosaiques caraibes — I. Les musiques et les dieux — II. Les musiques profanes — III. Les musiques

populaires. Accompanied by a CD of music linked to examples from the text.

185. Madiana. "The biguine of the French Antilles." In *Negro anthology, 1931–1933*, ed. Nancy Cunard. London: Published by Nancy Cunard at Wishart, 1934, pp. 401–402. Short piece on the biguine in Martinique, Guadeloupe and French Guiana.

186. Manuel, Peter, et al. *Caribbean currents: Caribbean music from rumba to reggae*. Rev. and exp. ed. Philadelphia: Temple University Press, 2006. First published: 1995. Partial contents: Haiti and the French Caribbean. Offers an introduction to the region and its musics aimed at general readers and college level music courses.

187. Maxime, Antoine, and Jack Corzani. "Chorales." In *Dictionnaire encyclopedique Desormeaux*, ed. Jack Corzani. Fort-de-France: Ed. Desormeaux, 1992, v. 2, pp. 599–603. Survey article covering choral music traditions from the French Antilles.

188. *The Penguin encyclopedia of popular music*. London: Viking, 1989. See entries for "Beguine" and "Cadence".

189. *Performing the Caribbean experience* / edited by Malena Kuss. Austin: University of Texas Press, 2008. (Music in Latin America and the Caribbean; v. 2). Major survey of musical traditions from the Caribbean region. Includes two essays on Haiti, one devoted to Vodou music, another on Martinique, and another on St. Lucia. Accompanied by two CDs of musical examples keyed to the text.

190. *Rythmes du monde francophone: celebrating 10 years of Festival International de Louisiane* / Herman Mhire, editor. Lafayette, La.: Festival International de Louisiane, 1996. Copiously illustrated program book celebrating the 10th anniversary of the Festival International de Louisiane, the francophone world music festival held annually in Lafayette, Louisiana. Includes numerous photos of French Antillean performers.

191. *Sans visa: le guide des musiques de l'espace francophone et du monde: 12000 addresses, artistes, lieux, medias, institutions* / [redaction, coordination Frank Tenaille]. [2. ed.]. [France]: Zone franche, 1995, pp. 294–324. Partial contents: Caraibes. Guadeloupe / Jean-Michel Denis — Guyane / Pascal Letellier — Haiti / Ralph Boncy — Martinique / Jean-Michel Denis. A French version of *World Music: the Rough Guide*. Consists of brief sketches, each including an introductory text followed by contact

listings for music organizations, artists, press, radio, and television.

192. Schmidt, Nelly. "Chansons des 'nouveaux libres' de Guadeloupe et de Martinique, 1848–1851." In *Chansons d'Afrique et des Antilles.* Paris: L'Harmattan, 1988, pp. 107–135. On post-emancipation songs written by Victor Schoelcher and Charles Auguste Cyrille Bissette representing the two dominant perspectives of the time— one which celebrated the newly-won freedom of the blacks and another decrying the changes as wrongheaded and unnecessary.

193. *South America, Mexico, Central America, and the Caribbean* / Dale A. Olsen and Daniel E. Sheehy, editors. New York: Garland Pub., 1998. (Garland encyclopedia of world music; v. 2). Partial contents: Popular music in the English-, French-, and Creole-speaking Caribbean / Gage Averill — French Guiana / Jean-Michel Beaudet — Dominica / Jocelyne Guilbault — St. Lucia / Jocelyne Guilbault — Guadeloupe / Jocelyne Guilbault — Haiti / Gage Averill and Lois Wilcken — Martinique / Monique Desroches. Accompanied by a CD of musical examples.

194. Wagner, Christoph. *Das Akkordeon oder die Erfindung der populären Musik.* Mainz: Schott, 2001, pp. 188–200. Chapter surveying the use of accordions in Caribbean popular music from 'merengue tipico' groups of the Dominican Republic to kwadril groups of the French Antilles.

195. *World Music: the rough guide* / edited by Simon Broughton, et al. London: Rough Guides, 2000, v. 2. Partial contents: Antilles-Zouk / Charles de Ledesma and Gene Scaramuzzo — Haiti / Sue Steward and Sean Harvey.

Dissertations and Theses

*196. Bermond, Marie-Pierre. "La danse, une musique corporelle." Thesis (M.A.)—Universite de Montreal, 1993. [viii], 121 leaves + 1 videocassette.

*197. Cardinal, Josee. "La flute de bambou dans quatre iles des Antilles (Martinique, Guadeloupe, Dominique et Sainte-Lucie)." Thesis (M.A.)—Universite de Montreal, 1989. xviii, 156 leaves: ill., music.

198. Hill, Edwin C. "Black soundscapes, white stages: the meaning of sound in the black francophone Atlantic." Dissertation (Ph.D.)— UCLA, 2007. xi, 232 leaves: ill. Explores the way ideas about black sound define aesthetic values, represent transnational

dynamics, and position the meaning of imperialism in the French West Indies.

*199. Kilgore, Christopher Aaron. "Music as identity in French Caribbean literature and culture." Thesis (M.A.)—University of Georgia, 2001. vi, 40 leaves.

200. Lekis, Lisa. "The origin and development of ethnic Caribbean dance and music." Dissertation (Ph.D.)—University of Florida, 1956. vi, 282 leaves. Contents: People of the Caribbean: the cultural and historical background of Caribbean dance — The significance and function of dance among the Afro-Caribbeans — Islands of the Caribbean: form and function of dances of specific areas [Haiti, French Antilles, etc.] — Status and destiny of Caribbean dance. Published in revised form as 182.

Journals

201. *Afiavi Magazine*. Bordeaux [France]: SARL Afiavi, 1991–. Alt. title: Afiavi music. Some articles also available online at: http://afiavi.free.fr/e_magazine. Glossy French-language periodical covering musics from Africa and the African diaspora.

202. *The Beat*. Los Angeles, CA: Bongo Productions, 1988–. Vol. 7, no. 5 (1988)–. Continues: The Reggae & African Beat. Website: www.getthebeat.com. Excellent fanzine offering news, interviews, and reviews of reggae, Caribbean and world music styles. Includes a regular column by Brian Dring offering coverage of new developments from the francophone Caribbean and its diaspora.

*203. *Mizik: la musique et la vie culturelle aux Antilles*. Fort de France: s.n., 1976–1977. [Held by the University of Amsterdam Library, The Netherlands]

Articles

204. Bar-David, Gerard. "Ragga des iles, ragga des villes." *Vibrations* (Lausanne), n.s. No. 5 (dec 1994–janv 1995): 46–47. Feature on recent developments in ragga/dancehall from the French Antilles. Discusses work by Kali and Metal Sound, Master Dji, Wailing Roots, JND, and others.

205. Bensignor, Francois. "Aux racines des musiques antillaises." *Hommes & Migrations*, No. 120 (sept 1996): 58–61. Focuses on two roots music idioms of the French Antilles—*gwo-ka* from Guadeloupe and belair (*bele*) from Martinique.

206. Bernabe, Jean. "Chronique d'une fin de vacances." *Antilla*, No. 209 (sept 24–oct 1 1986): 15–16; No. 210 (oct 1–8 1986): 10–11, 13. Two-part essay on the French Antillean dance music known as zouk.

207. Bowermaster, Jon. "Zouk, rattle, and roll; The hip-shaking music of the French Antilles is now going global." *Elle*, Vol. 4, No. 2 (October 1988): 120, 122. Short feature on zouk.

208. Caloc, Rene. "La zoukification du son et du sens: avis aux musiciens." *Antilla*, No. 437 (juin 6–13 1991): 33. Lament about the growing sameness and overly commercialized nature of zouk from the French Antilles.

209. Daniel, Yvonne. "Come with me and let's talk about Caribbean quadrilles." *Cariso!*, No. 6 (2006): 12, 6–11. Offers a look at the history and contemporary performance practice of quadrille dances and music in the English, French, Dutch and Spanish-speaking Caribbean. Among the variants mentioned are the *seis*, *jacana*, belair, quadrille, *kuadria*, *bele* and *haut-taille*, and *kadril*.

210. "De A a Zouk." *Echo Jeunesse*, No. 21 (Dec. 1988–Jan. 1989): 13–21. Special section on zouk.

211. Desroches, Monique. "Creolisation musicale et identite culturelle aux Antilles francaises." *Canadian Journal of Latin American and Caribbean Studies*, Vol. 17, No. 34 (1992): 41–51. Overview of the 'creolization process' whereby musical traditions from Europe, Africa and India are transformed into new, uniquely Antillean, traditions.

212. ———. "Les pratiques musicales: image de l'histoire, reflet d'un contexte." *Historial Antillais* (Fort-de-France), t. 1 (1980): 491–500. History of music in the French Antilles, with an emphasis on Martinique.

213. Donnart, Reynaldo. "Vive la Francehall: a brief history of dancehall in France." *The Beat*, Vol. 19, No. 4 (2000): 46–47, 49. Looks at the history of dancehall music in France and the French Antilles.

214. Dring, Brian. "Interview with Patrick Joseph-Pauline from Zoukarchive.com." *The Beat*, Vol. 22, No. 2 (2003): 55. Brief interview with the creator of the website Zoukarchive.com about its origins and purpose.

215. Dubouille, Gisele. "Nouveaux disques de musique negre = New records of Negro music." *La Revue du Monde Noir*, No. 3 (1932): 55–58. Comments on recent recordings of French Antillean dance music by Maurice Charlery, Maurice Banguio, Alexandre Stellio, and others.

216. Epstein, Dena J. "African music in British and French America." *Musical Quarterly*, Vol. 59, No. 1 (January 1973): 61–91. Account of African music and dance traditions in the former British and French colonies of Barbados, Jamaica, Antigua, Martinique, Haiti, Guadeloupe, Virginia, South Carolina and Louisiana from the 17th to the 19th centuries.

217. Florentin, Yves. "'Kadans': musique populaire des peuples creolophones facteur d'integration regionales?" *Antilla*, No. 11 (janvier 1982): 45–48; No. 12 (fevrier 1982): 42–45. Two-part feature on the Antillean dance music known as *kadans* (cadence) and its potential for unifying the Creole-speaking peoples of the French Caribbean.

218. Gerstin, Julian. "Tangled roots: kalenda and other neo-African dances in the circum-Caribbean." *Nieuwe West-Indische Gids*, Vol. 78, No. 1–2 (2004): 5–41. Examines the evolution of colonial-era choreography, musical instruments, and instrumental practices based on evidence from the historical literature. Includes discussion of the limitations and biases of these sources.

219. Goines, Leonard. "Latin-American and Caribbean music-IV: Black music of the French-speaking islands." *Allegro* [New York] (December 1972): 4, 24. Brief survey article.

220. Grenier, Line, and Jocelyne Guilbault. "Creolite and francophonie in music: socio-musical repositioning where it matters." *Cultural Studies* (London), Vol. 11, No. 2 (May 1997): 207–234. Examines the role of zouk and Quebecois chanson in helping to define national identity for members of the Creolite and Francophonie movements of the French West Indies and Quebec.

221. Guilbault, Jocelyne. "Creolite and the new cultural politics of difference in popular music of the French West Indies." *Black Music Research Journal*, Vol. 14, No. 2 (Fall 1994): 161–178. Looks at the ways in which zouk serves to embody a new generation's pride in its 'Creole,' as opposed to French, cultural heritage.

222. ———. "Interpreting out of contradiction: a world of music in the West Indies." *Canadian University Music Review*, No. 14 (1994): 1–17. 'Condensed and revised version of the main arguments presented in two chapters of (Part II) *Zouk: world music in the West Indies*' (156). Discussion of popular music in the French Antilles.

223   ———. "On interpreting popular music: zouk in the West Indies." *Bulletin / Folk Research Centre (St Lucia)*, Vol. 2, No. 2 (July–Dec. 1991): 4–31. Analysis of the idiom's cultural background and meaning based on fieldwork conducted in the Creole-speaking islands of Guadeloupe, Martinique, Dominica, and St. Lucia. Also includes a discussion of zouk supergroup Kassav and its role in disseminating the music both at home and abroad (p. 12–15).

224. ———. "Sociopolitical, cultural, and economic development through music: zouk in the French Antilles." *Canadian Journal of Latin American and Caribbean Studies*, Vol. 17, No. 34 (1992): 27–40.

225. Hazael-Massieux, Marie-Christine. "Vers une analyse des parties chantees dans les contes creoles." *Etudes Creoles* (Montreal), Vol. 8, No. 1–2 (1985): 40–63. Analysis focusing on children's game and story-songs of the French Antilles.

226. Jourdain, E[lodie]. "Trinidad calypso not unique." *The Caribbean*, Vol. 7, No. 10 (May 1954): 221–222, 232. Response to an earlier piece by Andrew Carr on the uniqueness of Trinidad's calypso music. Argues that since Carnival song traditions are well-established elsewhere in the Caribbean, particularly in the French West Indies, it is inaccurate to refer to calypso as unique.

227. Labat, Jean Baptiste. "Labat en 1698." *Fouyaya*, No. 58 (sept. 1987): 40–41. Excerpt from a reprint of the 1742 ed. of Labat's *Nouveau voyage aux isles de l'Amerique* (Fort de France: Edition des horizons caraibes, 1974). Offers a description of calenda drum and dance performances and their popularity among the slave communities of the French West Indies.

228. Labesse, Patrick. "Africa Fete 94: un tremplin pour les musiques du sud." *Rythmes* (Montreal), Vol. 2, No. 4 (1994): 9–10. Feature on the 1994 edition of a festival devoted to musics from francophone Africa and the African diaspora.

229. Lamy, Laurent. "Notes: Pour le zouk." *Percussions*, No. 48 (nov.–dec. 1996): 12–14. Introductory analysis.

230. Lastel, M. "Musique et danse—: realite antillaise." *Tropiques* (Paris), Vol. 48, No. 327 (Dec. 1950): 96–100. Impressionistic reflections on the music and dances of the French Antilles, more specifically, Guadeloupe and Martinique.

231. Laurence, Philippe. "Pauvre musique antillaise." *Antilla*, No. 400 (sept 13–20 1990): 35–38. Discusses a variety of issues pertaining to the pop music scene in the French Antilles, e.g. weak lyrics, etc.

232. Lee, Robert. "Reggae, calypso, soca...: now it's 'Cadence' from the 'little islands.'" *Caribbean Contact*, Vol. 5, No. 10 (Feb. 1978): 3. Survey of recent developments in Caribbean popular musics such as cadence (Dominica/French Antilles), soca (Trinidad), and spouge (Barbados).

233. Lee, Simon. "Mizik a nou—our music: World Creole Music Festival '99, Roseau, Dominica." *The Beat*, Vol. 19, No. 2 (2000): 36–39. In-depth report on the third annual World Creole Music Festival, a celebration of musics from the French Antilles and beyond.

234. Lurel, Roger. "Antilla-Kilti: Defense de la biguine." *Antilla*, No. 102 (mai 11–18 1984): 31–32.

235. Megenney, William W. "And the beat goes on: post-colonial Afro-Caribbean music." *Journal of Caribbean Studies*, Vol. 12, No. 2–3 (Fall 1997–Spring 1998): 171–183. Surveys traditions from Cuba, Haiti, the Dominican Republic, Jamaica, the French Antilles, and Trinidad.

236. "La musique aux Antilles francaises." *Paralleles*, No. 28 (1968). Partial contents: Notes sur une definition du folklore antillais / Anca Bertrand — Recensement des rythmes anciens de campagne / Anca Bertrand — Notes for a definition of West Indian folk music / Anca Bertrand — Quelques melodies creole de 1880 Martinique: texte et partitions extraits du 'Two Years in French West Indies' / Lafcadio Hearn — Le quadrille de la Guadeloupe [texts of dancers commands for the quadrille of Marie-Galante] / Anca Bertrand — Paulette Nardal: un compositeur pour chorale antillaise. Special issue on vernacular music traditions of Guadeloupe and Martinique. Includes numerous illustrations.

237. "Musiques Caraibes: la trace noire." *Africultures*, No. 8 (mai 1998). Special Caribbean music issue.

238. Nardal, Andree. "Etude sur la beguine creole = Notes on the biguine creole." *La Revue du Monde Noir* (Paris), No. 2 (1932): 51–53. Describes the key elements of the biguine dance craze of the early 1930s.

239. Nettel, R. "Historical introduction to 'la calinda.'" *Music & Letters*, Vol. 27, No. 1 (January 1946): 59–62. Introduction to the Caribbean drum and dance music known variously as calinda, kalinda, or kalenda. Based in part on descriptive accounts by Pere Labat from Martinique (1698) and Moreau de Saint-Mery from Haiti (1789).

240. Roberts, Peter. "Calenda: the rise and decline of a cultural image." *Sargasso* (Rio Piedras), No. 1 (2005–2006): 51–68. Examines the history and geographical distribution of a Caribbean dance and music idiom.

241. ———. "Labat's 'calenda': origin and associations." *La Torre*, ano 9, no. 32 (abril–junio 2004): 239–249. Discusses historical references to an African-derived drum and dance idiom of the West Indies.

242. Sager, Rebecca. "Letter from a CBMR Resident Rock[e]feller Fellow." *Cariso!*, No. 5 (2006): 14, 10–13. Sager describes the possibilities (and limitations) of using Peak-Motus digital motion capture technology to document and transcribe Caribbean music and dance styles. Based on the author's fieldwork in Haiti, the Dominican Republic and Martinique during 2005.

243. Scaramuzzo, Gene. "Magic music of the French Antilles. Part 3: The roots." *The Reggae & African Beat*, Vol. 6, No. 1 (1987): 20–23. Surveys the non-zouk offerings of Guadeloupe and Martinique— chouval bwa, gwo ka, biguine, jazz, folkloric groups, old-style dance orchestras, and more.

244. ———. "The other Caribbean: L'annee du zouk." *The Beat*, Vol. 12, No. 6 (1993): 32–35. Round-up of the top zouk recordings of 1993 followed by comments on the new Euzhan Palcy film *Simeon* which features a score by zouk supergroup Kassav.

245. ———. "The other Caribbean: Bitter medikamen." *The Beat*, Vol. 9, No. 2 (1990): 42, 44. Column on the steady decline of zouk recordings due to an overreliance on drum machines and formulaic production values.

246. ———. "The other Caribbean: Papa's got a brand new zoukcase." *The Beat*, Vol. 8, No. 5 (1989): 38–39, 56. Survey of recent zouk releases.

247. ———. "The other Caribbean: Zouk fever, latest outbreak." *The Reggae & African Beat*, Vol. 7, No. 2 (1988): 26–27. Snapshot of the current zouk scene followed by a round-up of recent releases.

248. ———. "The other Caribbean: Zouk galore." *The Beat*, Vol. 8, No. 2 (1989): 35, 48. Column on the current zouk scene and new releases from Michel Godzom, Guy Vadeleux, Serge Remion, the Zouk Allstars, and others.

249. ———. "The sounds of Summer." *The Beat*, Vol. 14, No. 5 (1995): 36–38. Round-up of Summer '95 Antillean recordings.

250. ———. "Zouk: magic music of the French Antilles." *The Reggae & African Beat*, Vol. 5, No. 4 (1986): 27–31, 33. The first major English-language feature on zouk and its rise in Guadeloupe, Martinique, and beyond, with particular attention to its best-known exponent, Kassav.

251. Snyder, Jared M. "Pumping and scraping: accordion music in the Caribbean." *Kalinda* (Summer 1995): 6–8. Describes a variety of folk and popular music traditions from the Caribbean and Latin America which use the accordion, e.g. Puerto Rican plena and Dominican merengue, Colombian vallenato, Haitian meringue, jing ping music from Dominica, and others.

252. Sommier, Claude. "Wa-bap: jazz et biguine." *Jazzman*, No. 175 (mars 1994): 4. Traces the history of Afro-Antillean biguine dance music and jazz from the 1930s to the 1990s.

253. Stapleton, Chris. "Kassav-a-go-go!" *Blues & Soul* (London), No. 481 (April 14–27 1987): 32–33. Conversation with Kassav keyboardist Jean-Claude Naimro about the reciprocal influence between Cameroonian makossa, Zairean soukous, and zouk.

254. Sueiro, Marcos. "Indecent kalinda." *Kalinda* (Summer 1994): 1–3. On a music and dance genre found throughout the Caribbean.

255. Weiss, Jason. "French-Caribbean music: an introduction." *Review: Latin American Literature and the Arts*, No. 58 (Spring 1999): 75–76. Brief review essay on recordings of French Antillean dance music released between the 1930s and the 1990s.

256. "Les zouks ont la part belle." *Fouyaya*, No. 52 (1986): 45–47. Looks at the economics of the music industry in the French Antilles.

Media Materials

*257. *La Musique Antillaise [videorecording]* / produced and directed by Tony Hall, et al. Port of Spain, Trinidad & Tobago: Banyan, c1991. 1 videocassette (ca. 30 min.). (Caribbean eye; [program 3]). Alt. title: Musique Antillean. Documentary surveying the roots of, and current trends in, French Antillean cadence and zouk.

Regional Studies

CANADA

258. Amedee, Alourdes. "Les chanteuses haitiennes a Montreal: des temoins d'une culture." *Canadian Folklore*, Vol. 15, No. 2 (1993): 95–106. Explores the role of singing in the lives of six Haitian women living in Montreal. Shows how traditional lullabies, story songs, and Vodou chants are used to connect the women with their Haitian past, to assist in child rearing and daily tasks, and finally, to give a sense of emotional and psychic solace in times of stress.

259. Juste-Constant, Voegeli. "Haitian popular music in Montreal: the effect of acculturation." *Popular Music*, Vol. 9, No. 1 (January 1990): 79–85.

*260. ———. "La musique populaire haitienne a Montreal." Thesis (M.A.)—Universite de Montreal, 1985. vii, 296 leaves: ill. + 1 audiocassette.

261. Villefranche, Robert, and Yves Bernard. "Petite histoire des musiques Afro-Montrealaises." *Canadian Folk Music Journal*, Vol. 17 (1989): 19–23. Short survey of Caribbean, Latin American and African musical activity in Montreal.

CUBA
See also 1246–1259

*262. Betancourt, Maria Teresa, and Florinda M. Sabido. "Influencia de la musica haitiana en la musica cubana." Trabajo de diploma—Instituto Superior de Arte (Cuba), 1987.

*263. Esquenazi Perez, Martha. "Apuntes para un estudio de la musica haitiana en Camaguey." In *Estudios etnologicos: 1989*, ed. Maria Elena Zulueta. La Habana: Editorial Academia, 1991.

264. ———. *Los cuentos cantados en Cuba*. Ciudad de La Habana, Cuba: Centro de Investigacion y Desarrollo de la Cultura Cubana Juan Marinello, 2002. Partial contents: Cuentos procedentes de Haiti. Study of Cuban story-songs, a tradition of storytelling in which songs play a key role.

265. Lapidus, Benjamin L. "An examination of the changui genre of Guantanamo, Cuba." Dissertation (Ph.D.)—City University of New York, 2002. xvi, 293 leaves: ill., music. Discography: leaves 287–291. Contents: Issues and claims surrounding the son's developmental and geographical trajectory; Historical overview of Guantanamo and changui — Como se toca se baila, como se baila se toca: the instruments and their roles in the changui ensemble — Styles of tres improvisation — The Afro-Haitian presence in eastern Cuba and its significance in the development of the Cuban son — Historicity and self-referencing in changui songs — The changui complex inside and outside of Guantanamo — Festivals, state-sponsored musical competitions for changui, and the process of folkloricization. Landmark ethnography of changui, a precursor to the Cuban son, based on fieldwork carried out in eastern Cuba during 1998.

266. ———. "Stirring the ajiaco: changui, son, and the Haitian connection." In *Cuban counterpoints: the legacy of Fernando Ortiz*, eds. Mauricio A. Font and Alfonso W. Quiroz. Lanham, MD: Lexington Books, 2005, pp. 237–246. Examines the contributions of Haitians brought to eastern Cuba during the 19th century to the evolution of Cuban son and changui.

267. Lapique, Zoila. "Aportes franco-haitianos a la contradanza cubana: mitos y realidades." In *Panorama de la musica popular cubana*, ed. Radames Giro. [2a ed.]. La Habana, Cuba: Editorial Letras Cubanas, 1998.

268. *Percussion Afro-Cubana. Vol. 1, Musica folklorica: percusion mayor y menor* / transcripcion, Adrian Coburg. 10. rev. ed. Bern, Suiza: A. Coburg, 2006, c2004. Partial contents: Toques haitiano-cubano — Tumba francesa. Transcriptions of a variety of folkloric rhythms for Afro-Cuban percussion instruments.

269. Ramos Venereo, Zobeyda. "Gaga. I. Cuba." In *Diccionario de la musica espanola e hispanoamericana*. [Madrid], 1999–2002, v. 5, pp. 302–303. Entry on Cuba's version of the Haitian music and dance style known as Rara.

270. Ruiz Miyares, Oscar. *Guia cultural de Santiago de Cuba*. Santiago de Cuba: Editorial Oriente, 1989 [i.e. 1990]. Includes entries on popular music (p. 52–54), folkloric troupes [Cutumba and De Oriente] (p. 55), and the tumba francesa (p. 72–73).

Articles

271. Barlow, Sean, and Christina Zanfagna. "Orienteering." *Folk Roots*, No. 241 (July 2003): 52–53, 55. Observations on the Franco-Haitian and African-derived musical traditions of Oriente province based on a recent trip to the island.

272. "Bohemia en Oriente: El Cocoye es el ultimo refugio de los descendientes de la esclavitud negra." *Bohemia*, ano 30, no. 3 (enero 16 1938): 40–41. Illustrated feature on the Haitian-Cuban Cocoye societies of Santiago de Cuba and their role as preservers of African-derived festival, music and dance traditions.

273. Chatelain, Daniel. "Musiques haitiennes a Cuba: influence et echanges." *Africultures*, No. 58 (janv–mars 2004): 87–98. Discusses the range of Haitian-derived musics found in Cuba today, i.e. tumba francesa, Vodu, Gaga.

*274. Esquenazi Perez, Martha. "Representacion cartografica de la musica popular tradicional en Holguin." *Anuario de Etnologia* [Havana] (1988): 148–174. Surveys the different types of folk musics currently performed in the urban and rural areas of eastern Holguin province. The area is notable for its concentration of descendants of Haitian and Jamaican sugar-cane workers who have each maintained their own musics.

275. Fals Castillo, Santiago. "Los complejos genericos de la musica cubana y sus fuentes." *Del Caribe*, No. 28 (1998): 53–57. On the various ethnic roots of Cuban music—Spanish, African, Franco-Haitian, Italian.

276. Gonzalez, David. "Transito cultural el tambor Assotor y su ritual de Benin a Haiti y a Cuba." *Del Caribe*, No. 50 (2007): 60–63. Traces the odyssey of a Vodou ritual drum from its origins in Benin to its New World homes of Haiti and Cuba.

277. Gonzalez Bello, Manuel. "Dahome, canto y danza de Haiti." *Bohemia*, ano 74, no. 43 (oct 22 1982): 20–21. Short feature on Haitian-derived music and dance traditions from Ciego de Avila in eastern Cuba.

278. Gutierrez, Pedro Juan. "Haitianos en Guantanamo: secretos bajo la piel." *Bohemia,* ano 87, no. 24 (nov 24 1995): 4–7. Feature on the Haitian cultural legacy in Guantanamo—Vodu and folk music and dance traditions such as the tumba francesa.

279. Morales Menocal, Alicia. "El bande rara haitiano." *Revolucion y Cultura* (agosto 1989): 32–39. Feature on Rara/Vodu music and dance traditions from the eastern Cuban town of Manati in Las Tunas province.

280. Pedro, Alberto. "La semana santa Haitiano-Cubano." *Etnologia y Folklore,* No. 4 (julio–dic. 1967): 49–78. Studies Easter week Rara/Vodu celebrations among the Haitian community of eastern Cuba (Camaguey/Oriente).

281. Rodriguez Valle, Juan Enrique. "Apuntes sobre un grupo de danzas haitianas en la provincia de Camaguey." *Signos* (Santa Clara), No. 17 (ano 6, no. 2–3) (mayo–dic. 1975): 50–58. Illustrated feature on folk music forms and musical instruments from Camaguey of Haitian origin.

282. Saenz, Carmen Maria. "Guantanamo, posibilidad sonora." *Revolucion y Cultura,* No. 3 (marzo 1985): 52–57. Feature on Afro-Cuban folk and popular music traditions from Guantanamo, e.g. changui, tumba francesa, and others.

Media Materials

*283. Daniel, Yvonne Payne. *Afro-Caribbean dance traditions: Cuba, Haiti, and Brazil, 1986–1992.* 35 hrs, 44 min. In-depth video documentation of Afro-Cuban dance traditions with a focus on rumba (with examples of professional, traditional, and general public performances by, among others, Danza Nacional, Conjunto Folklorico Nacional, Conjunto Folklorico de Oriente, and Cutumba). Also includes examples of Haitian traditions in Cuba such as the tumba francesa and Gaga, sacred dances derived from the Yoruba (Santeria), Kongo (Palo), Efik/Ejagham (Abakua), and Arara (Ewe-Fon) of West and Central Africa, and a few segments of dancing by carnival comparsas. [Held by the Smithsonian Institution, Human Studies Film Archives, Washington, DC / Call no.: HSFA 93.8.1]

Tumba Francesa

See also 270, 278, 282–283, 789–793, 1127–1129

284. Alen Rodriguez, Olavo. *La musica de las sociedades de la tumba francesa en Cuba.* Ciudad de la Habana, Cuba: Casa de las Americas, 1986. 271 p.: music. Contents: Introduccion historica — La observacion y descripcion de fiestas — Los instrumentos — El compose y su canto — El ritmo: duraciones temporales de los sonidos — El ritmo: distribucion de acentos. Detailed musicological study of tumba francesa music from eastern Cuba.

*285. ———. "Die Tumba-Francesa-Gesellschaften in Kuba." Gesellschaftswiss. Fak., Diss.—Humboldt Universitat (Berlin), 1979.

286. Armas Rigal, Nieves. *Los bailes de las sociedades de tumba francesa.* Ciudad de la Habana: Editorial Pueblo y Educacion, 1991. v, 34 p.: ill. Booklet on the folkloric dances and music of the Franco-Haitian tumba francesa groups of Santiago de Cuba and Guantanamo.

287. Boudreault-Fournier, Alexandrine. *The tumbas francesas societies in Cuba [electronic resource].* http://www.kanda7tumba.net/0000tumbafranc2.html. Essay based on fieldwork conducted in Guantanamo during July and August 2000.

*288. Tamames, Elisa. "La poesia en la tumba francesa." Tesis de grado—Universidad de La Habana (Cuba), 1955.

Book Sections

289. Alen Rodriguez, Olavo. "Afrikanische Musikeinfluesse in Kuba." In *Musikkulturen in Afrika*, ed. Erich Stockmann. Berlin: Verlag Neue Musik, 1987, pp. 292–304. Short essay on tumba francesa traditions in Santiago de Cuba.

290. ———. "Les afro-francais a Cuba." In *Les musiques guadeloupeennes dans le champ culturel Afro-Americain, au sein des musiques du monde: colloque de Pointe-a-Pitre, novembre 1986.* Paris: Editions Caribeennes, 1988, pp. 165–173. Conference paper on the Franco-Haitian tumba francesa societies of eastern Cuba.

291. ———. "Los afro-franceses en Cuba." In *Cuba et la France = Francia y Cuba.* Talence, France: Presses Universitaires de

Bordeaux, [1983], pp. 355–365. History of eastern Cuba's tumba francesa societies.

292. ———. "The Afro-French settlement and the legacy of its music to the Cuban people [tumba francesa]." In *Music and black ethnicity: the Caribbean and South America*, ed. Gerard H. Behague. New Brunswick, NJ: Transaction Publishers, 1994, pp. 109–117.

293. ———. *Pensamiento musicologico*. La Habana: Letras Cubanas, 2006. Partial contents: Tumbas para una fiesta de franceses — Las sociedades de tumba francesa en Cuba.

294. ———. "Tumba francesa." In *Diccionario de la musica espanola e hispanoamericana*. [Madrid], 1999–2002, v. 10, pp. 505–506.

295. ———. "The tumba francesa societies and their music." In *Essays on Cuban music*, ed. Peter Manuel. Lanham, MD: University Press of America, 1992.

296. Bettelheim, Judith. "The tumba francesa and tajona of Santiago de Cuba." In *Cuban festivals: a century of Afro-Cuban culture*, ed. Judith Bettelheim. Kingston: Ian Randle Publishers, etc., 2001, pp. 141–153. First published under title: *Cuban festivals: an illustrated anthology*. New York: Garland Pub., 1993.

297. Chatelain, Daniel. "Tumba francesa: permanece des 'noirs francais' dans la musique et la danse de Cuba." In *Musiques et societes en Amerique Latine*, ed. Gerard Borras. Rennes: Presses Universitaires de Rennes, 2000. (Mondes hispanophones; 25).

298. *Creoles de la Caraibe: actes du colloque international en hommage a Guy Hazael-Massieux, Pointe-a-Pitre, le 27 mars 1995* / sous la direction de Alain Yacou. Paris: Karthala, 1996, pp. 79–88, 143–145. Partial contents: Le creole de Saint-Domingue francais dans les tumbas francesas de Cuba / Alain Yacou — Remarques sur la musique des tumbas francesas de Cuba / Alex Petro. Two brief essays on tumba francesa, the Haitian-Cuban drum music from eastern Cuba.

299. Fernandez, Olga. *A pura guitarra y tambor*. Santiago de Cuba: Editorial Oriente, 1984, pp. 46–49. Reprint of a feature on the tumba francesa from *Cuba Internacional* (316).

300. *Fiestas populares tradicionales cubanas*. La Habana: Centro de Investigacion y Desarrollo de la Cultura Cubana Juan Marinello, etc., 1998. Includes section on tumba francesa traditions of eastern Cuba (p. 98–100).

301. Guanche, Jesus. *Procesos etnoculturales de Cuba.* Ciudad de La Habana: Editorial Letras Cubanas, 1983, pp. 279–283. Brief history of Cuba's tumbas francesas, the Afro-Haitian drum-dance societies found in Oriente province.

302. Johnson-La O, Sara Elizabeth. "Migrant recitals: Pan-Caribbean interchanges in the aftermath of the Haitian revolution, 1791–1850." Dissertation (Ph.D.)—Stanford University, 2001, pp. 84–123. Partial contents: Cinquillo consciousness: the formation of an inter-island consciousness. Chapter "explor[ing] musical production as a performative manifestation of regional integration. Using elements from Cuban tumba francesa, Puerto Rican bomba, and Martinican bele, I propose the existence of an inter-island musical aesthetic that was at the forefront of breaking colonial barriers"—Author abstract.

303. Kluge, Reiner. "Affektive Besetzungen von Trommel-Sehlag mustern in Tanzen der afro-kubanischen Tumba-francesa-Gesellschaften." In *Musikwissenschaft zwischen Kunst, Aesthetik und Experiment: Festschrift Helga de la Motte-Haber zum 60. Geburtstag.* Wurzburg: Konigshausen & Neumann, 1998, pp. 283–293.

304. Lammoglia, Jose A. "La tumba francesa: an Italian nun, a Haitian dance, Guantanamo City, and the new millenium." In *Dancing in the millenium: an international conference, proceedings.* Washington, D.C., 2000, pp. 277–281. Paper on the tumba francesa societies of Guantanamo.

305. Ramos Venereo, Zobeyda. "Bombo. V. Cuba." In *Diccionario de la musica espanola e hispanoamericana.* [Madrid], 1999–2002, v. 2, p. 601–602. Describes a drum used in the tumba francesa, tahona, and bembe ensembles of eastern Cuba.

Articles

306. Acosta, Alejandro G. "Contrapunto: La 'tumba francesa.'" *Cuba Internacional*, No. 175 (junio 1984): 84. A translation of this piece is also available in the English ed. of *Cuba Internacional* (Vol. 1, no. 1 (May 1985): 62).

307. Alen, Olavo. "Rhythm as duration of sounds in tumba francesa." *Ethnomusicology*, Vol. 39, No. 1 (Winter 1995): 55–71. Translation of chapter 5 from 284. Analysis of tumba francesa rhythmic patterns based on field recordings made by the author in Santiago de Cuba and Guantanamo in 1976.

308. ———. "Las sociedades de tumba francesa en Cuba." *Anales del Caribe del Centro de Estudios del Caribe*, No. 2 (1982): 223–230.

309. ———. "Las sociedades de tumba francesa en Cuba." *Santiago* (Santiago de Cuba), No. 25 (marzo 1977): 193–209. Looks at the historical circumstances under which the tumba francesa societies were introduced to Oriente province in the 19th century.

310. ———. "Die Tumba Francesa Gesellschaften in Kuba." *Beitrage zur Musikwissenschaft*, Jhrg. 28, Hft. 3 (1986): 167–188.

311. ———. "Tumbas para una fiesta de Franceses." *El Caiman Barbudo*, No. 75 (febrero 1974): 12–15. History of the tumba francesa and its leading exponents in eastern Cuba.

312. ———, and Laura Cruz. "La oralidad en la tumba francesa." *Oralidad* (La Habana), Vol. 13 (2005): 65–91. Also available online at: http://www.lacult.org/docc/REVISTA13.pdf. Special section devoted to the Haitian-Cuban tumba francesa tradition of Oriente province.

313. Bedia, Amanda. "Folklore: La tumba francesa." *Cuba Internacional*, No. 306 (mayo–junio 1997): 47.

314. Chatelain, Daniel. "Tradition: La tumba francesa." *Percussions*, No. 45 (mai–juin 1996): 39–47; No. 46 (juillet–aout 1996): 21–33. Very thorough history of eastern Cuba's tumba francesa tradition.

315. "De la tumba francesa." *Revolucion y Cultura*, No. 115 (marzo 1982): 55–56. Note on the history, past and present, of tumba francesa in Santiago de Cuba.

316. Fernandez, Olga. "Contrapunto: Fiesta de tambores." *Cuba Internacional*, No. 111 (febrero 1979): 65. Feature on the Franco-Haitian music-dance celebrations known as 'tumba francesa' from eastern Cuba. Reprinted in 299.

317. Gomez Ferrals, Marta. "La tumba francesa Pompadour." *Habanera: la revista de Cuba y sus amigos*, No. 20 (2001): 44–45. Feature on Asociacion Pompadour, the tumba francesa society from Guantanamo.

318. Gonzalez, Reynaldo. "Algo mas sobre la tumba francesa." *La Gaceta de Cuba*, No. 56 (marzo 1967): 11.

319. ———. "La tumba francesa." *Cuba Revolution et/and Culture* (La Habana), No. 4 (1966?): 26–45. Bi-lingual history (English/French)

of the Cuban-Haitian drum and dance groups found in eastern Cuba.

320. Marquez, Miguel Angel. "Las 'tumbas francesas.'" *Revista de Musica* (La Habana), ano 1, no. 2 (abril 1960): 62–67.

321. Martiatu, Ines Maria. "Costumbres y tradiciones: La tumba francesa." *Cuba Internacional*, No. 266 (feb. 1992): 69. On the Franco-Haitian dance-music tradition from eastern Cuba.

322. Martinez Gordo, Isabel. "Los cantos de las tumbas francesas desde el punto de vista linguistico." *Santiago*, No. 59 (sept. 1985): 33–71.

323. Munoz Lozano, Mario Jorge. "Tradiciones: De cuando el minue se fue de tumba." *Bohemia*, ano 96, no. 1 (enero 9 2004): 15–18. Feature on the Haitian-Cuban tumba francesa societies of Santiago de Cuba which have recently been named a 'cultural treasure' by UNESCO.

324. Nunes, Jorge, and Wilfredo Barban. "El seco sonar de los tambores." *Revolucion y Cultura*, No. 75 (nov. 1978): 78–80. Feature on the tumba francesa ensembles of Guantanamo and Santiago de Cuba.

325. Ortiz, Fernando. "Los bailes y cantos de las tumbas." *Bohemia*, ano 44, no. 6 (feb 6 1949): 20–22, 90–91, 97–98. Follow-up to an earlier feature by Ortiz (327) on the dances and songs of Guantanamo and Santiago de Cuba's tumba francesa groups.

326. ———. "Del folklore antillano afrofrances." *Bohemia*, ano 43, no. 34 (agosto 26 1951): 36–38, 116–117. Looks at the tumba francesa organizations of Guantanamo and Santiago de Cuba.

327. ———. "La musica de las tumbas." *Bohemia*, ano 41, no. 4 (enero 23 1949): 22–24, 93, 98, 105. Part one of a feature on the music of eastern Cuba's tumbas francesas.

328. Pelegrin Morales, Elsa. "La tumba francesa." *Verde Olivo*, ano 24, no. 4 (enero 27 1983): 62. On the tumba francesa tradition in Guantanamo.

329. Tamames, Elisa. "Antecedentes historicos de las tumbas francesas." *Actas del Folklore* (La Habana), ano 1, no. 9 (septiembre 1961): 7–13.

330. ———. "Antecedentes sociologicos de las tumbas francesas." *Actas del Folklore*, ano 1, no. 10–12 (oct.–dic. 1961): 25–32.

331. Viddal, Grete. "'Sueno de Haiti': danced identity in eastern Cuba." *Journal of Haitian Studies*, Vol. 12, No. 1 (Spring 2006): 50–64. Report on the tumba francesa societies of eastern Cuba with a focus on the work of Ballet Folklorico Cutumba.

DOMINICA
See also 154, 156, 183, 193, 197, 232–233, 251, 716, 885–886

332. Atwood, Thomas. *The history of the Island of Dominica, containing a description of its situation, extent, climate, mountains, rivers, natural productions, etc., together with an account of the civil government, trade, laws, customs, and manners of the different inhabitants of that Island, its conquest by the French, and restoration to the British Dominions.* London: F. Cass, 1971, p. 258, 262–263. Reprint of the 1791 ed. Brief observations on slave work songs and funeral music from Dominica.

*333. *Calypso Tempo.* [Roseau, Dominica?]: Movement for Cultural Awareness, 1997–. Dominican calypso journal.

334. Caudeiron, M.A. "Music and songs of Dominica." In *Our island culture* / by Lennox Honychurch. [Roseau: Dominica Cultural Council, 1982], pp. 26–31. Overview of the island's musical history and its multi-ethnic background—Amerindian, European (French, British), and West African. See also section on the island's dances (p. 36–38) which offers a survey of local folk idioms as well as drawings of the musical instruments used to accompany them.

335. *Chante dominitjen = Folk songs of Dominica* / collected by Alan Gamble. Roseau, Dominica: Dominica Institute, 1986. 64 p. of music: ill. Contents: Chante-mas and other social songs — Sa ki twavay: work songs — Hip hooray!: children's songs and games — Mese kwik...kwak!: songs in storytelling — Danse, danse, danse: dance tunes — Ouve pot la: sewinals and parish fetes — Gade nou: recent songs of development. Collection of Dominican folk songs.

336. Cyrille, Dominique. "Dance competition, tradition, and change in the Commonwealth of Dominica." *Cariso!: the newsletter of the Alton Augustus Adams Music Research Institute* (Spring 2004): 12, 8–11. Conversation with dancer Gilles Caban Jno Baptiste about quadrille and bele dance and music traditions in Dominica.

337. *Dominica's arts & culture magazine.* [Roseau, Dominica: Division of Culture, Commonwealth of Dominica, 2000?]. Partial contents:

Contemporary music in Dominica, 1950–2000 / Gregory Rabess — Steelband and calypso / Lan Jackson.

338. Henry, Steinberg D. "Language, music and the struggle for political and socio-economic change: the case of Dominica, 1974–1978." Thesis (M.A.)—University of Windsor, 1991. xxv, 136 leaves: ill. Analyses the contribution of calypso and cadence-lypso to the island's cultural and political resurgence during the mid-1970s.

339. ———. *A thick environment: [notes on Dominica's World Creole Music Festivals].* Roseau, Dominica: SHINC Productions, 2001. 51 p.: ill. Reflections on Dominica's World Creole Music Festival and what it means to the island's economy and sense of national identity.

*340. Louis, Cyrille. "Musical trends in Dominica: a survey of the evolution of Dominican music since the 1950s." Thesis (TER de maitrise)—Universite des Antilles et de la Guyane, Martinique, 2001. 91 leaves: col. ill.

341. Phillip, Daryl, and Gary Smith. *The heritage dances of Dominica.* Roseau: Govt. of Dominica, Division of Culture, 1998. viii, 181 p.: ill., music. Provides detailed analyses of Dominican bele and jing ping dances and their musical repertoires.

342. Stubbs, Norris. *A survey of the folk music of Dominica.* Roseau, Dominica: Dominica Arts Council, 1973. 17 p. Contents: Folk songs — Bele — Quadrille. Booklet surveying the major folk song styles of Dominica.

343. Thaly, Daniel. "Street cries of Martinique and Dominica." *West Indian Review*, Vol. 3, No. 8 (April 1937): 33–35. Describes the chants of island street vendors.

DOMINICAN REPUBLIC

344. Lizardo, Fradique. "Gaga. II. Republica Dominicana." In *Diccionario de la musica espanola e hispanoamericana.* [Madrid], 1999–2002, v. 5, pp. 303–304. On the music which accompanies Gaga, the Dominican Republic's version of Haiti's Rara processions.

FRANCE
See also 213, 700, 718, 911

345. Berliner, Brett A. *Ambivalent desire: the exotic black other in jazz-age France.* Amherst: University of Massachusetts Press, 2002, pp. 205–222. Discussion of the Paris nightclub Bal negre, a hot spot for French West Indian biguine music and dance during the late 1920s.

346. Birnbaum, Larry. "World music: The view from Paris." *Pulse!* [West Sacramento] (February 1996): 59–60, 62–63, 74. Feature on the world music scene in Paris with a focus on the cadence-lypso of Gordon Henderson and French Antillean zouk.

347. Decoret-Ahiha, Anne. "Danse sociale et interculturalite: la dansomanie exotique de l'entre-deux-guerres." In *Sociopoetique de la danse*, ed. Alain Montandon. Paris: Anthropos, 1998, pp. 505–519. Focuses on black social dances, both French Antillean and African American, performed in Paris between 1918 and 1940. Among the examples discussed are the houli, samba, black bottom, biguine, shimmy, and rumba.

348. ———. *Les danses exotiques en France: 1880–1940.* Pantin: Centre national de la danse, 2004, pp. 157–169. Section on French Antillean popular dances held in Paris during the 1920s and '30s.

349. Denis, Jacques. "L'esprit creole." *Vibrations* (Lausanne), No. 48 (novembre 2002): 48–55. Feature on the history of French Antillean musicians in Paris, past and present. Among the artists discussed are Al Lirvat, Ti Marcel, Henri Guedon, Roland Brival, and Guy Konket.

*350. Etienne, Jacob. "Les bals populaires des antillais en region Parisienne." Doctorat de 3e cycle—Universite de Paris 8, 1986. 247 leaves. Studies the ways in which popular dances held in French West Indian communities of Paris reflect upon ongoing cultural changes within French Antillean society as a whole.

351. Jattefaux, Maurice. *Apprenons a danser: tenue et maintien, principaux pas de la danse, rumba-biguine.* Paris: Librairie Garnier Freres, 1938. 351 p. Includes instructions on how to perform French ballroom versions of the biguine (p. 327–337), a dance from the French-speaking Caribbean.

352. Negrit, Frederic. *Musique et immigration dans la societe antillaise: en France metropolitaine de 1960 a nos jours* / prefaces

de Saul Escalona et Samuel Bordin. Paris: L'Harmattan, 2004. 400 p.: ill., music. Discography: p. [395]–397. These (doctorat)— Universite de Paris VIII, 2000. Scholarly study examining the post-1960 migration of French Antillean people and music to the Paris metropole.

FRENCH GUIANA (Guyane)
See also 56, 158, 168, 183, 185, 191, 193, 700

353. *Annou chante Nwel: recueil de cantiques traditionnels de Noel* / Bureau du Patrimoine Ethnologique; Conseil Regional de la Guyane. [French Guiana?]: The Bureau, 1994. 85 p. Collection of Christmas carol song texts from French Guiana.

354. Beaudet, Jean-Michel. "French Guiana." In *The new Grove dictionary of music and musicians*. 2nd ed. New York, 2001, v. 9, pp. 230–233. Survey article including sections on Creole and Maroon musical traditions.

355. Bilby, Kenneth M. "Making modernity in the hinterlands: new Maroon musics in the black Atlantic." In *Afrikanische Diaspora: out of Africa –into new worlds*, ed. Werner Zips. Munster: Lit, 2003, pp. [331]–359. Reprint of 364. Examines contemporary pop-influenced musics from Maroon communities in Colombia, French Guiana, and Suriname.

356. ———. "The remaking of the Aluku: culture, politics, and Maroon ethnicity in French South America." Dissertation (Ph.D.)—Johns Hopkins University, 1990. Ethnographic portrait of the Aluku (Boni) of French Guiana which includes a brief overview of their popular music styles—aleke and kaseko (p. 459–470).

357. Blerald-Ndagano, Monique. *Musiques et danses creoles au tambour de la Guyane Francaise*. Cayenne: Ibis Rouge Editions, 1996. 228 p.: ill. Study of the folk music and dances of French Guiana's black population. Includes illustrations of the dances being performed along with lyrics to the accompanying folk songs.

358. Bois, Pierre. "Franzosisch-Guayana." In *Festival traditioneler Musik '90: dhin dha tum tak = Trommler der Welt* / [Gesamtleitung, Habib H. Touma]. Berlin: Internationales Institut fur vergleichende Musikstudien, 1990, pp. 22–27. Essay on black drumming traditions in French Guiana.

359. Hurault, Jean. *Africains de Guyane: la vie materielle et l'art des noirs refugies de Guyane*. LaHaye: Mouton, 1970. Study of the

Boni maroon community of French Guiana. See plates 40, 42, 46 and 47 for illustrations of Boni apinti drums and drummers.

360. Jean-Louis, Marie-Paule. *Musiques en Guyane: 29 septembre–25 novembre 1989, Cayenne, Galerie de l'ARDEC.* [Cayenne]: Bureau du patrimoine ethnologique, Conseil regional Guyane, [1989]. 109 p.: ill. Partial contents: La musique aluku: un heritage africain / Kenneth Bilby — La musique creole: les formes de la tradition musicale en Guyane creole / Marie-Jose Jolivet — La musique guyanaise d'aujourd'hui: approche de la musique guyanaise / Christian Medus. Essays on Maroon and Creole musical traditions in French Guiana.

361. Lanou, Emile. *Itineraire de la musique instrumentale en Guyane.* Cayenne, Guyane francaise: Editions Anne C., 1999. 199 p.: ill., music. Contents: La periode classique: 1845–1881 — La periode creole: 1881–1945 — La periode moderne: 1945–1960 — La periode contemporaine: 1960. The first substantial history of dance music traditions in French Guiana from the mid-19th century to the present.

362. Pindard, Marie-Francoise. *Le graje de Guyane: musique traditionnelle creole.* Matoury, Guyane: Ibis Rouge, 2006. 122 p.: col. ill., music + 1 CD. Revision of author's thesis (master's)— Universite Francois Rabelais (Tours), 2002. Study of Graje, a creole folk dance music popular in towns north of Cayenne along the Atlantic coast of French Guiana.

Articles

363. Bilby, Kenneth. "Aleke: new music and new identities in the Guianas." *Latin American Music Review*, Vol. 22, No. 1 (Spring–Summer 2001): 31–47. Traces the development of Aleke, a form of Maroon popular music, in French Guiana and Suriname.

364. ———. "Making modernity in the hinterlands: new Maroon musics in the Black Atlantic." *Popular Music*, Vol. 19, No. 3 (October 2000): 265–292. Exploration of popular music production from the Maroon communities of French Guiana, Suriname, and Colombia. Includes discussion of work by the Wailing Roots and Anne Zwing. Reprinted in 355.

365. ———. "Maroons & reggae: the new music of French Guiana." *The Beat*, Vol. 10, No. 4 (1991): 34–38. Account of reggae produced by the Maroon community of French Guiana.

366. Chatillon, Marcel, et al. "Messe en cantiques pour les esclaves (1763)." *Bulletin de la Societe d'Histoire de la Guadeloupe*, No. 52 (1982): 39–63. Study of a mass performed for the slave population of French Guiana.

367. Planchet, Gael, and Emile Gana. "Musiques: Les Noirs marrons de Guyane." *Hommes & Migrations*, No. 1237 (mai–juin 2002): 125–130. Feature on music of the Maroon communities of French Guiana.

GUADELOUPE
See also 9, 12, 79, 154, 156, 158, 160, 168, 177–178, 185, 191–193, 197, 205, 216, 223, 230, 236, 243, 250

368. Benoit, Edouard. *Musique populaire de la Guadeloupe: de la biguine au zouk, 1940–1980*. Pointe-a-Pitre, Guadeloupe: Office regional du patrimoine guadeloupeen, etc., 1990. 127 p.: ill., music. French and Creole text.

369. Berard, Stephanie. "Au carrefour du theatre antillais: litterature, tradition orale et rituels dans les dramaturgies contemporaines de Guadeloupe et de Martinique." Dissertation (Ph.D.)—University of Minnesota, 2005, pp. 408–450. Chapter on the Afro-Guadeloupean drum and dance event known as 'lewoz.'

370. Blou, Lena. *Techni'ka: [recherches sur l'emergence d'une methode d'enseignement a partir des danses gwo-ka]*. Pointe-a-Pitre: Jasor, 2005. 221 p.: ill. Contents: De la gestation a l'analyse — La Techni'ka — Terminologie de la Techni'ka — Exercices adaptes en Techni'ka. Method illustrating the seven main dances of the gwo-ka complex, a drum-dance idiom of Guadeloupe, with details about their rhythms, musical accompaniment, terminology, and steps.

*371. Castry, Jean-Fred. *Le gwo-ka: de l'eveil musical a l'improvisation*. Le Moule [Guadeloupe]: Association DEFI-CEFRIM, 1997. 111 p. of music: ill. [Held by the Bibliotheque nationale de France]

*372. ———. *Gwoka: theorie de la musique: la methode moderne*. Le Moule [Guadeloupe]: Association DEFI-CEFRIM, 2005. 3 v.: ill. Contents: v. 1. Les reservoirs de notes dans la grande musique ka (modes, gammes) — v. 2. Exercices et etudes dans les gammes, modes et reservoirs de notes — v. 3. Tanbouka, la technique de base. Method for Afro-Guadeloupean gwo-ka drumming. [Held by the Bibliotheque nationale de France]

373. Chaudenson, Robert. *Des iles, des hommes, des langues: essai sur la creolisation linguistique et culturelle.* Paris: L'Harmattan, 1992, pp. 183–190. Discussion of Creole-language music traditions in Martinique and Guadeloupe.

*374. Divialle, Frederick. "Marche de la musique en Guadeloupe: quel poids dans l'economie et quelle place dans la poli[tiq]ue economique?" Thesis (Memoire de maitrise)—Universite des Antilles et de la Guyane, Guadeloupe, 2001. 115 p. Study of the music industry in Guadeloupe and its role in the economic and political life of the island.

375. Gabali, Joslen. *Diadyee.* Nouv. ed. Les Abymes [Guadeloupe]: Creapub', 2004. 190 p.: ill. First published: [Paris: Imprimerie Edit, 1980]. Note: In the 1980 ed. author's first name is spelled Jocelyn. Contents: Enumeration et explication des termes musicaux utilises par les paysans — Le gwoka dans d'autres occasions — Instruments de musique et formes musicales — Rapport entre la musique et la langue — L'etat actuel du gwoka. Study of Guadeloupean gwoka drum music.

376. Gerstin, Julian. "Martinique and Guadeloupe." In *The new Grove dictionary of music and musicians.* 2nd ed. New York, 2001, v. 15, pp. 929–932. Survey article.

377. Guilbault, Jocelyne. "Musique et developpement: le role du zouk en Guadeloupe." In *Musique et politique: les repertoires de l'identite,* ed. Alain Darre. Rennes [Ille-et-Vilaine]: Presses Universitaires de Rennes, 1996, pp. 305–321.

378. Hazael-Massieux, Marie-Christine. *Chansons des Antilles: comptines, formulettes.* Paris: L'Harmattan, 1996. 280 p.: music. First published: Paris: Editions du C.N.R.S., 1987. Contents: Berceuses ou jeux d'un adulte avec un enfant — Preliminaires et rites de jeu des enfants entre eux — Evocation ou description du monde environnant — Pieces pour divertissements collectifs avec meneur — La lanterne des magies. Study of folk songs for children (e.g. lullabies, counting and nursery rhymes, etc.) in Guadeloupe.

*379. Lancreot Uri, Francoise. "Recherche sur la musique populaire de la Guadeloupe." Doctorat (Nouveau Doctorat)—Universite de Paris IV, 1994. 2 v. (413, 263 leaves). History of popular music in Guadeloupe and its sources—African, Creole, European, and Amerindian.

380. Lockel, Gerard. *Traite de gro ka moden: initiation a la musique guadeloupeenne.* [Guadeloupe: G. Lockel, 1981]. 527 p.: ill. Contents: Les instruments — La gamme Gro Ka — Le phrase melodique — Les exercices en chiffres dans les intervalles de la gamme Gro Ka. Method book for learning Lockel's own version of gwoka which is a more formal, concert-oriented, version of Guadeloupe's traditional drum and dance idiom.

381. Mavounzy, Marcel Susan. *Cinquante ans de musique et de culture en Guadeloupe: memoires, 1928–1978.* Paris: Presence Africaine, 2002. 230 p.: ill. Discography: p. 227–230. First-person account of Guadeloupe's popular music scene and Carnival from the 1920s to the late 1970s. Also includes a biographical section with profiles of key musical figures (p. 195–220). An important resource.

382. *Les musiques guadeloupeennes dans le champ culturel afro-americain, au sein des musiques du monde: colloque de Pointe-a-Pitre, novembre 1986.* Paris: Editions Caribeennes, 1988. 261 p.: ill. Collection of conference papers devoted chiefly to folk music traditions from Guadeloupe.

383. Pentier, Fernand. *Musicalement de "La Creole" a "Musica."* [Saint-Claude: s.n., 1987]. 37 p.: ill. Traces the history of a Guadeloupean dance orchestra.

*384. Pitard, Eddy. *La musique Gwoka: elements de maitrise et de developpement.* [Guadeloupe]: KAribbean Music Art & Dance, [2004]. v.: ill. Contents: t. 1. Le Tanbouka: mieux connaitre l'instrument. Method for gwo ka drum music of Guadeloupe.

385. Pradel, Lucie. "Du ka au langage scenique: fondement esthetique." In *Les theatres francophones et creolophones de la Caraibe*, ed. Alvina Ruprecht. Paris: L'Harmattan, 2003, pp. 193–202. Essay on Guadeloupe's ka drum and its aesthetic as a possible foundation for Guadeloupean theatre practice.

386. Rey-Hulman, Diana. "Travailler pour les morts, chanter pour la vie a la Guadeloupe." In *Pour une anthropologie des voix*, eds. Nicole Revel and Diana Rey-Hulman. Paris: L'Harmattan, etc., 1993, pp. 141–171. Discussion of wake songs and music from Marie-Galante.

387. Rosemain, Jacqueline. *La musique dans la societe Antillaise: 1635–1902: Martinique Guadeloupe.* Paris: L'Harmattan, 1986. 183 p.: music. Contents: Les debuts de la colonisation (1635–1714) — L'age d'or de la colonisation (1714–1789) — La premiere

abolition de l'esclavage. La periode revolutionnaire francaise (1789–1802) — Le retour a l'esclavage (1802–1848) — La deuxieme abolition de l'esclavage et le Second Empire (1848–1870) — La Troisieme Republique (1870–1902).

*388. Sejor, Luc-Hubert, et al. *De la diversite des formes: Kakikateshisaka?* [Guadeloupe?: s.n., 199–?]. 44 p.: ill. On Gwoka music. [Held by the Universite des Antilles et de la Guyane, Pointe-a-Pitre, Guadeloupe]

*389. Solvet, Jean-Pierre. *Solfege du tambour ka: gwo-ka traditionnel.* Paris: L'Harmattan, 2007. 57 p.: ill. "Une methode simple pour jouer et ecrire tous les rythmes de Gwo-ka traditionnel de la Guadeloupe."

390. Succah, Frantz. "Le negre sans tambour." In *Guadeloupe: temps incertains*, eds. Marie Abraham et Daniel Maragnes. Paris: Autrement, 2001, pp. 161–167. (Autrement. Collection Monde; h.s. no. 95). Essay on gwoka drumming and dancing in Guadeloupe.

*391. Troupe, Georges. *Methode d'apprentissage des sept rythmes de Gwo Ka: graphie et musique.* [Guadeloupe]: I.G.E.S., [1988]. 16 p.: ill., music. Method illustrating the seven main rhythms of gwo ka drum music.

392. Uri, Alex, et Francoise Uri. *Musiques & musiciens de la Guadeloupe: le chant de Karukera.* Paris: Con Brio, 1991. 167 p.: ill. Oversize, beautifully illustrated, history of music in Guadeloupe.

Journals

393. *Son!* Abymes, Guadeloupe: Son, Residence les Quartiers, 1983–1984. No. 1–5 (1983–1984). "Magazine guadeloupeen d'informations: art, culture, musique."

Articles

394. Azoulay, Eliane. "Guadeloupe: l'ile des tambours." *Jazz Magazine* (Paris), No. 351 (juin 1986): 18–23. Feature on Batouka '86, a festival of world percussion traditions held in Guadeloupe, with a focus on the variety of styles found on the island.

395. Bensignor, Francois. "Musiques: Le gwo ka, nouvelle conscience des jeunes Guadeloupeens." *Hommes & Migrations*, No. 1214 (juil.–aout 1998): 105–113. Feature on gwo ka, the drum-dance music of Guadeloupe and its central role in the formation of

cultural nationalist identity on the island during the 1980s and 1990s.

396. Bertrand, Anca. "Folklore a la Guadeloupe: le Cercle de Culture Ansois." *Paralleles*, No. 14 (1966): 19–21. Report on folkloric music and dance traditions of the Guadeloupean countryside being studied and performed by the Centre Culturel Ansois' folklore division in Anse Bertrand.

397. Brisak, Nikol. "Mme Jacqueline Rosemain, 'notre musique va a la conquete du monde.'" *Jakata Magazine*, No. 7 (sept. 1987): 48. Conversation with Rosemain about her research into Antillean musics such as the gwo ka of Guadeloupe.

398. Cartagena, Juan. "Bomba in Puerto Rico, Lewoz in Guadeloupe: converging paths from the diaspora." *Guiro y Maraca*, Vol. 5, No. 3 (Fall 2001): 6, 9–10. Compares two forms of Afro-Caribbean drum music, Afro-Puerto Rican bomba and Guadeloupean gwoka.

399. Cesaire, Kristine. "La musique guadeloupeenne; est-elle en crise?" *Magazine Guadeloupeen*, No. 4 (fev–mars 1982): 7. Conversation with singer Hippomene Leauva about the state of the music scene in Guadeloupe. This is followed by an interview with record producer Henri Debs in which he is asked to respond directly to some of Leauva's complaints about local record companies and their practices regarding artists' rights and royalties.

400. Constant, Denis. "La route du rhum." *Jazz Magazine* (Paris), No. 355 (nov. 1986): 24–25. Impressions of the current folk and popular music scene in Guadeloupe.

401. Eli, Victoria. "Guadalupe: una de las islas sonantes." *Bohemia*, ano 82, no. 48 (nov 30 1990): 52–54. Description by a Cuban ethnomusicologist of a research trip to Guadeloupe and the types of music encountered.

402. Hazael-Massieux, Marie-Christine. "Des berceuses a la 'Lanterne des magies': regard sur le monde des comptines et refrains traditionnels en Guadeloupe." *Etudes Creoles*, Vol. 5, No. 1–2 (1982): 13–38. Study of Guadeloupean folk music for children, e.g. lullabies and counting rhymes.

403. Juraver, Jean. "Quadrille." *Son!* (Abymes), No. 3 (1984): 6. Looks at quadrille music in Guadeloupe.

404. Klein, Pamela. "Strong medicine: Guadeloupe's Zouk Radio gives zouk a home." *The Beat*, Vol. 19, No. 2 (2000): 34–35, 73. Feature on Zouk Radio, the Guadeloupean radio station.

405. Kurlansky, Mark. "Catching Guadeloupe's beat; Finding the island's musical heart at concerts, fairs and jam sessions." *New York Times* (August 5 1990): Sec. 5, pp. 8, 26. Travel feature on music in Guadeloupe, with a focus on zouk and gwoka activity in Pointe-a-Pitre and Basse-Terre. Includes a brief profile of gwoka moden guitarist and composer Gerard Lockel.

406. Lafontaine, Marie-Celine. "'Le carnaval de l''autre": a propos 'd'authenticite' en matiere de musique guadeloupeenne: theories et realities." *Les Temps Modernes* (Paris), Vol. 39, No. 441–442 (avril–mai 1983): "Antilles", pp. 2126–2173.

407. ———. "Le chant du peuple guadeloupeen, ou 'Plus c'est pareil et plus c'est different.'" *Cahiers d'Etudes Africaines*, No. 148 (1997): 907–942. Analysis of Guadeloupean 'lewoz' performances (verbal competitions) and wake songs.

408. ———. "Musique et societe aux Antilles: 'Balakadri' ou Le bal de quadrille au commandement de la Guadeloupe: un sens, une esthetique, une memoire." *Presence Africaine*, No. 121–122 (1982): 72–108.

409. ———. "Terminologie musicale en Guadeloupe: ce que le creole nous dit de la musique." *Langage et Societe*, No. 32 (juin 1985): 7–21. Also available online at: http://svr1.cg971.fr/lameca/dossiers/lafontaine-terminologie/index.htm. Examines creole terms and phrases used to describe folk idioms, musical instruments and performance practice in the Baie-Mahault region of Guadeloupe. Styles discussed include *lewoz*, *kadri* (Quadrille), *bigin* (Biguine), and *chante a veye* (wake songs).

410. Lancreot, Francoise. "Mizik: Es kadri e bigin se tan nou?" *Moun* (Pointe-a-Pitre), No. 1 (aout–oct. 1985): 19–21. Discusses the history and development of the biguine and quadrille in Guadeloupe.

411. ———. "Vaval: quelles musiques?" *Magwa* (Pointe-a-Pitre), No. 12 (jan.–fev. 1984): 27–28. Feature on Carnival music in Guadeloupe.

412. Lasserre, Karol. "Gwo-ka: ouvrir le debat." *Magazine Guadeloupeen*, No. 6 (juin 1982): 34–37. Outlines the history, structure and meaning of gwo ka drum music in Guadeloupe.

413. Lurel, Roger. "Yonnde pawol asou an mizik gwadloupeyen: 'Woule.'" *Antilla Kreyol*, No. 8 (juin 1987): 31–39. Offers a notational system for transcribing *woule*, a folk music and dance idiom from Guadeloupe.

414. Manuel, Sandra. "Bombance: groupe a pied et carnaval." *Le Naif* (Fort-de-France), No. 9 (mars–avril 1990): 23–24. Interview with the leaders of two Carnival bands from Martinique—La Sauss and Guanaval.

415. "Musicales: Syndicats des Auteurs Compositeurs [de Guadeloupe]." *Echo Jeunesse*, No. 23 (1989): 20. Report on a local musicians' rights organization in Guadeloupe.

416. Smith, CC. "The other Caribbean: Antilles encore." *The Beat*, Vol. 11, No. 1 (1992): 27–29, 60. Feature on the current music scenes of Martinique and Guadeloupe.

417. "Trois chansons guadeloupeennes." *Les Temps Modernes* (Paris), Vol. 5, No. 52 (February 1950): 1394–1396.

418. Virapin, Joce. "Construire un tambour ka." *Percussions*, No. 11 (mai 1991): 5–6. Instructions for making a ka drum.

419. Zandronis, Dannyck. "Gwo ka: le Boulaka, une nouvelle vibration." *Magazine Guadeloupeen*, No. 10 (jan–fev 1983): 25. Discusses an updated version of Guadeloupeen gwo ka known as *boulaka* (boula + ka).

Media Materials

*420. *Gwoka [videorecording]: l'ame de la Guadeloupe* / un film de Caroline Bourgine et Olivier Lichen. Paris: Home Sweet Home, 1995. 1 videocassette (55 min.). Documentary on the African-derived gwoka drum and dance music of Guadeloupe. See distributor's website for more information: www.zarafa-films.com. [Held by the Bibliotheque du Musee de l'Homme].

GUYANE
See **FRENCH GUIANA**

HAITI
See also 15–17, 32, 34, 92, 122, 124, 156, 168, 170, 176, 180, 182–183, 186, 189, 191, 193, 195, 200, 216, 235, 239, 242, 258–260, 262–331, 663, 667, 682–699, 701, 704–713, 1162–1163, 1272

421. Averill, Gage. *A day for the hunter, a day for the prey: popular music and power in Haiti.* Chicago: University of Chicago Press, 1997. xxviii, 276 p.: ill. Discography: p. 255–258. Contents: "Living from their own garden": the discourse of authenticity — "Konpa-direk for life": Francois Duvalier's dictatorship and konpa-direk — "Musicians are a single family": critical discourse in music under Baby Doc Duvalier — "Watch out for them!": Dechoukaj and its aftermath. Explores the interplay between political power and popular song in Haiti between 1915 and 1995.

422. *Brit kolobrit: introduction methodologique suivie de 30 chansons enfantines haitiennes: recueillies et classees progressivement en vue d'une pedagogie musicale aux Antilles* / Claude Dauphin. Sherbrooke, Quebec: Editions Naaman, 1981. 61 p. of music. Consists of a brief methodology for the teaching of Haitian children's songs followed by thirty song texts with music.

423. *Chansons de la montagne, de la plaine et de la mer* / [recueillies par] Rene Victor; preface de Jean Price-Mars; introduction et transcription musicale par Werner A. Jaegerhuber. Montreal: Memoire d'encrier, [2007]. 141 p.: ill., music. A collection of Haitian folk songs, with commentary by Rene Victor, completed during the late 1930s but published here for the first time. Contents: Introduction: Les origines de la musique folklorique haitienne / Werner A. Jaegerhuber — Chansons de nos mariniers — Transcriptions des chants de la mer — Chansons de la montagne et de la plaine — Transcriptions musicales des chants de la montagne et de la plaine.

424. Dauphin, Claude. *La chanson haitienne folklorique et classique.* Montreal, Canada: Societe de Recherche et de Diffusion de la Musique Haitienne, 1983. 25 p.: music. Analysis of Haitian folk (p. 3–10) and art song traditions (p. 11–23).

*425. ———. *Guide d'organologie haitienne.* Montreal: Centre de Recherches Caraibes, Universite de Montreal, 1980. 8 leaves: ill. [Copy held by the University of Montreal]

426. Denis, Lorimer, and Emmanuel C. Paul. *Essai d'organographie haitienne.* Port-au-Prince: Impr. V. Valcin, 1947. 38, [1] p.: ill. (Haiti. Bureau d'ethnologie. Publication. Serie II, no. 4). Contents: Instruments par percussion — Instruments par secouement — Instruments par frottement — Instruments a air — Instruments a cordes. Short survey of Haitian musical instruments.

427. Haiti. Bureau d'Ethnologie. *Folklore enfantin: chants et jeux des enfants haitiens.* Port-au-Prince: Imprimerie de l'Etat, 1949. 70 p.: ill., music. (Publication du Bureau d'Ethnologie de la Republique d'Haiti; Ser. II, No. 6). Collection of children's games and songs. Each song is accompanied by extensive notes discussing their respective meanings and method of performance.

428. Haiti. Bureau d'ethnologie. *Quelques aspects de notre folklore musical.* Port-au-Prince: Impr. de l'Etat, 1950. 48 p.: ill., music. (Publication (Haiti. Bureau d'ethnologie). Serie 2; v. 7). Surveys the various types of sacred and secular folk songs found in Haiti—historical, Vodou, lyric, children's, and Carnival.

429. Institut Musical d'Haiti. *Chansons populaires, composees en l'honneur du chef spirituel de la nation—.* Port-au-Prince: S. Bissainthe, [1958]. 62 p. Collection of song texts in tribute to Francois 'Papa Doc' Duvalier, the late Haitian dictator.

430. Jean-Pierre, Jean Sylvio. *30 ans de musique populaire haitienne: les moments de turbulence (1960–1990).* Port-au-Prince, Haiti: J.S. Jean-Pierre, etc., 2002. 155 p.: ill. Revision of author's thesis (licencie)—Universite d'Etat d'Haiti. Short survey of developments in Haitian popular music from 1960 to 1990.

431. Paul, Emmanuel. *Nos chansons folkloriques et la possibilite de leur exploitation pedagogique.* Port-au-Prince: Presses Libres, 1951. 38 p. Essay on the educational potential of Haitian folk songs.

432. Preval, Guerdy. *La musique populaire haitienne de Iere coloniale a nos jours.* Montreal: Histoires Nouvelles, 2003. viii, 325 p.: ill. "Meringue, calinda, troubadour, orchestre, jazz folklorique, mini-jazz, nouvelle generation, racines, ragga"—Cover. History of post-WWII developments in Haitian dance music from Nemours Jean-Baptiste to the present.

433. Vallon, Jean Lesly. *What you should know about Haitian music and the evolution of Compas Direct.* Bloomington, IN: AuthorHouse, 2007. xiii, 103 p.: ill. Useful English-language survey of Haitian popular music covering its evolution from 1955 to 2005.

434. *The voice of Haiti: an unusual collection of original native ceremonial songs, invocations, voodoo chants, drum beats and rhythms, stories of traditions, etc., of the Haitian people* / by Laura Bowman and Le Roy Antoine. New York: Clarence Williams Music

Publishing, 1938. 1 score (41 p.). Anthology of Haitian secular and sacred folk songs.

Book Sections

435. Averill, Gage. "Caribbean musics: Haiti and Trinidad and Tobago." In *Music in Latin American culture: regional traditions*, ed. John M. Schechter. New York: Schirmer Books, 1999. Introductory survey of Caribbean musics which includes details on Vodou and Rara musics in Haiti (p. 143–161) and the Haitian troubadour and politician Manno Charlemagne (p. 161–166).

436. ———. "Haiti." In *The new Grove dictionary of music and musicians*. 2nd ed. New York, 2001, v. 10, pp. 673–679. Detailed survey article offering an overview of folk and popular music traditions on the island.

437. ———. "Haitian music in the global system." In *The reordering of culture*, ed. Alvina Ruprecht. Ottawa: Carleton University Press, 1995, pp. 339–362. Examines the impact of the global 'world music' market on Haitian popular music.

438. ———. "'Mezanmi, kouman nou ye? My friends, how are you?': musical constructions of the Haitian transnation." In *Ethnomusicology: a contemporary reader*, ed. Jennifer C. Post. New York: Routledge, 2006.

439. ———. "Se kreyol nou ye'/'We're creole': musical discourse on Haitian identities." In *Music and black ethnicity: the Caribbean and South America*, ed. Gerard H. Behague. New Brunswick, NJ: Transaction Publishers, 1994, pp. 157–185.

440. ———, and Yuen-Ming David Yih. "Militarism in Haitian music." In *The African diaspora: a musical perspective*, ed. Ingrid Monson. New York: Garland Pub., 2000; New York: Routledge, 2003, pp. 267–293. Examines the influence of Haitian militarism in the island's music.

441. Barthelemy, Gerard. *Creoles – bossales: conflit en Haiti*. Petit-Bourg, Guadeloupe: Ibis rouge editions, 2000, pp. 153–177. Partial contents: Une societe du tambour: la danse de l'esclave. Covers dance and music traditions in colonial Haiti.

442. Bergman, Billy. "Rara." In *Hot sauces: Latin and Caribbean pop*. New York: Quill/Morrow, 1985, pp. 83–93. Overview of folk and popular music traditions in Haiti.

443. Butler, Melvin L. "Dancing around dancehall: popular music and Pentecostal identity in transnational Jamaica and Haiti." In *Constructing vernacular culture in the trans-Caribbean*, eds. Holger Henke and Karl-Heinz Magister. Lanham, MD: Lexington Books, 2008, pp. 63–99. Examines social tensions between secular youth-oriented musics such as Haitian compas and Jamaican dancehall and the religious music and culture of Pentecostalism in Haitian and Jamaican communities based in the Caribbean and the United States.

444. Courlander, Harold. *The drum and the hoe: life and lore of the Haitian people*. Berkeley: University of California Press, 1960. Partial contents: Songs of the peristyle [Vodou] — Mardi Gras and Rara — Songs of complaint, recrimination, and gossip — Comments on the mighty: political songs — Songs of bravado and boasting — Secret-society songs — Children's world: gage songs and games — Musical instruments — The music: musical notations by Mieczyslaw Kolinski of 186 songs and drum rhythms — Appendix 5: Translations of songs in Chapter 19. Landmark study of Haitian folk song, sacred and secular, based on fieldwork carried out between 1937 and 1955. *See also* 516–518.

445. ———. *Haiti singing*. New York: Cooper Square Publishers, 1973, pp. 62–[226]. Reprint. First published: Chapel Hill: University of North Carolina Press, 1939. Partial contents: Non-Vodoun sources of folk music — Haiti singing — Drum music for two dances — Music for the songs. Important early study of Haitian folk music.

446. Dash, J. Michael. *Culture and customs of Haiti*. Westport, CT: Greenwood Press, 2001, pp. 119–133. Contemporary overview of Haitian folk and popular musical styles.

447. Dauphin, Claude. "Genese et eclosion du metalanguage musical dans le conte-chante haitien." In *Ethnomusicology in Canada*, ed. Robert Witmer. Toronto: Institute for Canadian Music, 1990, pp. 271–276.

448. Dumerve, Constantin. "An annotated translation thesis of Constantin Eugene Moise Dumerve's Histoire de la musique en Haiti = The history of music in Haiti, 1968: from French to English" / by Jean Montes. Dissertation (D.M.A.)—University of Iowa, 2003. xi, 335 leaves: ill. English translation of 449.

449. ———. *Histoire de la musique en Haiti*. Port au Prince: Imprimerie des Antilles, 1968. Although Dumerve focuses on

Haitian art music traditions he does include two brief sections on sacred (p. 285–286) and popular musics [meringue] (p. 307–312).

450. Gradante, William. "Coumbite songs." In *The new Grove dictionary of music and musicians*. London, 1980, v. 4, pp. 832–833. Brief entry on a type of Haitian work song.

451. Kolinski, Mieczyslaw. "Haiti." In *The new Grove dictionary of music and musicians*. London, 1980, v. 8, pp. 33–37. Survey article which focuses on the sacred music of Haitian Vodou and work songs of the agricultural cooperatives known as coumbites.

452. ———. "Songs of Haiti." In *Suriname folk-lore* / Melville J. Herskovits and Frances S. Herskovits. New York: Columbia University Press, 1936, pp. 701–706. Transcriptions and analyses of songs based on field recordings made by Melville J. and Frances S. Herskovits. *See also* 600.

453. Lassegue, Frank. *Ciselures*. Albert [France]: Librairie R. Crossel, [1928], pp. [9]–33. Discussion of Vodou, classical and folkloric music traditions in Haiti.

454. Paul, Emmanuel C. *Notes sur le folk-lore d'Haiti: proverbes et chansons*. Port-au-Prince: Imp. Telhomme, 1946, pp. 33–80. Partial contents: Modalite d'une sanction sociale: nos chansons populaire — Place du chant dans notre folklore. Covers both sacred and secular song traditions.

455. ———. *Panorama du folklore haitien: presence africaine en Haiti*. Port-au-Prince: Impr. de l'Etat, 1962, pp. 29–93. Partial contents: Les chansons folkloriques — Les danses folkloriques — Les instruments de musique. Discussion of Haitian folk music and dance traditions, both sacred and secular.

456. Richman, Karen E. *Migration and vodou*. Gainesville: University Press of Florida, 2005, pp. 221–249. Revision of 470. Examines the social function of 'pwen songs' (songs of social criticism) in Leogane, a town in northern Haiti, and two communities of migrants from Leogane based in South Florida and Virginia. Accompanied by a CD of songs discussed in the book.

457. Romain, J.B. *Quelques moeurs et coutumes des paysans haitiens: travaux pratiques d'ethnographie sur la region de Milot a l'usage des etudiants*. [Folcroft, PA]: Folcroft Library Editions, 1974. Reprint. First published: Port-au-Prince: Imp. de l'Etat, 1959. (Revue de la Faculte d'Ethnologie; no. 2). Includes a section on

folk songs, secular and sacred, from Milot, Haiti, along with a
brief portrait of an Assotor drum (p. 134–147).

458. Schmiderer, Stephanie. "'Let's give thanks to all the Lwa':
Haitianische Gotter in der Hitparade. Vodou als Quelle fur
gesellschaftskritische Popmusik in Haiti und der US-Diaspora."
In *Afrikanische Diaspora: out of Africa –into new worlds*, ed.
Werner Zips. Munster: Lit, 2003, pp. [267]–290. Looks at Vodou as
a theme in the Haitian dance band music of Boukman
Eksperyans, Ram, Rara Machine, and others.

459. Smith, Jennie Marcelle. *When the hands are many: community
organization and social change in rural Haiti*. Ithaca: Cornell
University Press, 2001, pp. 45–68. Chapter examining the uses of
chante pwen (songs of derision and social criticism) in Grand'Anse,
Haiti. Explores their political impact in folk and popular contexts
such as the *konbit*, Rara, and civic organization meetings.

460. Steward, Sue. "Compas, carnival and Voodoo: Haiti's joyful dance
music transcends the island's troubles." In *World music: the rough
guide*, eds. Simon Broughton, et al. London: Rough Guides, 1994,
pp. 498–504.

461. Sweet, James H. "The evolution of ritual in the African diaspora:
Central African Kilundu in Brazil, St. Domingue, and the United
States, seventeenth-nineteenth centuries." In *Diasporic Africa*, ed.
Michael A. Gomez. New York: New York University Press, 2006,
pp. 64–80. Examines the origins and evolution of the *lundu* from
its earliest incarnation as a Kongolese divination/healing ritual to
its emergence as a secular drum and dance idiom with broad
popularity among Afro-Brazilians in the 19th century. Includes
speculation about the idiom's possible links to related drum and
dance styles in Haiti (calenda) and the United States (ring shout).

462. Wilcken, Lois. "Hosts, guests, and sacred souvenirs: the tourist-
drum as a measure of intergroup understanding in Haiti." In
*Come mek me hol' yu han': the impact of tourism on traditional
music*. Kingston: Jamaica Memory Bank, 1988. Conference paper
examining the effects of tourism on folk music traditions in Haiti.

Dissertations and Theses

*463. Averill, Gage. "Haitian dance band music: the political economy of
exuberance." Dissertation (Ph.D.)—University of Washington,
1989. xi, 362 leaves: ill., music + 1 audiocassette + 1 videocassette
(30 min.).

464. Boutros, Sandra Kathleen. "Altered states: travel, transcendence and technology in contemporary Vodou." Dissertation (Ph.D.)—McGill University (Canada), 2007, pp. 75–108. Partial contents: Vodou groove (or transnational tricks of transmission): the role of popular music in the dissemination of Vodou cosmology. Examines how Vodou imagery is conveyed to popular audiences via the music of Boukman Eksperyans, Vodu 155, D'Angelo, and Wyclef Jean.

465. Cancado, Tania Mara Lopes. "An investigation of West African and Haitian rhythms on the development of syncopation in Cuban habanera, Brazilian tango/choro and American ragtime (1791–1900)." Dissertation (D.M.A.)—Shenandoah University, 1999. xxi, 241 leaves: music.

*466. Dauphin, Claude. "La composition de la musique haitienne." Thesis (M.A.)—Universite de Montreal, 1981. iv, 143 leaves.

467. Greene, Barbara Joyce. "African musical survivals in the songs of the Negro in Haiti, Jamaica, and the United States." Thesis (M.A.)—University of Chicago, 1948, pp. 12–33, 70–76. Highly speculative analysis of African retentions in the songs of Haiti.

*468. Lefebvre, Genevieve. "Le 'compas' haitien: un pont musical entre le passe et le present." Thesis (M.A.)—Universite de Montreal, 1991. viii, 106 leaves: ill. + 1 audiocassette. Includes an analysis of music by Tabou Combo and Boukman Eksperyans.

469. Parker, Don Nigel. "An analysis of borrowed and retained West African, Cuban, and Haitian rhythms in selected percussion ensemble literature." Dissertation (D.M.A.)—University of Texas at Austin, 1996, pp. 343–465. Surveys the culture, music, musical instruments, and rhythms of Haiti before proceeding to a detailed analysis of Christopher Rouse's composition "Ogoun Badagris" and its use of elements from Haitian folkloric music.

470. Richman, Karen E. "'They will remember me in the house': the *pwen* of Haitian transnational migration." Dissertation (Ph.D.)—University of Virginia, 1992. Includes a discussion of *pwen* songs (songs of social criticism) and their use in the northern Haitian town of Leogane (p. 334–347, 360–368).

Articles

471. Amer, Michel, and Jean Coulanges. "Mini-Jazz: sens & significations." *Lakansiel*, No. 2 (1975): 8–21. Traces the

development of Haitian popular dance music from the 1940s to the 1970s. Among the groups and trends covered are the neo-folklore of Jazz des Jeunes and Haitian choral groups of the 1940s and '50s, the 'yeye' (Western-style pop) and 'compas direct' styles of the 1950s and '60s, and mini-jazz, a speeded up, guitar-based version of compas introduced in the mid-'60s.

472. Amoruso, Carol. "The return of the Haitian troubadours." *Global Rhythm*, Vol. 12, No. 7 (July 2003): 38–40. Feature on the recent revival of interest in twoubadou music among Haitian popular singers.

473. "Association des Producteurs (dossiers complets)." *Haiti Culture*, Vol. 5, No. 9 (oct. 1989): 4–5, 23, 27, 29–30. Feature on a meeting of leading Haitian record producers who have convened in order to air their complaints against the distributor African Records. Offers insights into some of the many problems facing the Haitian record industry and its artists.

474. Averill, Gage. "Haitian dance bands, 1915–1970: class, race, and authenticity." *Latin American Music Review*, Vol. 10, No. 2 (Autumn–Winter 1989): 203–235. Detailed social history of Haitian dance band music foregrounded by an analysis of the country's deep class and racial divisions. Includes discussion of styles such as the meringue, 1930s jazz bands, Cuban-influenced troubadour music, 1940s Vodou-jazz (Jazz des Jeunes, Orchestra Saieh), 1950s compas direct (Nemours Jean-Baptiste, Weber Sicot), combo and vocal jazz (late '50s/early '60s), yeye (Western-style rock) of the early '60s, and guitar-based mini-jazz bands of the mid-'60s and beyond.

475. ———. "Haitian fascination. All together now: sampling the samplers." *The Beat*, Vol. 8, No. 6 (1989): 42–44. Tells the story behind the making of "Konbit: burning rhythms of Haiti," a CD sampler compiled by Jonathan Demme, Fred Paul and Gage Averill.

476. ———. "Haitian fascination: New sounds for a new age." *The Beat*, Vol. 8, No. 4 (1989): 32–33, 56. Traces the genesis and development of the Nouvelle Generation movement in Haitian dance music led by artists such as Zekle, Emeline Michel, and others.

477. ———. "Haitian fascination: The season of living dangerously— elections, coups and carnival." *The Beat*, Vol. 10, No. 2 (1991): 20–

23, 69. Report on the musical soundscape accompanying Haiti's 1990 elections, the subsequent coup, counter-coup, inauguration and 1991 Carnival.

478. ———. "'Mezanmi, kouman nou ye? My friends, how are you?': musical constructions of the Haitian transnation." *Diaspora* (New York), Vol. 3, No. 3 (Winter 1994): 253–271. Reprinted in 438.

479. Barlow, Sean. "Elizabeth McAlister 2007 [electronic resource]." http://www.afropop.org/multi/interview/ID/120/Elizabeth+ McAlister+2007. Interview with McAlister, a scholar of Haitian religion at Wesleyan University, about the island's tumultous history and rich musical soundscape. Includes discussion of a wide range of idioms ranging from work songs and Vodou ritual music to Rara, *konpa* and the hiphop fusions of Wyclef Jean.

480. Birnbaum, Larry. "Voodoo on the jukebox." *Pulse!* [West Sacramento] (November 1992): 56–58. Feature on the Vodou rock and roots music (*mizik rasin*) movement in recent Haitian popular music. Gives special attention to work by Boukman Eksperyans, Rara Machine and Foula.

481. ———. "Voodoo roots, crossover dreams: Haiti's musical revolution." *Schwann Spectrum*, Vol. 6, No. 5 (Winter 1995–96): 6–9, 28–30.

482. Boncy, Ralph. "Haiti: les ondes tropicales." *Rythmes* (Montreal), Vol. 3, No. 2 (1995): 9–11. Feature on the popular music scene in Haiti.

483. ———. "Nouvelle musique haitienne: De Nemours ... a Bethova." *Conjonction*, No. 176 (1987): 160–176. Historical overview of Haitian popular music and its development between 1965 and 1985.

484. Comhaire-Sylvain, Suzanne. "La chanson haitienne." *Presence Africaine*, No. 12 (1951): 61–87. Essay on Haitian folk music, sacred and secular.

485. Courlander, Harold. "Haiti's political folk songs." *Opportunity; Journal of Negro Life*, Vol. 19, No. 4 (April 1941): 114–118.

486. ———. "Musical instruments of Haiti." *Musical Quarterly*, Vol. 27, No. 3 (July 1941): 371–383. Includes illustrations.

487. ———. "Profane songs of the Haitian people." *Journal of Negro History*, Vol. 27, No. 3 (July 1942): 320–344. On secular songs of Haiti's coumbites and bambouches.

488. Dauphin, Claude. "Le cont-chante comme lieu d'accumulation d'un savoir musical." *Yearbook of the International Folk Music Council*, Vol. 12 (1980): 77–83. Examination of Haitian story-songs for children.

489. ———. "Cuatro palabras sobre la musica haitiana." *Musica* (Casa de las Americas), No. 74–75 (enero–abril 1979): 11–17. Overview of Haitian musical idioms—folk, popular and art.

490. ———, and Liliane Devieux. "Conte et musique en Haiti: le cas de 'L'os qui chante.'" *Etudes Creoles* (Montreal), Vol. 8, No. 1–2 (1985): 23–39. Case study of a Haitian story-song.

491. Dorisca, Pierre-Antoine. "La musique a travers l'histoire d'Haiti." *Ecouter Voir*, No. 44–45 (aout–sept. 1995): 4–7. Short historical survey of music and its evolution in Haiti.

492. Fleischmann, Ulrich, and Alrich Nicolas. "Jedes Land soll seine Sprache sprechen: die Kadans-Musik aus Haiti." *Rock Session* (Reinbeck), No. 7 (1983): 33–43. Essay on popular dance music in Haiti.

493. Fleurant, Gerdes. "The song of freedom: Vodun, conscientization and popular culture in Haiti." *Compost* (Jamaica Plain), No. 5 (1995): 69–74; *Journal of Haitian Studies*, Vol. 2, No. 2 (Autumn 1996): 115–130. Looks at the interplay between politics and music in Haiti from the 18th century to the roots music (*mizik rasin*) movement of the late 1980s and '90s.

494. Franco, Jose L. "Tambores de Haiti." *Carteles*, ano 34, no. 10 (marzo 8 1953): 62. Short feature on an exhibition of Haitian drums held in Havana, Cuba.

495. Gonzalez, Fernando. "Mizik rasin: rhythm and roots of Haiti." *Miami Herald* (Apr. 10 1994): I6. Long feature on Haiti's roots music movement, a new arrival on the scene which merges elements of rock with folkloric rhythms from Rara and Vodou.

496. Gordon, Leah. "Letter from Haiti." *The Wire* (London), No. 125 (July 1994): 9. Looks at the problems facing Haiti's pop music scene due to the island's unsettled political situation.

497. Herard, Huguette. "Le theme de la femme dans la musique haitienne." *Les Cahiers de l'INAGHEI*, Vol. 2, No. 2 (avril–juin 1982): 12–19. On women as a theme in Haitian popular music.

498. Honorin, Emmanuelle. "La musique haitienne: grande histoire et petits dieux." *Africultures*, No. 58 (janv–mars 2004): 78–86.

499. Jaegerhuber, Werner A. "Les origines de la musique folklorique haitienne." *Cahiers d'Haiti*, Vol. 1, No. 5 (December 1943): 53, 55.

500. Laguerre, Ferere. "De la musique folklorique en Haiti." *Conjonction*, No. 126 (juin 1975): 9–31. Survey of Haitian folk idioms and instruments, sacred and secular.

501. Legros, Gloria. "Mini-jazz, maximum trouble." *Collusion* (London), No. 4 (Feb–Apr 1983): 37–39. Looks at the image of women in the lyrics of Haiti's mini-jazz dance groups.

502. McAlister, Elizabeth. "Ton Ton club." *Mirabella*, Vol. 1, No. 8 (January 1990): 56–57. Discusses the new openness in Haiti's pop music scene in the years following Baby Doc Duvalier's overthrow.

503. McLane, Daisann. "The Haitian beat thrives in times of suffering." *New York Times* (March 8 1992): Sec. 2, pp. 31–32. Surveys the range of musics coming out of contemporary Haiti and its diaspora—*mizik rasin*, Rara, *nouvel jenerasyon*, and compas, with a focus on current star Boukman Eksperyans.

504. Racine-Toussaint, Marlene, and Lois Wilcken. "Transcribing tradition: 'Rel pou Ayiti.'" *Journal of Haitian Studies*, Vol. 10, No. 2 (Fall 2004): 74–76. Transcription of a song written to commemorate the Haitian bicentennial.

505. Rohter, Larry. "Music returns to Haiti with the spirit of hope." *New York Times* (December 27 1994): C13, C18. On the return of popular music to Haiti's stages and airwaves following the ousting of the military junta which had banned and exiled many of the country's leading performers.

506. Schwartz, Timothy T. "Subsistence songs: Haitian 'teat' performances, gendered capital, and livelihood strategies in Jean Makout, Haiti." *Nieuwe West-Indische Gids*, Vol. 81, No. 1–2 (2007): 5–35. Examines how female sexuality and gender issues are addressed in songs performed by rural adolescent girls from Jean Makout in theatrical performances known as 'teat.'

507. Scott-Lemoine, Jacqueline. "Musique en Haiti." *Presence Africaine*, No. 169 (2004): 157–166. Personal tribute to the music of Haiti.

508. Simpson, George E. "Peasant songs and dances of northern Haiti." *Journal of Negro History*, Vol. 25, No. 2 (April 1940): 203–215. Documents songs performed as part of coumbite harvest activities and rural social dances known as 'bals.' Based on fieldwork conducted near the village of Plaisance in 1937.

509. Smith, CC, and Gerard Tacite Lamothe. "Legends of Haitian music." *The Reggae & African Beat*, Vol. 6, No. 2 (1987): 14–18; Vol. 7, No. 2 (1988): 30–37. Two-part history of Haitian dance band music starting in the late 1940s with pioneers such as Jazz des Jeunes, Nemours Jean-Baptiste and Weber Sicot, and continuing up to the 1980s.

510. Smith, Jennie M. "Singing back: the chan pwen of Haiti." *Ethnomusicology*, Vol. 48, No. 1 (Winter 2004): 105–126. Essay on songs of social critique known as *chan pwen*, literally 'pointing songs,' used to mock, taunt, chastise, shame or threaten.

511. Toro. "Music of Haiti." *Sing Out!,* Vol. 25, No. 5 (Jan–Feb 1977): 2–5.

512. White, Clarence Cameron. "A musical pilgrimage to Haiti, the island of beauty, mystery, and rhythm." *The Etude Music Magazine*, Vol. 47, No. 7 (July 1929): 505–506. Comments from a noted African American composer on the folk music of Haiti.

513. Widmaier, Mushi. "Musique haitienne." *Conjonction*, No. 206 (2001): 75–85. Historical survey intended for the as-yet-unpublished *Dictionnaire Encyclopedique d'Haiti*.

514. Wilcken, Lois E. "Emic and etic perspectives: Haitian children's songs." *Bulletin du Bureau National d'Ethnologie* (Port-au-Prince), No. 1 (1985): 27–33. Analysis of children's songs in Haiti with special reference to Claude Dauphin's collection *Brit Kolobrit* (422).

515. ———. "Staging folklore in Haiti: historical perspectives." *Journal of Haitian Studies*, Vol. 1, No. 1 (Spring 1995): 101–110. Examines the history of staged performances of Haitian folk music and dance—Vodou, Rara, Carnival, konbit.

Media Materials

*516. *[Haiti, 1939–1940] [sound recording]* / collected by Harold
       Courlander. 111 sound discs + documentation. Field recordings
       made at various locations in Haiti between 1939 and 1940.
       Accompanied by a complete catalog of the collection and song texts
       in Haitian Creole with English translations. Selected song
       transcriptions are included in Courlander's *The Drum and the Hoe*
       (444). Partial contents: Vodoun songs — Yanvalou dance songs —
       Loa songs — Kitta Mouille and Cheche songs — Petro ritual songs
       — Juba dance songs — Carnival songs — Ibo dance songs —
       Bumba songs — Damballa songs — Children's game songs —
       Songs for wakes — Secret society songs — Pinyique dance songs
       — Congo songs — Cuban cane-cutter's songs — Limba,
       carabienne, mascort, salongo and kanga drum rhythms —
       Mascaron (Carnival) songs — Tambour maringuin with songs —
       Vaccines (bamboo trumpets) — "Political" songs — Meringues —
       Haitian dance orchestra — Zepaule songs — Ba[m]boule songs —
       Calinda songs — Rada songs — Dahome songs — Songs with
       malimba — Moundongue songs — Bumba songs — Tikanbo music
       — Calebasse songs — Marimba music — Grinding songs —
       Woodcutter's songs — Fisherman's songs. [Held by the Archives of
       Traditional Music, Indiana University, Bloomington, IN]

*517. *[Haiti, ca. 1950–1954] [sound recording]* / collected by Harold
       Courlander. 18 sound tape reels + documentation. Field
       recordings made at various locations in Haiti. Selected song
       transcriptions contained in Courlander's *The Drum and the Hoe*
       (444). Partial contents: Workgang songs — Meringues — Popular
       music — Street singers — Songs for Ayida — Piano music —
       Songs to Legba — Carnival music — Discussion of loa —
       Discussion of instruments — Discussion of govi, hounfor,
       expeditions and other Vodoun ceremonies — Discussion of mange
       mort feast, mange yam festival, lave tete and other rituals —
       Discussion of Rara. [Held by the Archives of Traditional Music,
       Indiana University, Bloomington, IN]

*518. *[Haiti, 1975, 1979, 1983] [sound recording]* / collected by Harold
       Courlander. 8 sound cassettes. Contents: Discussion of Vodoun —
       Dance music (Rada and Petro) — Cult songs (mostly Rada) —
       Conversation about Legba — Ibo Combo (popular ensemble) —
       Rada ceremonial songs. [Held by the Archives of Traditional
       Music, Indiana University, Bloomington, IN]

*519. *Haitian dance: history and tradition. Conference, Haitian music from 1492 to today [videorecording] = Danse haitienne: histoire et tradition* / presented by the Haitian Committee of Art and Folklore (Comite Haitien Art et Folklore); seminar coordinator, Eileen Herzog-Bazin. 1 videocassette (67 min.). Lecture presented by Ronald "Mushy" Gousse Widmaier at the Haitian-American Academy of Ballet and Arts, Port-au-Prince, Haiti, April 4, 1997. [Held by the New York Public Library for the Performing Arts, Dance Division / Call no.: *MGZIA 4–3159]

*520. *[West Indies, Haiti, Haitian, 1947] [sound recording]* / collected by Laura Boulton. 5 sound tape reels. Field recordings made between Jan. 23 and 25, 1947. Contents: Reel 1: Yanvalous, zepaules, a hago, and a congo — Reel 2: Mascarons, a rabordage, Congos, Petros, an Ibo, Yanvalous, and zepaules — Reel 3: Zepaules, Yanvalous, lullabies, game songs, ochans, and bandas — Reel 4: Zepaules, a Yanvalou, Petros, a quitta, an Ibo, a kita, a bando, and a Nago — Reel 5: Yanvalous, a pas rigol, a monologue, and dioubas. [Held by the Archives of Traditional Music, Indiana University, Bloomington, IN]

*521. *[West Indies; various locations; Afro-Caribbean, Haitian, Jamaican, Cuban; 1936–1937] [sound recording]* / collected by Laura Boulton. 6 sound tape reels. Collection of field recordings made by ethnomusicologist Laura Boulton during a trip to the West Indies in 1936–1937. A finding aid to the collection, "Laura Boulton's Expeditions to Latin America and the Caribbean," is available for onsite usage. Partial contents: Reel 3: Game songs, ballads, lullabies, and dance music from Bahamas, Haiti, and Dominican Republic — Reel 4: Dance music from Port-au-Prince, Haiti — Reel 5: Ballad, game songs, and dance songs from Haiti, Jamaica, and Cuba. [Held by the Archives of Traditional Music, Indiana University, Bloomington, IN]

Genre Studies

*522. *Dances, chants and drum rhythms of Haiti with Jean Leon Destine* / presented by The New York Public Library for the Performing Arts. 1 videocassette (88 min.). Lecture-demo exploring the historical and cultural background of Haitian folk music and dance. The program includes: an invocation to Papa Legba and Papa Damballah, a work song and dance, contredanse/Juba, meringue (Angelico), compas, rabodaille, mazoune, Congo paillette, Yanvalou, Nago, Ibo, pas rigole, mahi, zepaules, Dahomey, Petro, and Banda. Performers are: Jean Leon Destine (speaker and performer), Nadia Dieudonne (dancer), Damas (Fanfan) Louis (master drummer), and Ti-Ga Jean Baptiste (drummer-accompanist). Videotaped: May 8, 2004. [Held by the New York Public Library for the Performing Arts, Dance Division / Call no.: *MGZIA 4–7278]

*523. *Haitian dance: history and tradition. Haitian social dance, Meringue and Compas [videorecording] = Danse haitienne: histoire et tradition* / presented by the Haitian Committee of Art and Folklore (Comite Haitien Art et Folklore). 1 videocassette (60 min.). Class in Haitian social dance presented at the Haitian-American Academy of Ballet and Arts, Port-au-Prince, Haiti, on April 3, 1997. Performers: Harry Policard (teacher), Jean Marie Brignol, Joseph Brignol, Jacques Fontilus, Saul Jean-Pierre, Julien Rodrique, Maurice Saintelus (musicians). [Held by the New York Public Library for the Performing Arts, Dance Division / Call no.: *MGZIA 4–3152]

CARNIVAL MUSIC
See also 85–124, 344, 428, 479, 516–517, 693

524. Averill, Gage. "'Anraje' to 'angaje': Carnival politics and music in Haiti." *Ethnomusicology*, Vol. 38, No. 2 (Spring–Summer 1994): 217–247. History of Haiti's Carnival music.

525. ———. "Haitian fascination: The whip and the whistle." *The Beat*, Vol. 10, No. 3 (1991): 24–27. Feature on the music of Haiti's Rara bands.

526. Hyppolite, Michelson. "Le carnaval: ses instruments et ses danses." *Optique*, No. 1 (March 1954): 35–39. Looks at the musical instruments and dances associated with Haitian Carnival.

527. Juste-Constant, Voegeli. "La musique dans le carnaval haitien: aspects urbains et ruraux." Dissertation (Ph.D.)—Universite de Montreal, 1994. xiv, 385 leaves: ill., music + 2 audiocassettes + 1 videocassette (24 min.). Contents: Origines historiques du phenomene carnavalesque — Le carnaval haitien, a proprement parler — Carnaval et societe — Carnaval et religion — Carnaval et philosophie — Carnaval et langue — Carnaval et deguisement — Le carnaval, l'humour et la peur — Carnaval et art — Carnaval et multiethnie — Le carnaval et les media — Les textes des chansons du carnaval — Carnaval et musique — Le Rara,

carnaval rural — Le prescriptif et le descriptif dans l'ecriture musicale populaire appliques au carnaval.

528. Largey, Michael. "Politics on the pavement: Haitian Rara as a traditionalizing process." *Journal of American Folklore*, Vol. 113, No. 449 (Summer 2000): 239–254. Examines the Haitian Lenten carnival known as Rara with a particular focus on its religious aspects and music.

*529. Phelps, Timothy Nicholas. "Music, politics, and carnival in Haiti: a masquerade of power." Senior honors thesis—University of Texas at Austin, 2005. 44 leaves.

COMPAS/KONPA
See also 421, 433, 443, 460, 468, 471, 474, 479, 503, 509, 523, 691, 694

530. Elongui, Luigi. "Aux sources de compa haitien: entretien avec Ralph Boncy." *Africultures*, No. 8 (mai 1998): 20–23. Short interview with Boncy, a leading Haitian record producer, about compas dance music and its history.

MERINGUE
See also 251, 448–449, 474, 516–517, 523

531. Dauphin, Claude. "La meringue entre l'oralite et l'ecriture: histoire d'un genre musical haitien." *Canadian University Music Review*, No. 1 (1980): 49–65.

532. Dickson, Katharine. "Magic of the meringue; a New Englander visits colorful Haiti and brings back new dance recipes." *Dance Magazine* (October 1956): 89–91. Describes the dance as performed in Haiti and how it differs from the Dominican merengue. Includes directions on how to perform the steps.

533. Elie, Justin. *Meringues populaires haitiennes*. New York: R. de la Rozierre, c1920. 1 score (6 p.). Piano arrangements of six meringues by a leading Haitian art music composer.

534. Fouchard, Jean. *La meringue: danse nationale d'Haiti*. [Montreal]: Lemeac, 1973. 198 p.: music. History of the idiom.

535. Ohl, Dorothea Duryea. "Dance cruise to Haiti; Discovering a meringue variation, the Ibo, on a Caribbean visit." *Dance Magazine* (Sept. 1957): 60–61. Offers a discussion of the dance and directions on how to perform it from dance instructor Jerry Thomas.

536. Saint Cyr, Jean. "La meringue haitienne." *Revista INIDEF* (Caracas), No. 5 (1981–82): 62–74.

537. Thomas, Jerry C. *Theory of the Haitian meringue.* [Port-au-Prince, Haiti: J.C. Thomas, c1957]. 34 p.: ill. Cover title: It's fun to dance the Haitian meringue. Booklet on how to dance the meringue by a Haitian dance instructor.

RARA
See **CARNIVAL MUSIC**

SACRED MUSIC
See also 90–92, 189, 428, 434, 443, 448–449, 451–458, 460, 464, 479–481, 484, 493, 495, 500, 516–518, 520, 522, 682–687, 695–699, 729–733, 889–890, 957, 1032, 1117, 1130

538. *Angels in the mirror: Vodou music of Haiti* / [editor, Elizabeth McAlister; written by Elizabeth McAlister and Y.-M. David Yih]. Roslyn, NY: Ellipsis Arts, 1997. 64 p.: col. ill. + 1 CD. (Musical expeditions)

539. Armstrong, James, and Travis Knepper. *Vodou drumset: drumset applications of traditional Afro-Haitian rhythms.* New York: C. Fischer, 2002. 79 p. of music: ill. + 1 CD. Discography: p. 78–79. Includes historical and instructional material. Method for adapting the traditional rhythms of Haitian Vodou (Yanvalou, Ibo, Nago) to the modern drumset.

540. Boulton, Laura. "Le culte Vaudou." In *Encyclopedie des musique sacrees*, ed. Jacques Porte. Paris: Editions Labergerie, 1968, v. 1, pp. 111–116. Sketch of the liturgical music, musical instruments and songs associated with Haitian Vodou.

541. Castor, Kesner. *Ethique Vaudou: hermeneutique de la maitrise.* Paris: Harmattan, 1999. 250 p. Contents: Pt. 1. Ethique du rite Rada — Pt. 2. Ethique du rite Petro — Pt. 3. Dualite — Conclusions et comparaisons. Exploration of ethics in Haitian Vodou via its song texts.

542. Daniel, Yvonne. *Dancing wisdom: embodied knowledge in Haitian Vodou, Cuban Yoruba, and Bahian Candomble.* Urbana: University of Illinois Press, 2005. xvi, 324 p.: ill. Masterful study of the liturgical dances and music of Vodou, Santeria, and Candomble by a noted dance ethnologist.

543. Dauphin, Claude. *Musique du Vaudou: fonctions, structures et styles*. Sherbrooke, Quebec: Editions Naaman, 1986. 182 p.: ill., music. Musicological analysis of the music used in Vodou ritual ceremonies.

544. Deren, Maya. *Divine horsemen: the living gods of Haiti*. New Paltz, NY: McPherson, [1983], pp. 225–246. Reprint. First published: London: Thames and Hudson, 1953. Chapter on the music and dances of Haitian Vodou. *See also* 597.

545. Fleurant, Gerdes. *Dancing spirits: rhythms and rituals of Haitian Vodun, the Rada rite*. Westport, CT: Greenwood Press, 1996. xii, 209 p.: ill., music. Revision of author's Ph.D. thesis (561). Discography: p. [205]–206. Contents: Vodun as a religious system and way of life — The music of the Rada rite — Drums, drummers, and Oungenikon in Haitian Rada — The music of the Rada battery — The song texts in the ritual context — Analysis of song tunes — Dancing spirits.

546. ———. "The music of Haitian Vodun." In *African spirituality*, ed. Jacob K. Olupona. New York: Crossroad, 2000, pp. 416–449. Provides a sketch of Vodou and its cosmology followed by a detailed analysis of the music—its social function, structure, songs, symbolism, instrumentation, and rhythms, both Rada and Kongo-Petro. A good introduction to the subject.

547. ———. "The song of freedom: Vodou, conscientization and popular culture in Haiti." In *Vodou in Haitian life and culture*, eds. Claudine Michel and Patrick Bellegarde-Smith. New York: Palgrave Macmillan, 2006, pp. 51–63.

548. *Haitian Vodou: spirit, myth, and reality* / edited by Patrick Bellegarde-Smith and Claudine Michel. Bloomington: Indiana University Press, 2006, pp. 45–69. Partial contents: Vodun, music, and society in Haiti: affirmation and identity / Gerdes Fleurant — Vodoun, peasant songs, and political organizing / Renald Clerisme.

549. Honorin, Emmanuelle. "Retour sur des notes de collectage sonore." In *Vodou*, eds. Jacques Hainard, et al. Gollion: Infolio, etc., 2008, pp. 199–210. Notes on field recordings of Vodou ritual music made by the author in southern Haiti between 1997 and 2000.

550. Jaegerhuber, Werner A. *Complaintes Haitiennes = Haitian folklore songs = Canciones del folklore Haitiana*. 2e ed. [Port au

Prince, Haiti?], 1950. 1 score ([20] p.): ill. Reedition of Jaegerhuber's *Chansons folkloriques d'Haiti*. Port-au-Prince: Valerio Canez, 1945. Collection of Vodou songs collected and arranged by Werner Jaegerhuber.

551. Laguerre, Michel S. *Voodoo heritage*. Beverly Hills, CA: Sage Publications, 1980. 231 p.: ill. Chiefly an analysis of songs and prayers used in Haitian Vodou rituals. Based on fieldwork carried out in Haiti between 1974 and 1976.

552. Largey, Michael D. *Vodou nation: Haitian art music and cultural nationalism*. Chicago: University of Chicago Press, 2006. Partial contents: Performing the nation: musical constructions of Haitian cultural identity — The politics of musical ethnography: Jean Price-Mars and the ethnological movement — Ethnography and music ideology: the music of Werner A. Jaegerhuber — Epilogue: roots music and cultural memory. Essay collection focusing on the use of Vodou sacred music as source material for several generations of Haitian and American composers.

553. Ramsey, Kate. "Vodou, nationalism, and performance: the staging of folklore in mid-twentieth-century Haiti." In *Meaning in motion: new cultural studies of dance*, ed. Jane C. Desmond. Durham: Duke University Press, 1997, pp. 345–378. Essay on staged versions of Vodou dance-music rituals, which function, much as in Cuba and Jamaica, as officially sanctioned representations of the religion, as opposed to the private, oft demonized, ritual ceremonies practiced by Haiti's masses.

554. Roumain, Jacques. *Le sacrifice du tambour-Assoto(r)*. Port-au-Prince: Impr. de l'Etat, [1943]. 71 p.: ill. (Publications du Bureau d'ethnologie de la Republique d'Haiti; no. 2). Description of the Vodou ceremony held to consecrate the Rada drum known as Assotor. Includes detailed information about songs and music used to accompany each phase of the event.

555. Simmons, Victoria. "The voice of Ginen: drums in Haitian religion, history, and identity." In *Turn up the volume!: a celebration of African music*, ed. Jacqueline Cogdell DjeDje. Los Angeles: UCLA Fowler Museum of Cultural History, 1999, pp. 158–169.

556. Welch, David B. *Voice of thunder, eyes of fire: in search of Shango in the African diaspora*. Pittsburgh, PA: Dorrance, 2001, pp. 110–139. Examines music used to worship the Yoruba deity Shango in

the New World contexts of Trinidad, Haiti, and Northeastern Brazil.

557. ———. "West African cult music retentions in Haitian urban Vaudou: a preliminary report." In *Essays for a humanist: an offering to Klaus Wachsmann*. Spring Valley, NY: Town House Press, 1977, pp. 337–349.

558. Wilcken, Lois, and Frisner Augustin. *The drums of Vodou*. Tempe, AZ: White Cliffs Media Co., 1992. 128 p.: ill. (Performance in world music series; no. 7). Contents: Social and historical context — The instruments — The rhythms — Song and dance — On becoming a master drummer: excerpt from interview with Frisner Augustin. Excellent introduction to the liturgical drum music of Haitian Vodou. Offers transcriptions and analysis, based on the Port-au-Prince style, for each of the music's major rhythms.

Dissertations and Theses

559. Butler, Melvin Lloyd. "Songs of Pentecost: experiencing music, transcendence, and identity in Jamaica and Haiti." Dissertation (Ph.D.)—New York University, 2005. 2 v.: ill., music. Transcriptions: v. 2, leaves 380–493. Study of Pentecostal music traditions in Jamaica and Haiti based on fieldwork conducted between 2000 and 2004.

560. Devlin, Eileen Bonnie. "'Vwa Guine': an original performance piece derived from the Haitian 'Vodu Coucher Tambour' ceremony: the sacred and the aesthetic in ritual and performance." Dissertation (Ph.D.)—New York University, 1986. 2 vols. (x, 2, 514 leaves): ill. Contents: The Vodu religion: structures, beliefs and ritual — The sacred and the authentic in Vodu — From the roots of Vodu: creative manifestations and aesthetics from the indigenous perspective — "Vwa Guine": an original performance piece derived from the Haitian Vodu Coucher Tambour ceremony — "Vwa Guine": the aesthetics of ritual and performance.

561. Fleurant, Gerdes. "The ethnomusicology of Yanvalou: a study of the Rada rite of Haiti." Dissertation (Ph.D.)—Tufts University, 1987. xv, 307 p.: ill., music. Published in revised form as 545.

*562. Hernandez-Mergal, Luis A. "The relationship between music and possession-trance in Haitian Vodun." Thesis (M.A.)—UCLA, 1990. v, 136 leaves.

*563. Lyon, Caroline Sidway. "Kase: the intersection of music, dance, and spirit in Haitian Vodun ritual and staged folklore contexts." Report (M.M.)—University of Texas at Austin, 1996. vii, 60 leaves: ill.

564. Sager, Rebecca Darlene. "Musical meaning of Haitian Vodou singing: an ethnography of musical and ritual discourse at a Lakou Ginen in northern Haiti." Dissertation (Ph.D.)—University of Texas at Austin, 2002. xi, 604 leaves: ill., music. Detailed ethnographic study.

*565. Washington, Kera M. "Vodou in a strange land: re-territorialization by others." Thesis (M.A.)—Wesleyan University, 1995. 161 leaves: ill., music.

*566. Yih, Yuen-Ming David. "Liturgical Yanvalou drumming in Port-au-Prince, Haiti." Thesis (M.A.)—Wesleyan University, 1988. i, 82 leaves: music.

567. ———. "Music and dance of Haitian Vodou: diversity and unity in regional repertoires." Dissertation (Ph.D.)—Wesleyan University, 1995. vii, 690 leaves: ill., music. Contents: Regionalism in Haitian culture — Vodou — Oppression and resistance — Militarism in Haitian folklore — Guide to the transcriptions and analysis of Vodou drumming — Cap-Haitien — Gonaives — Les Cayes — Vodou song: text and form. Appendix A: Construction and assembly of Vodou drums — Appendix B: Field recordings — Appendix C: Vodou song texts — Appendix D: Song form data tables. Descriptive survey based on fieldwork carried out between 1985 and 1991.

Articles

568. Beaudry, Nicole. "Le langage des tambours dans la ceremonie Vaudou haitienne." *Canadian University Music Review*, No. 4 (1983): 125–140.

569. Bensignor, Francois. "La memoire musicale du Vaudou haitien." *Hommes & Migrations*, No. 1210 (nov–dec 1997): 153–159.

570. Butler, Melvin L. "'Nou kwe nan Sentespri' (We believe in the Holy Spirit): music, ecstasy, and identity in Haitian Pentecostal worship." *Black Music Research Journal*, Vol. 22, No. 1 (Spring 2002): 85–125.

571. Courlander, Harold. "Reflections on the meaning of a Haitian cult song." *Bulletin du Bureau National d'Ethnologie*, No. 1–2 (1986):

53–56. Discusses the ways in which interpretations of Vodou songs can change over time, particularly as knowledge about their origins and meanings begin to fade.

572. Daniel, Yvonne Payne. "Tourism dance performances: authenticity and creativity." *Annals of Tourism Research*, Vol. 23, No. 4 (October 1996): 780–797. Comparative study of folkloric music and dance traditions as a lure for tourists, e.g. Vodou dances in Haiti (p. 786–787, 791–792) and Cuban street rumba (p. 787–789, 792–794).

573. Denis, Lorimer, and Francois Duvalier. "La culture populaire: de la poesie, du chant et des danses dans l'esthetique vodouesque." *Bulletin du Bureau d'Ethnologie*, Ser. 2, No. 12 (1955): 1–29.

574. Dumerve, Constantin. "Musique et danse vaudouesques." *Les Griots* (Port-au-Prince), Vol. 3, No. 3 (jan–mars 1939): 411–414. Discusses the rhythms, songs and musical instruments associated with Haitian Vodou.

575. ———. "Musique vaudouesque." *Les Griots* (Port-au-Prince), Vol. 4, No. 4 (avril–sept 1939): 559–564. Focuses on Vodou musical motifs found in the work of composer Justin Elie.

*576. Fleurant, Gerdes. "Ethnomizikoloji rit Rada an Ayiti." *Perfiles* [Somerville, MA] (1984): 49–61.

577. Gonzalez, David. "Transito cultural el tambor Assotor y su ritual de Benin a Haiti y a Cuba." *Del Caribe*, No. 50 (2007): 60–63. Traces the odyssey of a Vodou ritual drum from its origins in Benin to its New World homes of Haiti and Cuba.

578. Grenier, Robert. "La melodie vaudou – Voodoo art songs: the genesis of a nationalist music in the Republic of Haiti." *Black Music Research Journal*, Vol. 21, No. 1 (Spring 2001): 29–74. Examines the use of motifs from Vodou liturgical music in the work of art music composers from Haiti.

579. Grohs-Paul, Waltraud. "Notes sur les chants vodouesques de Werner A. Jaegerhuber." *Bulletin du Bureau National d'Ethnologie* (Port-au-Prince), No. 2 (1985): 73–76. Prefatory notes on the Jaegerhuber collection below (580).

580. Jaegerhuber, Werner A. "Chants vaudouesques." *Bulletin du Bureau National d'Ethnologie* (Port-au-Prince), No. 2 (1985): 77–101. Previously unpublished collection of 24 Vodou songs, with

music and descriptive notes, collected by Jaegerhuber between 1937 and 1945.

581. ———. "Contribution a la musique vodouesque." *Conjonction*, No. 10–11 (Aug.–Oct. 1947): 63–64. Discussion of the song 'Cibao.'

582. Juste-Constant, Voegeli. "Approche ethnomusicologique du Vodou haitien." *Folklore Americano*, No. 21 (junio 1976): 95–140. Outlines the function, meaning, and musical structure of Vodou liturgical music in Haiti.

583. Laguerre, Michel. "The drum and religious dance in Christian liturgy in Haiti." *Freeing the Spirit*, Vol. 1, No. 2 (Spring 1972): 10–15.

584. ———. "Le tambour et la danse religieuse dans la liturgie chretienne en Haiti." *Revue du Clerge Africain*, Vol. 27, No. 6 (Nov. 1972): 587–603.

585. Marcelin, Milo. "Danses et chants Vodou." *Optique*, No. 12 (February 1955): 29–37.

586. Maximilien, Louis, and Werner Jaegerhuber. "Hersulie Freda Dahomey." *Cahiers d'Haiti*, Vol. 1, No. 8 (mars 1944): 22–27. Essay on the sacred songs associated with Vodou and its gods. Includes musical transcriptions.

587. Merwin, B.W. "A Voodoo drum from Hayti." *The Museum Journal* (University of Pennsylvania), Vol. 8, No. 2 (June 1917): 123–125. According to Merwin's account this drum was acquired by the University of Pennsylvania Museum after being 'confiscated and [having] its head punctured because the beating of a drum was the signal to assemble the Voodoo devotees and to incite them to a religious race war' during a Haitian insurrection in 1916.

588. Metraux, Alfred. "Chants Vodou." *Les Temps Modernes* (Paris), Vol. 5, No. 52 (February 1950): 1386–1393.

589. Paul, Emmanuel C. "Les chansons folkloriques haitiennes." *Optique*, No. 8 (October 1954): 28–35. Discussion of sacred songs associated with Vodou.

590. Pradines, Emerante de. "Instruments of rhythm." *Tomorrow*, Vol. 3, No. 1 (Autumn 1954): 123–126. Discusses the musical instruments and songs used in Vodou ceremonies.

591. Ramsey, Kate. "Without one ritual note: folklore performance and the Haitian state, 1935–1946." *Radical History Review*, No. 84

(Fall 2002): 7–42. Detailed examination of the somewhat schizophrenic cultural policies of the Haitian government in the years immediately following the American occupation (1915–1934) of the island. Describes how, in order to avoid 'embarrassing the nation' the government banned any and all performances of Vodou ritual ceremonies, including their music and dances, in an attempt to rid the country of its 'superstitious' African past. At the same time they initiated a government-supported 'mouvement folklorique' in which Haitian folkloric troupes were created to perform secularized versions of the very same Vodou rituals which they had banned.

592. Serpa, Enrique. "Tambores del Vodu." *Bohemia*, ano 41, no. 23 (junio 5 1949): 36–38, 88–90. Illustrated feature on Haitian sacred music traditions.

593. Starry, David Edward. "Come with me to Antoine's in Jacmel where the mysterious Voodoo drums are made." *Etude* (Philadelphia), Vol. 68, No. 5 (May 1950): 20, 51. Account of the author's visit to a Jacmel-based maker of Vodou drums.

594. Vonarx, Nicolas. "Les chants de oungan: un incontournable dans la pratique de soins Vodou." *Journal of Haitian Studies*, Vol. 11, No. 2 (Fall 2005): 59–74. Discusses songs used for healing in Haitian Vodou.

595. Webb, John. "The primal roots of jazz: rediscovering the music of Vodou." *Jazz Research Papers* (1995): 128–135. Introductory look at the sacred music of Haitian Vodou.

596. Welch, David B. "Um melotipo Ioruba/Nago para os canticos religiosos da diaspora negra." *Ensaios/Pesquisas*, No. 4 (julho 1980): 1–8. Portuguese version of 556 using examples from SW Nigeria, Bahia and Haiti.

Media Materials

597. *Divine horsemen [videorecording]: the living gods of Haiti* / filmed by Maya Deren. New York: Mystic Fire Video, 1985. 1 videocassette (52 min.). Classic documentary shot in Haiti by Deren between 1947 and 1951 and edited posthumously by Teiji and Cherel Ito. Includes footage of Rada, Petro, and Congo ritual dances and music. *See also* 544.

*598. *[Haiti, Port Bendet and Leogane, 1951] [sound recording]* / collected by Alan Lomax. 4 sound tape reels. Field recordings of

Haitian ritual music recorded in Leogane and Port Bendet.
Contents: Pt. 1. Port Bendet. A ceremony, including a section of
'full Vodun drum accompaniment' and 10 drum rhythms — Pt. 2.
Leogane. 8 Rara songs. [Held by the Archives of Traditional
Music, Indiana University, Bloomington, IN]

*599. *[Haiti, Saut d'Eau, 1985] [sound recording]* / collected by Michael
D. Largey. 6 sound cassettes. Field recordings of Haitian sacred
music made in June and July of 1985. Partial contents: Oungan
dance — Prayers and songs from the Stations of the Cross (Kalve).
[Held by the Archives of Traditional Music, Indiana University,
Bloomington, IN]

*600. *[Surinam, Bush Negroes, and Haiti, 1928–1929] [sound recording]*
/ collected by Frances and Melville Herskovits. 100 cylinders +
documentation. Collection including field recordings of Haitian
Vodou songs made by the Herskovitses in Port-au-Prince, Haiti.
Accompanied by notes on the music. [Held by the Archives of
Traditional Music, Indiana University, Bloomington, IN]. See 452
for transcriptions of several of these songs.

*601. *[West Indies, Haiti, Haitian, 1966] [sound recording]* / collected by
Laura Boulton. 4 sound tape reels. Contents: Reel 1: Mange Loa
(Feast of the gods) Vodoun ceremony — Reel 2: Mange Loa
ceremony, cont'd — Reel 3: Mange Loa ceremony, concl. Reel 4:
Interview with Horace Ashton, and Laura Boulton tells of her
1937–38 expedition to the West Indies. [Held by the Archives of
Traditional Music, Indiana Univ.]

MARTINIQUE
See also 132, 144, 154, 156, 158–159, 163–164, 176–177, 180, 185, 189,
191, 193, 197, 205, 212, 216, 221–224, 230, 236, 239, 242–250,
345–352

602. *Asou chimen danmye: propositions sur le danmye, art martial
martiniquais.* Fort-de-France: Association Mi Mes Manmay
Matinik, A.M.4, 1994. 112 p.: ill. Treatise on the *danmye* (aka
ladja kokoye wonpwen), a Martinican martial art/dance and music
akin to the kalinda stick fighters of Trinidad.

603. Cally, Sully. *Musiques et danses afro-caraibes: Martinique.* Gros-
Morne, Martinique: Sully-Cally/Lezin, 1990. 221 p.: ill., music.
History of folkloric and popular music styles from Martinique.

604. Cesaire, Ina. "La voix des boeufs: chants de labours a la Martinique." In *Pour une anthropologie des voix*, eds. Nicole Revel and Diana Rey-Hulman. Paris: L'Harmattan, etc., 1993, pp. 173–195. An earlier version of this essay may be found in 382. Discussion of plowing songs in Martinique.

605. Chaudenson, Robert. *Des iles, des hommes, des langues: essai sur la creolisation linguistique et culturelle.* Paris: L'Harmattan, 1992, pp. 183–190. Discussion of Creole-language music traditions in Martinique and Guadeloupe.

606. Coridun, Victor. *Le carnaval de Saint-Pierre (Martinique): chansons creoles d'avant 1902.* 2e ed. Fort-de-France, Martinique: August Flaun, 1980. 1 v. (various pagings): ill., music. Reprint. First published as: *Le Carnaval de St.-Pierre (Martinique) folklore martiniquais. 45 chansons creoles recueilles de 1920 a 1925.* Fort-de-France: R. Illemay, 1930. Contents: Anthologie (texte) — Chansons politiques — Les masques defilent (chansons satiriques) — Chansons d'amour (biguines et mazurkas). Collection of 45 songs associated with Martinique's Carnival collected between 1920 and 1925.

607. Cyrille, Dominique. *Recherche sur la musique rurale de la Martinique.* Villeneuve d'Ascq: Presses universitaires du Septentrion, [2001]. 666 p.: ill., music. (These a la carte). Thesis (nouveau doctorat)—Universite Paris-Sorbonne-Paris IV, 1996. Contents: A. Les premiers contacts. Les origines — La musique originelle des negres de la Martinique — La musique negre dans la societe esclavagiste. B. Emergence de la musique creole. Naissance des traditions musicales. C. L'Heritage. Fusions d'elements heterogenes — L'epoque contemporaine. Examines the fusion of European and African elements in *bele, lassote* and *kont kweyol*-story-songs from rural Martinique and the ways in which these traditions are passed on from one generation to another.

608. Desroches, Monique, et al. *Les instruments de musique traditionnelle.* Fort-de-France: Bureau du Patrimoine du Conseil Regional de la Martinique, [1989]. 87 p.: ill. Ethnomusicological study of Martinican musical instruments.

*609. ———. *La musique traditionnelle de la Martinique.* Montreal: Universite de Montreal, Centre de Recherches Caraibes, 1985. v, 177 p.: ill., music. (Rapport de recherche (Universite de Montreal. Centre de Recherches Caraibes); no 6) [Held by the University of Montreal]

*610. Donatien, Fernand. *Musique en Martinique: English version inside*. Fort de France: Sim'ln, 1999. 79 p. (Sim'ekol. Melodie Creole).

611. Gabriel-Soime, Leona. *Ca! C'est la Martinique*. [Fort de France: s.n.], 1966. 1 score (215 p.): ill., music. Arrangements of Martinican dance and folk music idioms, e.g. biguine, mazurka, lagya, and others, with lyrics by Leona Gabriel and music by Victor Coridun.

612. Gerstin, Julian. "The allure of origins: neo-African dances in the French Caribbean and the southern United States." In *Just below South: intercultural performance in the Caribbean and the U.S. South*, eds. Jessica Adams, et al. Charlottesville: University of Virginia Press, 2007, pp. 123–145. Comparative study of kalenda dances and music from Martinique with African American folk dance idioms of the American South.

613. ———. "Martinique and Guadeloupe." In *The new Grove dictionary of music and musicians*. 2nd ed. New York, 2001, v. 15, pp. 929–932. Survey article.

614. ———. "Musical revivals and social movements in contemporary Martinique: ideology, identity, ambivalence." In *The African diaspora: a musical perspective*, ed. Ingrid Monson. New York: Garland Pub., 2000; New York: Routledge, 2003, pp. 295–327. Examines the *bele* music revival and Carnival as two examples of recent social movements on the island.

615. Gilles, Clotilde. *Un univers musical martiniquais: les swares bele du Nord atlantique*. Paris: L'Harmattan, 2001. 252 p.: ill., music. Discography: p. 251–252. Contents: Approche generale de la musique bele — Les expressions du bele — Analyse des materiaux sonores — Les repertoires principaux: caracteristiques musicales et choregraphiques — Les repertoires damie et lalink'le. Study of *bele* set dances and music from the northern coast of Martinique.

616. Hearn, Lafcadio. *Two years in the French West Indies*. New York: Harper & Brothers, 1890. Includes a description of a kalinda/*bele* performance (p. 143–147) and Carnival songs (p. 424–431) performed in St. Pierre, Martinique ca. 1887.

*617. Jean-Baptiste, E., and M. Lechevalier. *Met a bele: methode de tambour Bele*. Fort de France [Martinique]: SIM'LN, 1992. (Collection Sim'ekol). Method for Martinican *bele* drumming.

618. Kubayanda, Josaphat Bekunuru. *The poet's Africa: Africanness in the poetry of Nicolas Guillen and Aime Cesaire.* New York: Greenwood Press, 1990, pp. 89–108. Revision of author's thesis (Ph.D.)—Washington University, 1981. Chapter on drum language in the poetry of Cuba's Nicolas Guillen and Martinique's Aime Cesaire. An earlier version of this essay appears as 652.

619. Laferl, Christopher F. *"Record it, and let it be known": song lyrics, gender and ethnicity in Brazil, Cuba, Martinique and Trinidad and Tobago from 1920 to 1960.* Wien: Lit, 2005. 380 p. + 1 CD. Discography: p. 353–357. Revision of the author's habilitation: A mulata e a tal—University of Vienna, 2002. Textual analysis of more than a thousand songs (sambas, sones, beguines, calypsos, etc.) with 'special attention ... to ... topics [such as] the relations between ethnicity and national identity; the presence of Africa and slavery; the presentation of the gendered and ethnically marked body; and, finally, the description of cultural blackness.'

620. Meyer, Andreas. "On rural and urban musics in Afro-Caribbean cultures." In *Historical studies on folk and traditional music*, eds. Doris Stockmann and Jens Henrik Koudal. Copenhagen: Museum Tusculanum Press, etc., 1997, pp. 191–196. Short essay on black music traditions in the Caribbean with reference to styles from Trinidad, Cuba and Martinique.

621. *Notes techniques sur les instruments tibwa et tanbou dejanbe: musique danmye-kalennda-bele de Martinique.* Fort-de-France: Association Mi Mes Manmay Matinik, A.M.4, 1992. 68 p.: ill., music. Discography: p. 12–13. Contents: Presence de tanbou et tibwa dans la litterature et l'histoire — Ti bwa matinik — Tanbou dejanbe — Les kout tanbou les plus frequents (essai de transcription). Method for the *tibwa* and *tanbou dejanbe*, percussion instruments used to accompany Kalennda-Bele dances in Martinique. Includes details on how to construct both instruments.

*622. *Piano creole: musique et chants d'hier et d'aujourd'hui /* [transcription pour piano par Louis-Jose Lancry]. Fort de France: Sim'ln, 1994. 2 v.: ill., music. (Collection Sim'ekol; 1–2). Collection of piano music. Includes portraits and biographical information for eight Martinican musicians.

623. *Pour le renouveau du kalennda-bele: danses nationales martiniquaises.* Fort-de-France: Association Mi Mes Manmay Matinik, A.M.4, 1992. 103 p.: ill. Discography: p. 3–4. Study of two

Martinican folk dance-music genres. The first, known elsewhere
in the Caribbean as calinda or kalinda, is a stick fighting dance,
while the second is a set dance derived from the European belair.
Includes details on the drum and vocal accompaniment for both.
The work is organized in four parts with part one describing the
positions, gestures, and rhythms of the dances and parts two
through four their history, cultural context, and regional
variations.

624. Rosemain, Jacqueline. *La musique dans la societe Antillaise:
1635–1902: Martinique Guadeloupe.* Paris: L'Harmattan, 1986.
183 p.: music. Contents: Les debuts de la colonisation (1635–1714)
— L'age d'or de la colonisation (1714–1789) — La premiere
abolition de l'esclavage. La periode revolutionnaire francaise
(1789–1802) — Le retour a l'esclavage (1802–1848) — La
deuxieme abolition de l'esclavage et le Second Empire (1848–1870)
— La Troisieme Republique (1870–1902).

625. Terrine, Jean. *La ronde des derniers maitres du bele: la musique
traditionnelle dans le nord de la Martinique.* Paris: HC, 2004. 191
p.: ill. Discography: p. 185–189. Oral history account of *bele* dance
and music traditions from the town of Sainte-Marie on the
northern end of Martinique.

Dissertations and Theses

*626. Dorina, Sonia. "Le mouvement dancehall reggae en Martinique."
Thesis (Memoire de maitrise)—Universite des Antilles et de la
Guyane, Martinique, 2004. 102 p.: ill.

627. Gerstin, Julian Harris. "Traditional music in a new social
movement: the renewal of bele in Martinique (French West
Indies)." Dissertation (Ph.D.)—University of California, Berkeley,
1996. xiii, 372 leaves: ill., music. Discography: leaves 371–372.
Contents: Art and opposition: why not in Martinique? —
Martinican ideas and ideologies in context — Bele from slavery to
the 1980s renewal — Kalenda, or the conundrum of origins — The
urban bele renewal, 1981–1995 — Conclusions: the bele renewal
and new social movements in Martinique. Postscript: Ti Kascot, or
the continual balancing — Appendix 1: Martinican traditional
dance and music: a survey — Appendix 2: Transcripts. Includes
discussion of the following artists: Les Ballets Folkloriques
Martiniquais (p. 138–148), Eugene Mona (p. 155-157), Ti Emile (p.
170–174), AM4 (p. 207–253, 292–301), Belenou (p. 258–260),
Wapa (p. 261–262) and Bel Alians (p. 264–271).

628. Johnson-La O, Sara Elizabeth. "Migrant recitals: Pan-Caribbean interchanges in the aftermath of the Haitian revolution, 1791–1850." Dissertation (Ph.D.)—Stanford University, 2001, pp. 84–123. Partial contents: Cinquillo consciousness: the formation of an inter-island consciousness. Chapter "explor[ing] musical production as a performative manifestation of regional integration. Using elements from Cuban tumba francesa, Puerto Rican bomba, and Martinican bele, I propose the existence of an inter-island musical aesthetic that was at the forefront of breaking colonial barriers"—Author's abstract.

*629. Pastel, Yves. "La musique traditionnelle martiniquaise: moment de conservation de la langue creole." Memoire de maitrise—Universite de Bordeaux 2 (France), 1992. 124 leaves.

*630. Sylvestre, Anique. "Reggae, rap, ragga, arts de la rue en Martinique: effets de mimetisme ou mode d'expression d'une jeunesse en mal-etre." Memoire DESS—Universite Pierre Mendes (Grenoble II), 1997. 218 leaves.

*631. Vert-Pre, Serge. "Creolite et identite: le paradoxe de la musique traditionnelle bele." Memoire DESS—Universite Pierre Mendes (Grenoble II), 2003. 199 leaves.

*632. Zobda-Zebina, Mylenn. "Les musiques dancehall: comparaison de deux societies caribeennes, la Martinique et la Jamaique." These (doctorat)—Ecole des hautes etudes en sciences sociales (EHESS), 2006. 3 v. (546 leaves): ill. Comparative study of dancehall reggae in Martinique and Jamaica.

Articles

633. Bertrand, Anca. "Les jeux de l'amour a Sainte-Marie: les orchestres populaires a la Martinique." *Paralleles*, No. 6 (1965): 20–21. Discusses a traditional type of mating dance from rural Martinique and its musical accompaniment. According to Bertrand the dance part seems to have died out while the songs and rhythms live on.

634. ———. "Love games at Sainte-Marie: folk orchestras in Martinique." *Paralleles*, No. 15 (1966): 18–19. Translation of 633.

635. "Biguines et autres chansons de Martinique." *Les Temps Modernes* (Paris), Vol. 5, No. 52 (February 1950): 1397–1407. Song texts with commentaries. Most songs are from the Victor Coridun collection *Le carnaval de Saint-Pierre* (606).

636. "Comment faire un disque?" *Antilla*, No. 345 (aout 7–13 1989): 6–
7. Interview with the director of Studio Hibiscus, the top recording
studio in Martinique, about the costs of making a record,
percentages received by the artist, the different types of contracts
offered, and more.

637. Delsham, Tony. "Artiste, tourisme, patrimoine culturel
et...politique." *Antilla*, No. 240 (mai 7–14 1987): 27–28.
Commentary on a recent decision by the Conseil Regional de la
Martinique to begin offering financial support to local musicians.
Explores how the social status and training of Martinican
musicians has changed since the 1970s.

638. ———. "Piraterie musicale." *Antilla*, No. 269 (janvier 7–13 1988):
16–19. Feature on musical piracy in Martinique. Includes
comments from several leading musicians as to its negative
impact on their work and careers.

639. Desroches, Monique. "Musical tradition in Martinique: between
the local and the global." *TRANS: Transcultural Music Review* [e-
journal], No. 2 (November 1996). http://www.sibetrans.com/trans/
trans2/desroches.htm. Short essay discussing Martinican popular
music styles such as biguine, kadans, and zouk.

640. ———. "Les pratiques musicales, image de l'histoire, reflet d'un
contexte." *Historial Antillais* (Fort-de-France), Vol. 1 (1980): 491–
500.

641. Donatien, Fernand. "Musique: Conseils et rappel d'un maitre."
Antilla, No. 376 (mars 29–avril 4 1990): 36–38. Reflections on the
influence of France's S.A.C.E.M. recording industry awards on the
Martinican music scene.

642. Eda-Pierre, A. "Danses et chansons." *Horizons Caraibes*, Vol. 3,
No. 22–24 (juin–aout 1955): 1–4. General discussion of folk idioms
from Martinique—ladja, biguine, bele, etc.

643. Elongui, Luigi. "Aux sources de la biguine: tambours Allada et
violons tziganes." *La Lettre des Musiques et des Arts Africains*, No.
26 (jan. 5 1996): 4–7; No. 27 (fev. 5 1996): 5–9. Rambling two-part
essay tracing the social, historical and musical roots of
Martinique's biguine, from West Africa (Benin) and colonial
Martinique to Paris in the 1920s and beyond. Part two also
includes a sidebar article by Gerald Arnaud on the history of
'Begin the Beguine' and the beguine's development in Paris from
the 1920s to the present.

644. ———. "La Martinique de Dede Saint-Prix et les sources du chouval-bwa." *Africultures*, No. 8 (mai 1998): 8–11. Discusses African influence in the musics of Martinique.

645. Erwan, Jacques. "Chanson des Antilles: A la Martinique, Martinique, Martinique...." *Paroles & Musique*, No. 27 (fevrier 1983): 35–38. Profile of the island's popular music scene and some of its leading artists.

646. Fortune, Fernand Tiburce. "Nouveaux propos sur notre musique." *Antilla*, No. 329 (avril 17–23 1989): 33–34. Reflections on the state of the Martinican pop music scene.

647. Gallo, William K. "Creole music and dance in Martinique." *Revista/Review Interamericana*, Vol. 8, No. 4 (Winter 1978–79): 666–670. Discusses the two different forms of the Martinican biguine—*bele* and St. Pierre style—and their popular cousin, the mazurka, or *mazouk*.

648. Gerstin, Julian. "Interaction and improvisation between dancers and drummers in Martinican bele." *Black Music Research Journal*, Vol. 18, No. 1–2 (Spring–Fall 1998): 121–165.

649. ———. "Reputation in a musical scene: the everyday context of connections between music, identity and politics." *Ethnomusicology*, Vol. 42, No. 3 (Fall 1998): 385–414. Discussion of contemporary *bele* music in Martinique and two of its leading exponents, Bel Alians and AM4 [Association Mi Mes Manmay Matinik].

650. "Interview d'Yves-Marie: a propos d'une experience de cafe-theatre." *Antilla*, No. 30 (nov 10 1982): 31–32. Interview with Martinican journalist Yves-Marie Seraline about his new Fort-de-France-based 'Cafe-Theatre,' a performance space for Martinican music, poetry and and related arts.

651. J., Patricia. "Non le tambour n'est pas mort." *Fouyaya*, No. 58 (sept. 1987): 38–39. Brief history of the *ka* drum and its role in Martinican music from the 19th century to the 1980s.

652. Kubayanda, Josaphat B. "The drum poetics of Nicolas Guillen and Aime Cesaire." *Prismal/Cabral*, No. 7–8 (Spring 1982): 37–55. Appears in revised form as 618. Study of drum language in the poetry of Guillen and Cesaire.

653. "Quelques grans noms de famille 'bele.'" *Fouyaya*, No. 58 (sept. 1987): 40–41. List some of the key names—singers, drummers, and dancers—in the history of Martinican *bele*.

654. Ravaud, Daniel. "'Notre musique doit vivre.'" *Antilla*, No. 67 (sept. 9–16 1983): 16–17. Laments the many problems facing the contemporary music scene in Martinique, i.e. an over-reliance on imported music, monopolisation of the local market by a few promoters, limited record distribution, etc.

655. Scaramuzzo, Gene. "The other Caribbean: Martinique carnival." *The Beat*, Vol. 15, No. 2 (1996): 58–59. Discusses musical highlights of the 1996 Carnival in Martinique.

656. ———. "The other Caribbean: The ragga also rises." *The Beat*, Vol. 14, No. 6 (1995): 34–35, 82. Column about the ragga (dancehall) scene in Martinique and one of its leading producers, Don Miguel.

657. ———. "The other Caribbean: Taxi dancing." *The Beat*, Vol. 14, No. 3 (1995): 32. Report on music from Martinique's 1995 Carnival.

658. ———. "Return to Martinique: the magic music of the French Antilles." *The Beat*, Vol. 9, No. 6 (1990): 27–33. Snapshot of the contemporary music scene in Martinique with a focus on the musicians Marce, Kali, and Djo Dezormo.

659. Sirot, Guy. "Plaidoyer pour la musique martiniquaise." *Bulletin d'Information du CENADDOM*, No. 74 (1984): 63–68. Discusses a report by the Commission de la Musique Martiniquaise on the state of intellectual property rights and the music business in Martinique.

660. Smith, CC. "The other Caribbean: Antilles encore." *The Beat*, Vol. 11, No. 1 (1992): 27–29, 60. Feature on the current music scenes of Martinique and Guadeloupe.

661. ———. "Report from Martinique: Ile entre deux mondes (Island between two worlds)." *The Reggae & African Beat*, Vol. 7, No. 1 (1988): 22–25. Report on the pop and roots music scene in Martinique ca. 1988.

662. Thaly, Daniel. "Street cries of Martinique and Dominica." *West Indian Review*, Vol. 3, No. 8 (April 1937): 33–35. Describes the chants of each island's street vendors.

663. Tiburce, Fernand. "Musique Haitienne: le mauvais alibi des musiciens Martiniquais." *Antilla*, No. 7 (sept. 1981): 36–39. Looks at the dominance of Haitian dance music styles in the popular music scene of Martinique.

664. Watrous, Peter. "Arts abroad: Finding cultural roots in the rhythms of carnival." *New York Times* (March 3 1998): E2. On the music of Martinique's Carnival and its cultural background.

Media Materials

*665. *Bele [videorecording]: an instructional examination of the Caribbean folk dance form* / written and narrated by Elizabeth O'Brien. Port of Spain, Trinidad & Tobago: Banyan, 1979. 1 videocassette (28 min.). Summary: Anthropologist Beth Ryan explores the traditions of the belaire dance in the rural village 'Bele feasts' of Trinidad and Tobago and Martinique.

*666. *Biguine [videorecording]* / director, Guy Deslauriers; script, Patrick Chamoiseau. Paris: Kreol Productions - RFO, 2005. 1 DVD (90 min.). In French and Creole with English subtitles. Format: [PAL] zone 2. Documentary on a Martinican popular dance music.

PUERTO RICO

667. Dufrasne-Gonzalez, J. Emanuel. "La homogeneidad de la musica caribena: sobre la musica comercial y popular de Puerto Rico." Dissertation (Ph.D.)—UCLA, 1985. In Spanish with chapter summaries in English. Partial contents: Haiti, las Antillas francesas y la musica puertorriquena. Chapter on the Haitian legacy in Afro-Puerto Rican folk traditions such as *bomba*.

ST. LUCIA
See also 146–150, 154, 156, 183, 189, 193, 197, 223

668. Dalphinis, Morgan. "Saint Lucian Lawoz and Lamagwit songs within the Caribbean and African tradition." In *Framing the word: gender and genre in Caribbean women's writing*, ed. Joan Anim-Addo. London: Whiting and Birch, 1996, pp. 86–92. Short essay on songs from the island's La Rose and La Marguerite flower societies.

*669. Guilbault, Jocelyne M. *Instruments musicaux a Sainte-Lucie: contexte d'apparition et transmission d'un savoir musical*. [Paris]: Agence de cooperation culturelle et technique, 1983. 47 p.: ill.

670. ———. "Musical events in the lives of the people of a Caribbean island, St. Lucia." Dissertation (Ph.D.)—University of Michigan, 1984. xxiv, 377 leaves: ill., music. Contents: The La Rose and the La Marguerite organizations — Jwe ('play') activities during beach parties, full moon gatherings, and 'debut' evenings — A 'kwadril' evening — Wake celebrations. Ethnography of folk music traditions from the southern part of St. Lucia. Based on fieldwork conducted between 1980 and 1983.

671. Norville, Frank. *Songs of St. Lucia: "folk songs".* [Castries, St. Lucia]: F. Norville, 1983. 50 p. of music: ill. In English and Creole. Contents: Santa Lucia — Shabeen la — Harry — Amelina — Pa touche moin — Oui nous dit sa vre — Madrie leve — Sa nai dit mama moin — We welcome you here — Jeune ti fille — Oil Bill la — Doo do darling — La rose/la margarite mele — She say — Happy Christmas. Collection of folk and popular songs by Norville and others.

672. Simmons, Harold F.C. "Notes on folklore in St. Lucia." In *Iouanaloa: recent writing from St. Lucia*, ed. Edward Brathwaite. Castries: Dept. of Extra Mural Studies, [University of the West Indies], 1963, pp. 41–49. Discusses various forms of St. Lucian folk music—hymns, drinking songs, the music of the La Rose and La Marguerite flower societies, work songs, and folk dances.

673. *St. Lucia sings* / [compiled by] Joyce Auguste. St. Lucia: Lithographic Press, 1984. 48 p. of music: ill. Contents: La Marguerite songs — La Rose songs — Songs from folk musicals by Roderick Walcott — Konte — Saint Cecilia, patron saint of musicians — Contemporary songs — Traditional songs — Christmas songs. Folk song collection. Includes a profile of the choral group Hewanorra Voices led by Joyce Auguste (p. 38).

Journals

674. *Lucian kaiso.* Castries, St. Lucia: Folk Research Centre, 1990–. No. 1 (Feb. 1990)–. Annual. Issue for 1996 not published. Invaluable source of information on the local calypso/soca scene in St. Lucia. Covers the island's recording industry, leading performers, press, and more.

Articles

675. Charles, Patricia. "Saint Lucia music school: case study in collaboration." *CARICOM Perspective*, No. 56–57 (July–Dec 1992):

90, 92. Traces the development of the Saint Lucia School of Music from its inception in 1987.

676. Crowley, Daniel J. "Kinds of folk music differentiated according to social institution: St. Lucia." *Caribbean Society and Culture Notes*, Vol. 1, No. 2 (December 1955): [8–9]. List of St. Lucian folk music styles with brief descriptions for each.

677. ———. "Song and dance in St. Lucia." *Ethnomusicology Newsletter*, No. 9 (January 1957): 4–14. Covers music of the La Rose and La Marguerite singing societies, songs for family rituals, masquerade music, caliso (old-style calypso), and music for work and play.

678. Guilbault, Jocelyne. "Fitness and flexibility: funeral wakes in St. Lucia, West Indies." *Ethnomusicology*, Vol. 31, No. 2 (Spring–Summer 1987): 273–299. Ethnographic study of wakes in St. Lucia and the musical activities associated with them. Based on fieldwork conducted between 1980 and 1983.

679. ———. "Oral and literate strategies in performances: the La Rose and La Marguerite organizations in St. Lucia." *Yearbook for Traditional Music*, Vol. 19 (1987): 97–115. Ethnographic portrait of two rival social organizations, the La Rose and La Marguerite societies, and the music that helps define them and their place in St. Lucian society. Revision of chapter one of Guilbault's Ph.D. thesis (670).

680. ———. "A St. Lucian 'kwadril' evening." *Latin American Music Review*, Vol. 6, No. 1 (Spring–Summer 1985): 31–57. Descriptive and interpretive study of a quadrille (*kwadril*) performance event covering the history of the style in St. Lucia, the structure of the performance, and the event itself.

681. Midgett, Douglas K. "Performance roles and musical change in a Caribbean society." *Ethnomusicology*, Vol. 21, No. 1 (January 1977): 55–73. Ethnography of La Rose singing in St. Lucia, a genre of religious music associated with celebrations for St. Rose de Lima.

UNITED STATES
See also 443, 456

*682. Armstrong, James D. "Vodou drumming: an overview of Haitian ritual drumming in New York City." Thesis (M.M.)—Bowling

Green State University, 1997. iii, 47 leaves: music + 1 sound tape reel.

683. Burroughs, Joan H. "Haitian ceremonial dance on the concert stage: the contextual transference and transformation of Yanvalou." Dissertation (Ph.D.)—New York University, 1995. xiii, 296 leaves: ill. Contents: Historical overview — The symbolic dimension of Yanvalou — Serving the lwa — A ceremonial event — Yanvalou on the concert stage — Analysis. Offers an analysis of ritual and theatrical settings of Yanvalou, a Vodou ritual music and dance, based on examples from New York City.

*684. Keister, Jay Davis. "Vodou music and spirit possession in Washington, D.C." Thesis (M.A.)—UCLA, 1991. vi, 110 leaves: ill.

685. Wilcken, Lois E. "The changing hats of Haitian staged folklore in New York City." In *Island sounds in the global city: Caribbean popular music and identity in New York*, eds. Ray Allen and Lois Wilcken. New York: New York Folklore Society, etc., 1998, pp. 162–183.

686. ———. "Music folklore among Haitians in New York: staged representations and the negotiation of identity." Dissertation (Ph.D.)—Columbia University, 1991. ix, 331 leaves: ill., music. Contents: The pre-migration context: Haiti — The Haitian migration to New York — The cultural dimension: folklore — Close-up: La Troupe Makandal — Ambivalence and change in folklore. History and ethnography of Haitian folkloric music and dance in New York. Focuses on the contributions of choreographers and musicians such as Lavinia Williams, Jean-Leon Destine, Louines Louinis, Paulette St. Lot, Arnold Elie, and Frisner Augustin.

687. ———. "Vodou music among Haitians living in New York: a symbolic approach." Thesis (M.A.)—Hunter College, 1986. 134 leaves: ill., music. Offers a discussion of 'songs, percussion patterns, instruments, and performance practice in relation to one another and in the context of the religion.'

Journals

688. *Haiti Culture*. Brooklyn, NY: s.n., 1984–. Monthly magazine which includes extensive coverage of Haitian popular music activity and artists based in New York.

Articles

689. Averill, Gage. "Haitian fascination: Still the best in town." *The Beat*, Vol. 12, No. 3 (1993): 58–59. Conversation with Jeff Wainwright, a producer and part owner of the Miami-based Nouvel Jenerasyon label Melodie Makers, about the Haitian record industry.

690. ———. "Hey, Miami: listen up!; Meet the musicians and the music of Little Haiti." *New Times* (Miami), Vol. 2, No. 39 (Mar. 16–22 1988): 10–15. Long feature on the local Haitian popular music scene in Miami based on interviews with key figures such as Wagner Lalanne, Robert Martino and Dadou Pasquet.

691. Cobo-Hanlon, Leila. "The culture of Konpa; Haiti's most popular and best-known music thrives in South Florida, but few people other than Haitians known it." *Miami Herald* (Jan. 13 1999): 1E–2E. Feature.

692. Courlander, Harold. "Some New York recording episodes, 1940–41." *Resound* (Bloomington), Vol. 7, No. 4 (October 1988): 2–6. Includes details on recordings made with Haitian folkloric musicians in New York during the early 1940s.

693. McAlister, Elizabeth. "Rara: Haitians make some noise in Brooklyn." *The Beat*, Vol. 10, No. 4 (1991): 28–29. Feature on the revival of interest in Rara music among middle-class members of Brooklyn, NY's Haitian emigre community.

694. McDonnell, Evelyn. "Compas gets cool." *Miami Herald* (May 6 2001): 1M, 10M. Long feature on South Florida's compas scene and the challenges it faces in trying to extend its reach beyond its core Haitian audience.

695. Wilcken, Lois E. "Haiti cherie: journey of an immigrant music in New York City." *New York Folklore*, Vol. 14, No. 3–4 (1988): 179–189. Survey of folkloric and popular music traditions of New York's Haitian community with an emphasis on Vodou.

696. ———. "Haitian fascination: The spirits come to Brooklyn." *The Beat*, Vol. 10, No. 5 (1991): 26–28. Description of a Vodou initiation ceremony and its music.

697. ———. "One and one makes three: wisdom in the rhythmic organization of Vodou drumming." *Journal of Haitian Studies*, Vol. 10, No. 2 (Fall 2004): 68–73.

698. ———. "Power, ambivalence, and the remaking of Haitian Vodoun music in New York." *Latin American Music Review*, Vol. 13, No. 1 (Spring–Summer 1992): 1–32. Essay focusing on staged versions of Vodou performance in New York and the profound ambivalence of the area's Haitian community toward it.

Media Materials

*699. *Fet Gede in Little Haiti [videorecording]* / by Luke Wassermann. [United States?]: Ekulnamm Productions, 2006. 2 DVDs (140 min.). Subtitle on container: Festival of Vodou drumming. Summary: Depicts the drum and dance celebration of Fet Gede [Fete Guede], the Vodou festival of the dead, held at the Jakmel Art Gallery and the Jakmel Vodou Temple in the Little Haiti neighborhood of Miami, FL, Nov. 1, 3, and 5, 2005. Contents: Disc 1. Opening ceremony; Rara music; The night of Bawon Samedi. part 1 — Disc 2. Gede drumming; The night of Bawon Samedi, part 2.

IV

Biographical and Critical Studies

See also 1, 175, 381

*700. Bagoe, Aude-Anderson. *Encyclopedie de la musique traditionnelle aux Antilles-Guyane: musiciennes et musiciens ayant evolue en France metropolitaine*. Case Pilote [Martinique]: Editions Lafontaine, 2005. 271 p.: ill. Biographical dictionary of French Antillean musicians.

701. Boncy, Ralph, et al. *La chanson d'Haiti*. Montreal: CIDIHCA, 1992–. Contents: Tome 1 (1965–1985). Collection of Boncy's mini review essays on Haitian popular music recordings released between 1965 and 1985. Artists discussed are: G.M. Connection, Manno Charlemagne, Zekle, Scorpio, System Band, DP Express, Tabou Combo, Shleu-Shleu, Skah-Shah, Super Ensemble Weber Sicot, Ibo Combo, Volo-Volo de Boston, Mini All Stars, Bossa Combo, Orchestre Septentrional, Rodrigue Milien et Groupe Combite, Freres Dejean, 7 Vedettes, Gerald Merceron, Pirogue, Roger Colas, Magnum Band, Coupe Cloue, Orchestre Tropicana, Gypsies de Petionville, Difficiles, Marco Jeanty, and Raoul Guillaume.

702. Bordowitz, Hank. *Noise of the world: non-Western musicians in their own words*. Brooklyn, NY: Soft Skull Press, 2004. Includes interviews with Jocelyne Beroard/Kassav (p. 41–45); Fred Paul (p. 47–51); and Clifford Sylvain/Rara Machine (p. 57–61).

703. Cally, Sully. *Le grand livre des musiciens Creoles*. Gros Morne, [Martinique]: S. Cally, 1996. v. <1–>: ports. Contents: v. 1. Guadeloupe, Guyane, Martinique. Biographical dictionary

featuring sketches of most of the leading lights of French
Antillean popular music.

704. Louis-Charles, Thony. *Le compas direct: la vraie musique
entrainante haitienne de tous les temps.* Port-au-Prince: Thony
Louis-Charles, etc., 2003. 311 p.: ill. Collection of the author's
articles on Haitian popular music and musicians first published in
the Haitian dailies *Le Nouvelliste* and *Le Matin* between 1984 and
2002. Includes profiles of Jazz des Jeunes (p. 17–20), Nemours
Jean-Baptiste, Weber Sicot, Michel Pressoir (p. 97–108), Luc
Philippe (p. 111–114, 253–256), Wagner Lalanne (p. 117–122),
Anilus Cadet and Robert Molin (p. 125–130), Leconte Villevaleix
and Orchestre Citadelle (p. 147–152), Issa el Saieh (p. 170–175),
Antoine Charles Dessalines (p. 176–183), Gerard Dupervil (p.
185–191), Louis Lahens (p. 193–203), Emile Volel (p. 205–208),
Serge Rosenthal and Thony Moise of Shleu Shleu (p. 211–219),
Guy Durosier (p. 221–232), Fritz Duval (p. 235–241), Coupe Cloue
(p. 243–259), Ancy Dullon Joseph (p. 256–258), Pierre Michel
Pean (p. 261–264) and Jean Ledan (p. 264–269).

705. Sainvill, Ed Rainer, and Katia Millien Sainvill. *Tambours frappes,
Haitiens campes: la fabuleuse histoire de la musique haitienne de
la periode precolombienne a l'epoque contemporaine.* [New York]:
Heritage, [2001]. 570 p.: ill. A landmark biographical dictionary
on musicians and composers from Haiti and the Haitian diaspora.
Offers a wealth of data not available in any other source.

Articles

706. Averill, Gage. "Haitian fascination: Creme de la creme." *The Beat,*
Vol. 9, No. 1 (1990): 24–25. Column offering Averill's choices for
the 10 best Haitian recordings of 1989. Discusses releases by
Tabou Combo, Magnum Band, Farrah Juste, Emeline Michel,
Reginald Policard and le Caribbean Sextet, Zinglin, Orchestra
Tropicana d'Haiti, Skah Shah, and System Band.

707. ———. "Haitian fascination: Let me pass!" *The Beat,* Vol. 15, No.
4 (1996): 34. Reviews new releases by Emeline Michel (*Ban'M
Pase*), Kanpech (*Pale Yo*), and Tabou Combo (*Reference*).

708. ———. "Haitian fascination: The Miami magnet." *The Beat,* Vol.
9, No. 5 (1990): 38–39. Survey of recent recordings by Haitian
artists based in Miami, e.g. Skandal, Sakaj, Anderson Cameau,
Freres Dejean, and others.

709. ———. "Haitian fascination: Mizik san fwontie." *The Beat*, Vol. 15, No. 6 (1996): 36–37, 70–71. Discusses new recordings by Zshea (*n-o j-o-k-e*), Boukan Ginen (*Rev an Nou*), Ti Paris (*Anasilya*), and Magnum Band (*San Fwontie*).

710. ———. "Haitian fascination: 'Papa took a boat': the tragedy of the Haitian boat people." *The Beat*, Vol. 11, No. 4 (1992): 26–27, 74. Surveys two decades of songs about the plight of Haiti's boat people by Atis Endepandan, Rodrigue Milien, Farah Juste/Manno Charlemagne, Ti-Manno, and Dadou Pasquet.

711. ———. "Haitian fascination: Watering the roots." *The Beat*, Vol. 9, No. 3 (1990): 60–61. Column focusing on the roots movement in Haitian pop and some of its leading voices, e.g. Boukman Eksperyans, Foula, Sanba-yo, Rara Machine.

712. ———. "Haitian fascination: Where there's smoke...." *The Beat*, Vol. 13, No. 1 (1994): 36–37, 73. Discusses recent recordings by Boukan Ginen (*Jou a rive*), Emeline Michel (*Rhum et Flamme*), and Ram (*Aibobo*).

713. ———. "Haitian fascination: Women taking risks." *The Beat*, Vol. 11, No. 3 (1992): 62–64, 84. Column outlining women's contributions to Haitian popular music. Discusses singers Lumane Casimir, Martha Jean-Claude, Toto Bissainthe, Farah Juste, Carole "Maroule" Demesmin, Myriam Dorisme, Fedia Laguerre, and the all-female Nouvel Jenerasyon group Riske.

714. Cauver, J.G. "Chanson retro, l'album souvenir." *Antilla*, No. 220 (dec 10–17 1986): 6–9. Photo-feature on a concert showcasing a number of legendary singers from the French Caribbean.

715. Denis, Jean-Michel. "Les nouveaux looks du zouk." *Afrique Elite*, No. 23 (fevrier 1988): 24–25. Discusses the work of reigning zouk stars Experience 7 and Zouk Machine with Tanya Saint-Val.

716. Dring, Brian. "The other Caribbean: Definitely Dominica." *The Beat*, Vol. 17, No. 5 (1998): 34–35. Survey of recent dance music releases from Dominica. Among the groups discussed are the WCK Band, Exile One, Midnight Groovers, and others.

717. Galland, Stephane. "Le zouk-love, a-t-il un avenir?" *Afiavi*, No. 24 (mai–juin 2000): 12–13. Discusses the work of zouk singers Saxe, Jacky Rapon, Marie-Jose Gibon, and Jean-Michel Rotin.

718. Ponnamah, Michel. "Emigration: la musique martiniquaise a Paris." *Antilla*, No. 27 (oct. 1 1982): 35–38. Portrait of three

French Antillean musicians long resident in Paris—Alain Jean-Marie, Bibi Louison, and Henri Guedon.

719. Scaramuzzo, Gene. "The other Caribbean: Hot zouk in the summertime." *The Reggae & African Beat*, Vol. 7, No. 5 (1988): 41, 56. Survey of recent releases by Zouk Machine, Edith Lefel, Ralph Thamar/Malavoi, Sartana, Pascal Vallot, Les Aiglons, and others.

7 VEDETTES (Haiti)
See 701

AIGLONS, LES (Guadeloupe)
See 719

AKIYO (Guadeloupe)

720. Labesse, Patrick. "Les tambours de la grande terre." *Vibrations* (Lausanne), n.s. No. 14 (oct–nov 1996): 21–23. Feature on Akiyo, the Guadeloupean percussion group.

ALBICY, JEAN-MARC (Martinique)
See **MALAVOI**

ALEXANDRE, STEPHANE "STEF" (Haiti/US)
See **MIEL**

ALIE, MARIEJOSE (1951–) (Martinique)

721. Mandibele. "Marijose Ali: Fal-fret genyen, jodi-jou tout moun ka koute lanmizik-taa." *Antilla*, No. 329 (avril 17–23 1989): 15. In Kreyol. Interview.

722. "Musique: Marie-Jose Alie." *Antilla Kreyol*, No. 13 (octobre 1989): 8–9. Portrait of Alie accompanied by a selection of her song lyrics.

723. Pinalie-Dracius, Pierre. "Marie-Jose: ni vierge ni martyre." *Antilla*, No. 241 (mai 14–21 1987): 31–32. Profile.

724. ———. "Marijose derriere et devant la camera." *Antilla Kreyol*, No. 12 (fevrier 1989): 35–36. Short feature on the television actress and singer.

ALPHA, JENNY (1910–) (Martinique/France)

725. Bertrand, Anca. "Rencontre a Dakar: Jenny Alpha." *Paralleles*, No. 17 (1966): 21. Profile of the popular singer and actress from Martinique.

726. Migow, Erwan. "Jenny Alpha: la salut par les planches." *Divas* (Paris), No. 2 (aout–sept 1999): 28–29. Feature.

AM4 [Association Mi Mes Manmay Matinik] (Martinique)
See also 627, 649

727. "Hommage a Man Carmelite: premiere bamboula de l'ile." *Antilla*, No. 317 (janv. 20–30 1989): 32–33. Conversation with a representative of the Martinican dance and music collective AM4 about an upcoming tribute to veteran *bele* folksinger and dancer Man Carmelite. Includes a discussion of AM4's aims, aesthetic concerns and commitment to keeping idioms such as the *bele*, *kalenda*, and *danmye* alive.

ANTOINE, ALFRED (Martinique/France)

728. Mandibele. "Musique: Alfred Antoine nous revient." *Antilla*, No. 357 (nov 9–15 1989): 39–40. Short interview with a Martinican popular musician based in France.

ANTOINETTE, JEAN-CLAUDE (Guadeloupe)
See **VAN LEVE**

ATIS ENDEPANDAN (Haiti)
See 710

AUGUSTE, JOYCE (St. Lucia)
See 673

AUGUSTIN, FRISNER (1948–) (Haiti/US)
See also 558, 686

729. Amoruso, Carol. "Frisner Augustin, Vodou ambassador." *Rhythm Music*, Vol. 6, No. 12 (Dec 1997–Jan 1998): 20–23. Feature.

730. Govenar, Alan. *Masters of traditional arts: a biographical dictionary*. Santa Barbara, Calif.: ABC-CLIO, 2001, v. 1, pp. 36–38.

731. "Je suis le maitre du tambour." *Haiti Culture*, Vol. 3, No. 9 (janvier 1987): 2, 14. Feature.

732. Ridgeway, James, and Jean Jean-Pierre. "Haitian drums call from Port-au-Prince to Brooklyn." *Natural History*, Vol. 107, No. 10 (Dec 1998–Jan 1999): 30–37. Feature on Brooklyn-based drummer Frisner Augustin and his itinerant life as a master drummer/ educator and Vodou missionary.

733. Wadler, Joyce. "Public lives: An urban folk hero, captive to the drums." *New York Times* (November 17 1998): B2. Profile of Haitian master drummer Frisner Augustin.

AYIZAN (Haiti)

734. Pareles, Jon. "From Haiti, the rhythm of Ayizan." *New York Times* (December 12 1986): C23. Interview with the leader of Ayizan, Alix 'Tit' Pascal, about the group and its music.

AZEROT, NESTOR (Haiti)

735. "Nestor Azerot." *Haiti Culture*, Vol. 3, No. 9 (janvier 1987): 4, 13. Interview with the ex-Magnum Band singer.

BAGO [Pierre Michel Balthazar] (Martinique)
See 152

BAGOE, MICHEL (Martinique)

736. Lafontaine, Jeannine. "Rencontre avec Michel Bagoe." *Antilla Kreyol*, No. 14 (janvier 1990): 32–33. Interview with a trapset drummer from Martinique.

BAKA, GISELE (Martinique)

737. "Interview: Le come-back de Gisele Baka." *Antilla*, No. 322 (fev 27–mars 5 1989): 27, 26. Interview with the Martinican singer.

BA LAN (Martinique)
See 132

BALLETS FOLKLORIQUES MARTINIQUAIS (Martinique)
See also 627

738. Bertrand, Anca. "A propos des Ballets Folkloriques Martiniquais." *Paralleles*, No. 26 (1968): 74–77. Profile of a leading Martinican folk dance and music ensemble.

BANGUIO, MAURICE (1905–1965) (Martinique/France)
See 215

BAYARD, PIERRE "PEPE" (1945–2008) (Haiti/US)

739. Charles, Jacqueline. "Pierre 'Pepe' Bayard, 62; Pioneer in Haitian music, advocate." *Miami Herald* (Mar. 27 2008): B5. Obituary.

BAZILE, MICHEL-ANGE (1953–) (Haiti)

740. "Que promet Michel-Angel Bazile?" *Haiti Culture*, Vol. 2, No. 11 (mars 1986): 3. Interview with the Haitian singer-songwriter.

BEAUBRUN, DANIEL "DADI" (Haiti)
See also **BOUKMAN EKSPERYANS**

741. Dring, Brian. "The other Caribbean: Intertwining roots." *The Beat*, Vol. 24, No. 6 (2005): 44–45. Conversation with Beaubrun about *Tou Manbre*, his new recording with the group Lataye.

BEAUBRUN, MARJORIE (Haiti)
See **BOUKMAN EKSPERYANS**

BEAUBRUN, MIMEROSE (Haiti)
See **BOUKMAN EKSPERYANS**

BEAUBRUN, THEODORE "LOLO" (Haiti)
See also **BOUKMAN EKSPERYANS**

742. Charles, Jacqueline. "Sounds of change." *Miami Herald* (Feb. 8 2004): 1B–2B. Feature on Beaubrun's vocal opposition to the Haitian Presidency of Jean-Bertrand Aristide. Includes discussion of how that position is being reflected in his most recent song lyrics.

BECO [Moise Crespy] (Guadeloupe)

743. "Moise Crespy, un homme qui monte." *Antilla*, No. 108 (juin 22–29 1984): 38–39. Interview with the Guadeloupean musician and bandleader.

BEL ALIANS (Martinique)
See 627, 649

BELENOU (Martinique)
See also 627

744. Mandibele. "Antilla culture: Belenou vire." *Antilla*, No. 373 (mars 9–16 1990): 35. Profile of Belenou, a young ensemble which has helped to spur a resurgence of interest in *bele* music and dance in Martinique.

BERNABE, JOBY [Georges Bernabe] (1954–) (Martinique)

745. Galland, Stephane. "Paroles de Joby Bernabe, artiste meconnu."
Afiavi, No. 24 (mai–juin 2000): 22–23. Conversation with the
Martinican musician and poet.

BERNARD, ALEX (Martinique)
See **BERNARD BROTHERS**

BERNARD BROTHERS (Martinique)
See 152

BERNARD, JACKY (1952–) (Martinique)
See **BERNARD BROTHERS; WEST INDIES JAZZ BAND**

BERNARD, NICOL (1956–) (Martinique)
See **BERNARD BROTHERS; MALAVOI**

BEROARD, JOCELYNE (1954–) (Martinique/France)
See also 152, 702, 910–937

746. Schwarz-Bart, Simone, and Andre Schwarz-Bart. *Hommage a la
femme noire*. [Belgium]: Editions Consulaires, 1988–, v. 6, pp.
116–127. Biographical sketch.

Articles

747. Berrian, Brenda F. "Zouk diva: interview with Jocelyne Beroard."
MaComere, Vol. 2 (1999): 1–11. Interview with Beroard originally
conducted in May, 1995. Touches on her formative years as a
singer in Martinique, the ideas behind the songs on her solo
recordings, and her work with Kassav.

748. Bradshaw, Paul. "Zouk love." *Straight, No Chaser*, No. 3 (Spring
1989): 22–24. Conversation with Beroard about zouk, Kassav, and
her own rise to fame.

749. Dring, Brian. "The other Caribbean: Pawol Jocelyne." *The Beat*,
Vol. 23, No. 1 (2004): 49. Conversation with Beroard about her
new recording *Madousinay*, upcoming projects, and her move back
to Martinique.

750. Leymarie, Isabelle. "Jocelyne Beroard." *Unesco Courier* (April
1996): 48–49. Interview.

751. Pulvar, J. Marc. "Portrait: Jocelyne Beroard, 'Canaille, pas devergondee.'" *Antilla*, No. 382 (mai 11–17 1990): 36–41. Interview with the Antillean singing star.

752. Serbin-Thomas, Marie-Jeanne. "Jocelyne Beroard: quand la musique devient une famille." *Divas* (Paris), No. 9 (aout 2000): 20–21. Feature focusing on Beroard's humanitarian work with the organization Enfants et Partage.

753. "Succes: Jocelyn Beroard, la star qui monte...." *Antilla*, No. 225 (janv. 21–28 1987): 32–33. Short interview.

BIGGA HAITIAN [Charles Dorismond] (Haiti/US)
See **DORISMOND FAMILY**

BISSAINTHE, TOTO [Marie Clothilde Bissainthe] (1935–1994) (Haiti/France)
See also 713

754. "Decesos: Toto Bissainthe." *Canales*, ano 22, no. 385 (julio–agosto 1994): 48. Obituary.

755. Erwan, Jacques. "Chanson sans frontieres: Toto Bissainthe." *Paroles & Musique*, No. 5 (dec. 1980): 34–35. Feature.

756. Lucas, Rafael. "Toto Bissainthe, la transe tranquille de l'ame haitienne." *Afiavi Magazine*, No. 2 (mars–mai 2007): 42. Profile.

757. Schwarz-Bart, Simone, and Andre Schwarz-Bart. *Hommage a la femme noire*. [Belgium]: Editions Consulaires, 1988–, v. 6, pp. 40–50. Biographical sketch.

758. "Toto Bissainthe, actress and singer, 60." *New York Times* (June 9 1994): B20. Short obituary.

BIWA

759. "Biwa exclusif." *Antilla*, No. 41 (fevrier 18 1983): 21. Short profile which includes complete info on the group's personnel at the time.

BLANCHET, LINA MATHON [Lina Fussman-Mathon] (1902–1993) (Haiti)
See **HAITI CHANTE**

BOISDUR, ESNARD (Guadeloupe)
See **KATEL**

BOISLAVILLE, LOULOU [Louis-Lucien Boislaville] (1919–2001) (Martinique)
See also 158, 627, 738

*760. *Chants et compositions de Loulou Boislaville: un recueil de textes et partitions parmi les plus belles chansons traditionnelles de la Martinique* / realise par Jean-Luc Danglades. Fort-de-France: SOCIFAC, 1997. v.: ill. Contents: v. 1. Biguines, mazurkas, valses creoles, vides, cantiques de Noel et chants varies.

BONITO PATUA (Cuba)

761. Gonzalez Bello, Manuel. "Bonito Patua: fiesta en casa de Eva." *Bohemia*, ano 77, no. 10 (marzo 8 1985): 3–7. Feature on Bonito Patua, the Cuban-Haitian folkloric group from Camaguey, and its leader Eva Luben Ilien.

BOSSA COMBO (Haiti)
See 701

BOUKAN GINEN (Haiti/US)
See also 709, 712

762. Averill, Gage. "Haitian Fascination: The day has come." *The Beat*, Vol. 14, No. 2 (1995): 33. Review of Boukan Ginen's debut recording, *Jou A Rive* (Xenophile).

763. Perlich, Tim. "Boukan Ginen: Haiti's Rara-rock renegades dance toward democracy." *Now On* (Online), Vol. 15, No. 48 (Aug. 1–7, 1996). http://www.now.com/issues/15/48/Ent/cover.html. Conversation with the group's leader, Jimmy Jean-Felix.

764. Waters, Alan. "Boukan Ginen: new roots music of Haiti." *Rhythm Music Magazine*, Vol. 4, No. 3 (1995): 14–17. Feature on the Haitian roots band.

BOUKMAN EKSPERYANS (Haiti)
See also 458, 464, 468, 480, 503, 711

765. Lipsitz, George. *Dangerous crossroads: popular music, postmodernism, and the poetics of place*. London: Verso, 1994. Includes a section on the Haitian roots music of Boukman Eksperyans (p. 7–12).

766. White, Timothy. *Music to my ears: the Billboard essays: profiles of popular music in the '90s*. New York: Henry Holt, 1996, pp. 81–84. Reprint of a profile first published in *Billboard* (Nov. 21 1992).

Articles

767. Averill, Gage. "Haitian fascination: A day for the hunter, a day for the prey." *The Beat*, Vol. 14, No. 3 (1995): 28. Column on Boukman and their new recording *Libete (Pran Pou Pran'L)* on Mango Records.

768. Baehler, Jean-Marc, and Fred Bernard. "Croisement." *Vibrations* (Lausanne), No. 9 (fevrier–mars 1993): 25–26. Interview.

769. Burr, Ty. "Behind the scenes: Eksperyans counts." *Entertainment Weekly*, No. 148 (December 11 1992): 19. Short feature.

770. Cullman, Brian. "Vodou rising: Boukman Eksperyans build the rhythm of resistance." *Village Voice* (June 6 1995): 33–36. Feature on Haiti's leading *mizik rasin* (roots music) group.

771. Eyre, Banning. "Africa Fete." *Rhythm Music*, Vol. 4, No. 6 (July 1995): 33. Short feature.

772. Gonzalez, Fernando. "Haitian group explores the sound of Voodoo." *Boston Globe* (May 17 1991): 42. Feature on Boukman Eksperyans based on a conversation with the group's leader, Theodore "Lolo" Beaubrun.

773. Gordon, Leah. "Racines rockin' in Haiti." *Folk Roots*, No. 138 (December 1994): 34–35, 37, 39. Feature on Boukman Eksperyans and the roots music movement in Haitian pop.

774. "Hard Hittin" Harry. "Boukman Eksperyans: Haiti's political refugees and modern day heroes; A conversation with Theodore "Lolo" Beaubrun, Jr. (lead singer)." *Black Diaspora*, Vol. 21, No. 6 (September 2000): 22–24. Interview with Boukman's founder and leader, preceded by a profile of Beaubrun himself (p. 20).

775. Heilig, Steve. "Boukman Eksperyans, Haiti's real revolutionaries." *The Beat*, Vol. 18, No. 2 (1999): 42–44, 46. Interview with the group's leader, Theodore 'Lolo' Beaubrun.

776. Moody, Shelah. "World riddims: Boukman Eksperyans." *Reggae Report*, Vol. 10, No. 9 (1992): 32–33. Feature.

777. Nixon, Richard. "Are you Eksperyansed?" *Reflex Magazine*, No. 30 (December 1992): 25–27. Feature.

778. Pareles, Jon. "Haitian band revitalizes tradition." *New York Times* (April 29 1990): 60. Review of the group's New York concert debut.

779. Rochlin, Brian E. "Boukman Eksperyans: fighting the hate that Haiti produced." *Option* (Los Angeles), No. 46 (Sept–Oct 1992): 82–86. Feature.

780. Silver, Vernon. "Souls in a bottle; 'Roots music' is the music of Haitian revolution. One group, Boukman Eksperyans, plays it in spite of the danger it could bring." *New York Times* (Nov. 28 1993): Sec. 9 (Styles), p. 6. Interview with Boukman's leader Theodore "Lolo" Beaubrun as the group prepares to head back to an uncertain future in Haiti.

781. Sofranko, Denise. "Boukman Eksperyans: soundtrack for a revolution." *Dirty Linen*, No. 63 (April–May 1996): 40–43. Feature.

782. Spencer, Peter. "The Vodou pulse of Boukman Eksperyans." *Sing Out!*, Vol. 38, No. 3 (Nov. 93–Jan. 1994): 25–28.

BRIVAL, ROLAND (Martinique/France)
See 349

CADET, ANILUS (Haiti)
See 704

CALLY, SULLY (1955–) (Martinique)
See 152

CAMEAU, ANDERSON (Haiti/US)
See 708

783. "Anderson Cameau: sa vie a travers la musique." *Haiti Culture*, Vol. 1, No. 9 (janvier 1985): 5–6. Interview with the veteran Haitian trumpeter.

784. "Des Skah Shah aux Caribbean Stars." *Haiti Culture*, Vol. 2, No. 3 (juillet 1985): 5, 16. Interview with the ex-Skah Shah trumpeter about his newly formed group, Caribbean Stars.

785. "Le souffle puissant de Anderson Cameau." *Haiti Culture*, Vol. 4, No. 1 (mai 1987): 13–14. Interview with the trumpeter best known for his work with the dance band Skah Shah.

CANONGE, MARIO (1960–) (Martinique)
See also 152

786. Bowe, Bela. "Mario Canonge: des claviers bien tropicaux." *Jazzman*, n.s. No. 3 (mai 1995): 18–19. Feature.

787. Cauver, J.G. "Decouverte: Mario Canonge, jeune pianiste Martiniquais, leader du groupe Ultra-Marine." *Antilla*, No. 261 (nov 5–11 1987): 12–13. Interview.

788. Perraudin, Jean-Baptiste. "Mon batteur et moi: Mario Canonge." *Batteur Magazine*, No. 179 (mars 2005): 16–17. Conversation with the pianist about his relationship with various drummers.

CARABALI ISUAMA [also Izuama] (Cuba)

789. Ante, Gilberto. "Santiago de Cuba: en visperas del carnaval." *Bohemia*, ano 64, no. 29 (julio 21 1972): 42–45. Interview with representatives from the Santiago comparsas Carabali Izuama and Carabali Oluga.

790. *El Cabildo Carabali Isuama* / Nancy Perez ... [et al.]. Santiago de Cuba: Editorial Oriente, 1982. 104 p.: ill. History of a leading comparsa from Santiago de Cuba. Includes an analysis of their songs (p. 37–56).

791. "Las comparsas: Carabali Izuama y Carabali Olugo." *Revolucion y Cultura*, No. 115 (marzo 1982): 60–61. Profile of two leading Afro-Cuban Carnival groups from Santiago de Cuba.

792. Gonzalez Freire, Nati. "Entre tumbas y carabali." *Bohemia*, ano 69, no. 20 (mayo 20 1977): 10–13. Feature on Santiago de Cuba's Carabali Izuama and the Afro-Cuban music and dance idioms, e.g. tumba francesa, they are known for preserving.

793. Hearn, Adrian Hugh. "Viven los cabildos: el caso de la Carabali Isuama." In *Actas: VII Conferencia Internacional de Cultura Africana y Afroamericana*, eds. Yadine Yara Gonzalez, Zaylen Claveria Centurion. Santiago de Cuba: Centro Cultural Africano Fernando Ortiz, [2002?], pp. 107–111. Paper on Carabali Isuama, a comparsa group which has long been a cornerstone of Santiago's Carnival.

CARAIBANA (Guadeloupe)

794. "The Bouillante gros-cas group." *Paralleles*, No. 15 (1966): 16–17. English translation of Hilaire piece below.

795. Hilaire, Francisque. "Le groupe gros-cas de Bouillante." *Paralleles*, No. 6 (1965): 14. Conversation with the manager of Caraibana, a folkloric music and dance group from Bouillante, Guadeloupe, about their repertoire.

CARAIBE JAZZ ENSEMBLE (French Antilles)

796. Larade, E., and J. Lanoir. "Caraibe Jazz Ensemble au carrefour des musiques caraibeennes." *Son!* (Abymes), No. 3 (1984): 28–29. Interview with the group's manager, Charlie Chomereau Lamotte.

CARIBBEAN STARS
See 784

CARMELITE, MAN (Martinique)
See 727

CARNOT [Francois Moleon] (1919–1998) (Guadeloupe)

797. Carnot. *Alors ma chere, moi—* / Carnot par lui-meme; propos d'un musicien guadeloupeen recueillis et traduits par Marie-Celine Lafontaine. Paris: Editions Caribeennes, 1986. 159 p.: ill. Q&A transcript of Marie-Celine Lafontaine's oral history interviews with Carnot about his life as a gwo ka drummer in Guadeloupe.

798. Halley, Michel. "Karno e Halley ka pale." *Moun* (Pointe-a-Pitre), No. 2 (juil.–sept. 1986): 53–55. Conversation with Carnot, the gwo ka master drummer.

CASERUS, EMMANUEL
See **TI-EMILE**

CASIMIR, LUMANE (1917–1955) (Haiti)
See 713

CAUDEIRON, MABEL "CISSIE" (1909–1968) (Dominica)

799. Warner, Paula. "Music and songs of Dominica: 'Cissie' Caudeiron." *Caricom Perspective*, No. 52–53 (July–December 1991): 46. Profile celebrating the contributions of activist and folk singer Mabel Caudeiron to Dominican culture.

CEDIA, SYLVIANE (1955–) (French Guiana)

800. "Originaire de la Guyanne, Cedia chante en creole, en Francais, en anglais, en espagnol, c'est une chanteuse auteur compositeur." *Amina*, No. 123 (sept 1982): 63. Interview.

CELESTIN, LOUIS (1922–1986) (Haiti)

801. "Louis Celestin: a travers le temps." *Haiti Culture*, Vol. 2, No. 9 (janv. 1986): 11. Profile of the Haitian folkloric drummer.

802. "Louis Celestin est mort." *Haiti Culture*, Vol. 2, No. 10 (fev. 1986): 7, 9. Report on Celestin's death from cancer on Jan. 10 1986.

CELIA

See **MANGA, CELIA**

CHANCY, LOUBERT (Haiti)
See 1012

CHARLEMAGNE, MANNO [Joseph Emmanuel Charlemagne] (1948–) (Haiti)
See also 435, 701, 710

803. Chalmay, Manno. *Manno Charlemagne: trente ans de chansons = thirty years of songs*. Port-au-Prince, Haiti: Edition Special Fokal, 2007. [47] p.: ill. Consists of a bi-lingual introduction by Joanne Biondi on Charlemagne's career and his importance as a political singer in Haiti followed by an anthology of his song lyrics.

804. ———, et al. "Five songs." In *The archipelago: new writing from and about the Caribbean*, eds. Robert Antoni and Bradford Morrow. Annandale-on-Hudson, NY: Bard College, 1996, pp. 142–166. Translations of five Charlemagne songs, with accompanying notes by Gage Averill and an afterword by Mark Dow offering a portrait of the man.

805. Jacobson, Robert R. "Manno Charlemagne." In *Contemporary Black biography*. Detroit: Gale Research, 1996, v. 11, pp. 39–41. Biographical sketch of the twoubadou/angaje singer-songwriter.

Articles

806. Averill, Gage. "Haitian fascination: Mayor Manno." *The Beat*, Vol. 14, No. 5 (1995): 31. Profile of Charlemagne as he transitions from protest singer to Mayor of Port-au-Prince.

807. ———. "Manno Charlemagne imprisoned twice by the Haitian army." *The Beat*, Vol. 10, No. 6 (1991): 29. Report on the angaje singer's imprisonment following his attacks on the men responsible for overthrowing Jean-Bertrand Aristide.

808. ———, and Mark Dow. "Konpa demokrasi-a: the rhythm of democracy." *The Beat*, Vol. 13, No. 6 (1994): 54–55, 82. Consists of a profile of Charlemagne by Gage Averill followed by an interview conducted by Mark Dow.

809. Birnbaum, Larry. "Rockbeat: Haiti crimes." *Village Voice* (November 19 1991): 90. Brief report on Charlemagne's beating and detention in Port-au-Prince following the 1991 coup against Jean-Bertrand Aristide.

810. French, Howard W. "Haitian chronicles." *New York Times* (March 8 1992): Sec. 2, p. 32. Short profile of Charlemagne and his repeated battles with the military government of Haiti.

811. Gonzalez, Fernando. "The Bob Dylan of Haiti." *Miami Herald* (Jan. 27 1994): 1G, 7G. Feature on Charlemagne.

812. "Progressistes!" *Haiti Culture*, Vol. 5, No. 3 (dec. 1988): 4, 18. Interview.

813. Rohter, Larry. "Port-au-Prince journal: Protest singer is now mayor, but still protesting." *New York Times* (October 17 1995): A4. Profile of ex-troubadour Charlemagne in his new role as Mayor of Port-au-Prince.

814. "Vie artistique a NY...." *Haiti Culture*, Vol. 2, No. 9 (janvier 1986): 3, 15. Interview with the protest singer.

Media Materials

*815. *Dans la gueule du crocodile [videorecording]: un portrait de Manno Charlemagne* / un film de Catherine Larivain et Lucie Ouimet. [Paris]: Mediatheque des trois mondes, 1998. 1 videocassette (52 min.). Utilizes the memories and reflections of Charlemagne's many musical collaborators to sketch his life and career.

CHARLERY, MAURICE (1909–) (Martinique/France)
See 215

CHASSEUR, TONY (1962–) (Martinique/France)

816. Dring, Brian. "The other Caribbean: The alphabetical islands." *The Beat*, Vol. 21, No. 6 (2002): 31. Short interview with the Martinican zouk singer.

817. Jerome, Patrick. "Tony Chasseur, faire une musique originale." *Fouyaya*, No. 58 (sept. 1987): 36–37. Interview.

CHOMEREAU-LAMOTHE, CHARLY (Guadeloupe)

818. Ducosson, Dany. "Interview-musique: Un moment avec Charly Lamothe." *CARE* (Paris), No. 13 (fevrier 1988): 124–133. Interview with the veteran Guadeloupean percussionist.

CILLA, MAX (1944–) (Martinique)

819. "Max Cilla, fluter les mornes." *Antilla*, No. 342 (juillet 17–23 1989): 10. Brief interview.

820. Sebas, J. "Kaleidoscope: Max Cilla." *Antilla*, No. 160 (juillet 19–26 1985): 7. Portrait of the flautist and bandleader.

CIMBER, ALPHONSE (ca. 1899–1981) (Haiti/US)

821. "Alphonse Cimber, drummer, is dead; Master of U.S. African music played for dancers." *New York Times* (March 19 1981): B14. Obituary for the Haitian master drummer best known for his work with folkloric dance companies of the 1940s and '50s.

COLAS, ROGER (1937–1986) (Haiti)
See also 701

822. Camille, Jacques. "En memoire de Roger Colas." *Haiti Culture*, Vol. 4, No. 5 (sept. 1987): 30. Memorial tribute to the veteran Haitian dance band singer.

823. "Roger Colas." *Haiti Culture*, Vol. 3, No. 6 (oct. 1986): 8. Obituary.

COMBETTE, CHRIS (ca. 1956–) (French Guiana)

824. Birnbaum, Larry. "Chris Combette, pan-Caribbean pop." *Rhythm Music*, Vol. 7, No. 7 (July 1998): 38–39. Feature on the French Antillean pop singer.

825. Dring, Brian. "The other Caribbean: interview with Chris Combette." *The Beat*, Vol. 23, No. 2 (2004): 27.

COMPAGNIE CREOLE, LA (France)
See 156

CORIDUN, VICTOR (1895–1973) (Martinique)
See 611

COUPE CLOUE [Jean-Gesner Henri] (1925–1998) (Haiti)
See also 701, 704

826. Averill, Gage. "Coupe Cloue discography." *The Beat*, Vol. 12, No. 1 (1993): 28.

827. ———. "Haitian fascination: Old grooves, new directions." *The Beat*, Vol. 8, No. 2 (1989): 20–21. Review of the Coupe Cloue recording *Racine*.

828. ———. "Passings: Coupe Cloue 1925–1998." *The Beat*, Vol. 17, No. 2 (1998): 59. Obituary.

829. Cadet, Henry. "Chanson: Coupe Cloue et la societe haitienne." *Demain-Haiti*, Vol. 1, No. 1 (aout 1982): 19. Column reflecting on the songs of Coupe Cloue and their critique of contemporary Haitian society.

830. "Coupe Cloue." *Haiti Culture*, Vol. 2, No. 6 (oct. 1985): 3, 11, 13. Interview with Cloue, Assade Francoeur, one of his singers, and Ernest Louis, his manager.

831. Miles, Milo. "King Cut's treasures." *Village Voice* (June 15 1993): 67, 70. Discographical profile focusing on Coupe Cloue's Earthbeat CD *Maximum Compas from Haiti*.

CREOLE PROJECT (France)
See 1007

CULTIER, MARIUS (1942–1985) (Martinique)
See also 152, 159

832. "Marius Cultier." *Antilla Kreyol*, No. 7 (janvier 1987): 21–49. Special memorial tribute to one of Martinique's leading musicians and composers. Includes reminiscences from friends and colleagues.

833. "Marius Cultier." *Paralleles*, No. 32 (1969): 65. Profile.

834. "Marius Cultier: on aurait du foutre un monument a ce con-la!" *Fouyaya*, No. 45 (janvier 1986): 8–9. Excerpt from an interview with the pianist first published in *Fouyaya*, No. 18 (sept. 1983). Followed by a selection of commentary on Cultier's work from the French press accompanied by photos of his Dec. 1985 funeral (p. 9–10).

CUTUMBA (Cuba)
See also 270, 283, 331

835. Leon, Barbara A. "Construccion de la afrocubanidad a traves de las artes espectaculares cubanas despues de 1959." Dissertation (Ph.D.)—University of California, Irvine, 1998, pp. 179–202. Chapter on Cutumba, the Afro-Cuban folk music and dance ensemble from eastern Cuba.

836. Pola, J.A. "El Cutumba y La Tajona." *Bohemia*, ano 74, no. 31 (julio 30 1982): 21–22. Interview with company director Juan Bautista about Cutumba's history and its specialty, a Cuban-Haitian dance known as tajona.

DANTIN, DENIS (1947–) (Martinique)
See **MALAVOI**

DAO, ADELAIDE [Adelaide Darius] (Guadeloupe/France)

837. Epaminondas, Guy. "Adelaide Darius: du football a la musique." *Antilla*, No. 222 (dec. 25 1986–janv. 5 1987): 11–13. Interview with the Paris-based gwo ka musician.

†**DEBS, GEORGES** (ca. 1943–2002) (Guadeloupe/France)
See also 159

838. Cadet-Petit, Alexandre. "George Debs faisons connaissance." *Fouyaya*, No. 58 (sept. 1987): 31–35. In-depth interview with Debs, a leading French Antillean record producer during the zouk boom of the 1980s.

839. Seraline, Yves-Marie. "Georges Debs: la passion du disque." *Antilla*, No. 93 (mars 2–9 1984): 14–15. Interview.

†**DEBS, HENRI** (1932–) (Guadeloupe)

840. Mapolin, Harry. "Une belle fete pour Henri Debs." *Antilla*, No. 296 (juillet 15–21 1988): 25–26. Report on a dinner celebrating the 30th anniversary of Production H. Debs, one of the leading record and concert production companies in the Antilles. Followed by an interview with Debs himself.

DECIMUS, GEORGES (1955–) (Guadeloupe)
See **KASSAV**

DECIMUS, PIERRE-EDOUARD (1947–) (Guadeloupe)
See **KASSAV**

DELOS, ALAIN (Guadeloupe)

841. "Salut d'artiste: Alain Delos, le plus experimente des salseros guadeloupeens." *Grin Fos*, No. 1 (aout–sept. 1987): 5–7. Interview.

DEMESMIN, CAROLE "MAROULE" (Haiti/US)
See 713

DEROSE, ANSY [Arntz Derose] (1934–1998) (Haiti)

842. Derose, Ansy. *Ansy Derose: a fleur de coeur—* / [conception et montage: Rudy Derose]. [Port-au-Prince, Haiti: Musee d'art haitien du College Saint-Pierre, 2001]. 76 p.: ill. Portrait of the Haitian popular singer. Consists of a brief biographical sketch followed by an extensive selection of song texts (p. 22–72).

DESSALINES, ANTOINE CHARLES (1932–) (Haiti)
See 704

DESTINE, JEAN-LEON (1925–) (Haiti/US)
See 522, 686

DESVARIEUX, JACOB (1955–) (Guadeloupe/France)
See **KASSAV**

DEZORMO, DJO [Joseph Gros-Desormeaux] (1943–) (Martinique)
See also 152, 658

843. Chamoiseau, Patrick. "Musique: L'arriere-pays de Michel Godzom, un chef-d'oeuvre de creolite." *Antilla*, No. 323 (mars 6–12 1989): 30–32. Review of a new recording pairing musicians Michel Godzom and Djo Dezormo.

844. Delsham, Tony. "Beee...mach! Le phenomene Loup." *Antilla*, No. 373 (mars 9–16 1990): 9–10. Feature on Dezormo's 1990 nationalist hit "Voici les Loups," an acerbic commentary on an agreement by the European Union which would provide citizens of any member country the right to buy land in any other member country, thus opening Martinique's doors to the economic 'wolves' of Europe.

845. Mandibele. "Voici le loup: analyse d'une chanson-symbole." *Antilla*, No. 373 (mars 9–16 1990): 11–13. Critical essay on Dezormo's 1990 Carnival hit, "Voici les Loups."

846. Pulvar, Jean-Marc. "Djo Desormo, mode d'emploi d'un succes." *Antilla*, No. 374 (mars 15–21 1990): 11–14. Interview with Dezormo about his song "Voici les Loups."

847. Restog, Serge. "Jo Dezormo, 'sa pe chanje.'" *Antilla*, No. 296 (juillet 15–21 1988): 13–14. Interview with the popular singer-songwriter from Martinique.

DIFFICILES (Haiti)
See 701

DOMINIQUE, HANS (Haiti)
See **BOUKMAN EKSPERYANS**

DONATIEN, FERNAND (1922–2003) (Martinique)
See 158

DONATIEN, FRANCK (Martinique)
See 152

DON MIGUEL (Martinique)
See 656

DORISME, MYRIAM (1943–2004) (Haiti/US)
See 713

DORISMOND, ANDRE (Haiti/US)
See **DORISMOND FAMILY**

DORISMOND FAMILY (Haiti/US)

848. Barstow, David. "Shooting victim bore famous name." *New York Times* (March 22 2000): B6. Profiles the family of New York shooting victim, Patrick Dorismond, which includes such illustrious Haitian performers as father Andre, a star vocalist with the Weber Sicot band of the 1950s and '60s, and brother, Charles, a reggae singer known as Bigga Haitian.

D.P. EXPRESS (Haiti)
See 701

DUPERVIL, GERARD (1932–1994) (Haiti)
See also 704

849. "Gerard Dupervil aveugle et livre a lui-meme." *Haiti Culture*, Vol. 5, No. 7 (juin 1989): 16–17, 30. Interview with the longtime Jazz des Jeunes vocalist.

850. Preval, Gerard. *Gerard Dupervil, ou, La voix d'une generation.* [Saint-Leonard, Quebec]: Ilan-Ilan, 1995. 184, [2] p.: ill. Biographical portrait of the well-known Haitian singer-songwriter followed by an appendix with Creole-to-French translations of his songs.

DUROSIER, GUY (1932–1999) (Haiti/US)
See also 704

851. Pierre-Pierre, Garry. "Guy Durosier, 68, Haitian singer and composer." *New York Times* (August 24 1999): B11. Obituary.

DUVAL, FRITZ "TOTO" (1943–2003) (Haiti)
See 704

DUVIELLA, SERGE (Haiti)

852. "L'expertise de Serge Duviella." *Haiti Culture*, Vol. 4, No. 8 (janvier 1988): 16–19. Interview with a leading Haitian sound engineer.

ELIE, ARNOLD (1929–1990) (Haiti/US)
See 686

ELIE, JUSTIN (1883–1931) (Haiti)
See 533, 575

EL SAIEH, ISSA
See **SAIEH, ISSA EL**

EMERAUDE (Guadeloupe)

853. Lara, Bottino. "La manifestation artistique du groupe folklorique Emeraude." *Revue Guadeloupeenne*, No. 44 (avril–juin 1961): 43–47. Describes the repertoire of a folkloric music and dance troupe from Basse-Terre, Guadeloupe.

EMILE, DERNST (Haiti)

854. "Dernst Emile, un arrangeur." *Haiti Culture*, Vol. 4, No. 6 (November 1987): 6, 28. Interview with the Haitian popular music arranger.

EUGENE, ROGER M.
See **SHOUBOU**

EXILE ONE (Dominica)
See also 716, 855

855. Aribo, Tony. "Exile One: depuis 14 ans." *Antilla*, No. 252 (aout 3 1987): 16. Short interview with Exile One founder-leader Gordon Henderson about the group's history from 1973 to 1987.

EXPERIENCE 7 (Guadeloupe)
See 715

FAL FRETT (Martinique)
See 152

FANFANT, JEAN-PHILIPPE (1966–) (Guadeloupe/France)

856. Menu, Thierry. "Thierry & Jean-Philippe Fanfant: poigne de freres et seduction." *Batteur Magazine*, No. 181 (mai 2005): 40–42. Interview with the Fanfant brothers, trombonist Thierry and drummer Jean-Philippe, about their careers on the French Antillean music scene in France.

FANFANT, THIERRY (1964?–) (Guadeloupe/France)
See 856

FELINE, REGINE (Martinique)

857. Delsham, Tony. "Portrait de femme: Regine Feline, a coeur ouvert." *Antilla*, No. 318 (jan 30–fev 6 1989): 26–28. Interview with the Martinican pop singer.

858. Kozman. "Filinman Regine Feline." *Antilla Kreyol*, No. 14 (janvier 1990): 4–6. In Kreyol. Interview.

FELIX, VLADIMIR JEAN (Haiti)
See **BOUKAN GINEN**

FLERIAG, CELINE (1961–) (Martinique)
See also 152

859. "Musique: Banboch lespri pawol nou." *Antilla Kreyol*, No. 13 (octobre 1989): 10–11. Short Kreyol-language interview with the Martinican popular singer.

FLO ET DOUCE 'IN (Martinique/France)

860. Cooper, Mike. "Flo charts." *Folk Roots*, No. 111 (September 1992): 17, 19. Profile of the Martinican trio Flo et Douce 'in.

FORTERE, JACQUES
See **WAWA**

FOSTIN, JANE (1970–) (Guadeloupe/France)

861. Nogbou, Christophe. "Jane Fostin: ni-ange, ni demon." *Divas* (Paris), No. 4 (dec 1999–jan 2000): 40–41. Feature on a former member of Zouk Machine and her new solo career.

FOUBAP (Guadeloupe)

862. "Salut d'artiste: Le groupe Foubap's, une valeur sure de la musique populaire guadeloupeenne." *Grin Fos*, No. 1 (aout–sept. 1987): 33–36. Interview with Foubap, a leading gwo ka ensemble from Guadeloupe.

FOULA (Haiti)
See also 480, 711

863. "Gwoup Foula." *Haiti Culture*, Vol. 4, No. 10 (avril 1988): 19. Interview with Fritz Vivien, a Foula member, about the group's music and history.

FRANCISCO [Frantz Mathurin Charles-Denis] (1932–) (Martinique)

864. Cyrille, Dominique. *Francisco* / avec une preface d'Andre Lucrece. Fort-de-France [Martinique]: Sim'LN, [1997]. 76 p.: ill., music. (Collection Sim'Ekol). Discography: p. 37–40. Biographical portrait. Includes transcriptions of six Francisco compositions (p. 43–60).

865. ———. "Popular music and the Martinican-Creole identity." *Black Music Research Journal*, Vol. 22, No. 1 (Spring 2002): 65–83. Examines the music and careers of Martinican musicians Francisco and Eugene Mona.

*866. Francisco. *Ainmin la vie*. Paris: Euro Trajectoire, 2005. 239 p. Memoir.

867. "Francisco, une des racines du pays Martinique." *Le Naif* (Fort-de-France), No. 27 (avril 1992): 5–6. Profile.

868. Juliard, P. "Portrait: Un batisseur nomme Francisco." *Antilla*, No. 202 (juin 23–29 1986): 3–4, 42. Profile of the Martinican pianist

and bandleader with a focus on his longtime involvement with the sport of judo.

FRANCK, RICARDO
See **TI PLUME**

FRANCOIS, EDDY (Haiti)
See **BOUKAN GINEN**

FRANCOIS, LUTHER (1952–) (St. Lucia)
See also 1138

869. Gatto, Gerlando. "Intervista: Luther Renaldo Francois." *Blu Jazz* (Roma), Vol. 3, No. 19 (1991): 20–22. Interview with the St. Lucian jazz saxophonist.

870. Lee, Simon. "Features: Luther's jazz." *Nou Magazine* [e-journal], Vol. 1, No. 1 (2002?). http://www.nou-caribbean.com/v1n1/ fea_jaz1.shtml. Extended feature on Francois, one of the Caribbean's leading jazz exponents.

871. Loupien, Serge. "Dans la presse: 'Liberation et Luther Francois.'" *Antilla*, No. 427 (mars 29–avril 4 1991): 16. Reprint of a profile first published in the French newspaper *Liberation*.

FRERES DEJEAN, LES (Haiti)
See 701, 708

GABRIEL-SOIME, LEONA (1891–1971) (Martinique)
See 152, 611

GAIS TROUBADOURS (Haiti)

872. Camille, Jacques. "Souvenez-vous des Gais Troubadours?" *Haiti Culture*, Vol. 5, No. 5 (mars 1989): 23–24, 26–27. Interview with two members of the group, singer Ulysse Cabral and saxophonist Hermane Camille, about the heyday of the ensemble's popularity in the 1940s.

GALVA, LEA (Martinique)
See 152

GIBON, MARIE-JOSE
See 717

G.M. CONNECTION (Haiti)
See 701

GODZOM, MICHEL [Michel Gros-Desormeaux] (1949–) (Martinique)
See also 248

873. Chamoiseau, Patrick. "Musique: L'arriere-pays de Michel Godzom, un chef-d'oeuvre de creolite." *Antilla*, No. 323 (mars 6–12 1989): 30–32. Review of a new recording pairing musicians Michel Godzom and Djo Dezormo.

GROCRAVLA, JOJO (Martinique/France)

874. Cauver, J.G. "Antilla culture: Jojo Grocravla en concert." *Antilla*, No. 378 (avril 12–18 1990): 37. Review of Grocravla's first Martinican concert in two decades.

875. ———. "Musique: Jojo vire." *Antilla*, No. 375 (mars 23–29 1990): 36–38. Interview with the veteran Martinican percussionist.

GRUPO FOLKLORICO DE AFICIONADOS CAIDIJE (Cuba)

876. Espinosa Hechevarria, Luisa. "La cultura en Camaguey: Caidije." *Bohemia*, ano 72, no. 8 (feb 22 1980): 30–31. Feature on the Camaguey-based Cuban-Haitian folkloric ensemble.

877. "Un grupo folklorico camagueyano: Caidije retona sus raices culturales." *Bohemia*, ano 67, no. 4 (enero 24 1975): 8–9. Profile.

GUANAVAL (Martinique)
See 414

GUEDON, HENRI (1944–2005) (Martinique/France)
See also 152, 349, 718

878. Cauver, J.G. "Antilla culture: Henry Guedon, 'un artiste ne prend pas le pouvoir, il est au service de l'art.'" *Antilla*, No. 301 (sept. 23–29 1988): 30–34. Interview.

879. Guedon, Henri. "Antilla culture: Henri Guedon chante la Marseillaise." *Antilla*, No. 339 (juin 26–juillet 2 1989): 28. Discusses Guedon's plan for a musical spectacle featuring a series of variations on the Marseillaise.

880. Milepak, Gustave. "Antilla-kilti: Rencontre avec Henri Guedon." *Antilla*, No. 89 (fevrier 10–17 1984): 33–35. Interview.

881. Ponnamah, Michel. "Henri Guedon: un foissonnement de sons et de couleurs." *Antilla*, No. 27 (oct 1 1982): 36–38. Interview with Guedon about his activities as an Antillean musician and artist based in Paris.

882. "Rencontres: Henri Guedon." *Son!* (Abymes), No. 5 (1985): 27. Profile.

GUILLAUME, RAOUL (1927–) (Haiti)
See 701

GYPSIES DE PETIONVILLE (Haiti)
See 701

HAITI CHANTE (Haiti)

883. Santos, Benedicta Quirino dos. "Haiti sings." *Americas*, Vol. 3, No. 6 (June 1951): 30–31. Feature on the folkloric troupe Haiti Chante and its leader, music teacher Lina Blanchet.

HALIAR, PAUL-EMILE (Guadeloupe)

884. Emmanuel, M. "Musicales: Paul-Emile Haliar ou la longevite musicale." *Echo Jeunesse*, No. 24 (1989): 12, 14. Interview.

HENDERSON, GORDON (Dominica/France)
See also 346

885. Henderson, Gordon. *Zoukland*. [S.l.]: G. Henderson, 1998. 90, 86 p.: ill. + 1 CD. French and English. First-hand account of pop music developments in the French Antilles during the 1970s and '80s by bandleader and Exile One founder, Gordon Henderson.

886. Meschino, Patricia. "Gordon Henderson: creole crusader." *Rhythm* (New York), Vol. 8, No. 3 (March 1999): 40. Feature on the cadence-lypso innovator from Dominica.

HEWANORRA VOICES (St. Lucia)
See 673

IBO COMBO (1962–1966) (Haiti)
See also 518, 701

887. Averill, Gage. "Haitian fascination: The legacy of Ibo Combo." *The Beat*, Vol. 8, No. 3 (1989): 49, 64. Traces the history of the group and its influence on several generations of Haitian dance bands.

IPOMEN (Guadeloupe)

888. "Ipomen." *Son!* (Abymes), No. 3 (1984): 7, 30. Interview with the popular musician from Guadeloupe.

JAEGERHUBER, WERNER (1900–1953) (Haiti)
See also 552, 579

889. Largey, Michael D. "Musical ethnography in Haiti: a study of elite hegemony and musical composition." Dissertation (Ph.D.)— Indiana University, 1991, p. 166–184. Chapter on the work of an art music composer best known for his adaptations and arrangements of Haitian Vodou songs.

*890. Procopio, Mary J. "Haitian classical music, Vodou and cultural identity: an examination of the classical flute compositions by Haitian composer Werner A. Jaegerhuber." Dissertation (D.M.A.) —Michigan State University, 2005. xvii, 144 leaves: music.

JAZZ DES JEUNES (Haiti)
See also 474, 509, 704, 849, 1042

891. Beaubrun, Rene Ch. *Initiation a la musique avec le super Jazz des Jeunes.* [Port-au-Prince?]: Editions du Tambour, [1961–1962]. 2 v. (278 p.): ill. "125 chansons populaires, 100 devinettes, 20 charades, 10 enigmes, 50 fables comiques, photos et gravures humoristiques." Collection of Jazz des Jeunes song texts accompanied by brief biographical sketches of the group's members. [No library is known to have v. 1 of this set]

892. "Le Jazz des Jeunes fete ses 42 ans." *Haiti Culture*, Vol. 2, No. 5 (sept. 1985): 8–9. Chronicles the legendary career of Haiti's Jazz des Jeunes, a dance band founded in 1943 by Rene St Aude. Includes several portraits.

JEAN, WYCLEF (1972–) (Haiti/US)
See 464, 479

JEAN-BAPTISTE, NEMOURS (1918–1985) (Haiti)
See 474, 509, 704

JEAN BAPTISTE, SMITH (Haiti)
See 1095–1096

JEAN-CLAUDE, MARTHA (1919–2001) (Haiti/Cuba)
See also 713

893. Gonzalez, Waldo. "Mujer de dos islas; el amor de Martha Jean-Claude por Cuba la hace tambien nuestra." *Bohemia*, ano 91, no. 8 (abril 9 1999): 58. Profile.

*894. *Martha Jean-Claude: mujer de dos islas [videorecording]* / guion y direccion, Marlene Gomez. [New York]: Crowing Rooster Arts, etc., 2000. 1 videocassette (57 min.).

895. *Martha Jean-Claude: mwen se fanm de peyi = femme de deux iles* / [textes, Nicole Arcelin, Richard Mirabal]. Montreal: Editions du CIDIHCA, 1999. 59 p.: ill. Sub-title from cover: Une retrospective en images de l'itineraire de Martha. Photo portrait of Jean-Claude's singing career in Haiti and Cuba.

896. Ramos, Zobeida. "Porque esta region es parte de mi vida." *Clave* (Havana), No. 5 (1987): 57–60. Interview with the legendary Haitian vocalist.

897. Rivero, Angel. "Madame, ou lib: entrevista con Martha Jean Claude." *Revolucion y Cultura*, No. 74 (oct. 1978): 54–57. Interview with the Haitian-born, Cuba-based songstress.

JEAN-FELIX, JIMMY [Vladimir Jean-Felix] (Haiti)
See also **BOUKAN GINEN**

898. Birnbaum, Larry. "Jimmy Jean-Felix: the Voodoo Van Halen." *Guitar Player*, Vol. 29, No. 11 (November 1995): 22. Profile of Jean-Felix, lead guitarist and musical director of Boukan Ginen.

JEAN-MARIE, ALAIN (1945–) (Guadeloupe/France)
See also 718

899. Anquetil, Pascal. "Piano biguine: Alain Jean-Marie, l'ile aux tresors." *Jazzman*, No. 172 (dec. 1993): 10. Interview with the Guadeloupean jazz pianist.

JEANTY, MARCO (Haiti)
See 701

JEHELMAN, CHYCO [Lucien Jehelman] (1951–) (Martinique)

900. Cauver, J.G. "Festival: Chyco Jehelman joue Aime Cesaire." *Antilla*, No. 205 (juillet 14–23 1986): 8–10. Interview with Jehelman about his musical career.

901. Leno, Georges. "Musique: Chico sort de l'ombre." *Antilla*, No. 43 (mars 3 1983): 41–42. Profile.

JESOPHE, KRISYAN (Martinique)
See **PAKATAK**

JND (France)
See 204

JOSEPH, ANCY DULLON (d. 1993) (Haiti)
See 704

JU BAPTISTE, MAQUEL (Haiti)
See **BOUKMAN EKSPERYANS**

JU-LOUIS, MARGARETTE (Haiti)
See **BOUKMAN EKSPERYANS**

†**JURAD, SIMON** (1951–) (Martinique)

902. Delsham, Tony. "Cinq questions a Simon Jurad." *Antilla*, No. 252 (aout 3 1987): 14–15. Short interview with a leading popular singer from Martinique.

JUSTE, FARAH (1952–) (Haiti/US)
See also 706, 710, 713

903. Leroy, Felix Morisseau. "Farah Juste, symbole de la chanson patriotique." *Haiti Culture*, Vol. 3, No. 10 (fev. 1987): 3, 16.

904. Mapou, Jan. "Farah Juste a signe son dernier disque." *Haiti Culture*, Vol. 1, No. 3 (juillet 1984): 9. Creole-language profile.

905. "La vie artistique de Farah: est-elle menacee en Haiti?" *Haiti Culture*, Vol. 4, No. 2 (juin 1987): 2, 4. Interview with Haitian singer Farah Juste.

KAJOU
See **KING KINO; SYLVAIN, CLIFFORD**

KALI [Jean-Marc Monnerville] (1959–) (Martinique)
See also 152, 159, 204, 658

906. Caloc, Rene. "Rasin Kali an te Matnik." *Antilla*, No. 443 (juillet 19–25 1991): 39–40. Report on a recent Kali concert in Martinique followed by a short interview.

907. Dring, Brian. "Beguine to reggae, a dreadlocked banjoist leads a Martinican roots revival." *Rhythm* (New York), Vol. 8, No. 7 (July 1999): 36–37. Interview.

908. Medeuf, Serge. "Musique: Kali-Banjo en quete du 6eme continent." *Antilla*, No. 362 (dec. 14–20 1989): 37–38. Feature on the up-and-coming Martinican singer and banjo player.

909. Scaramuzzo, Gene. "The other Caribbean: Kali flowers." *The Beat,* Vol. 14, No. 4 (1995): 33. Overview of Kali's recorded work beginning with his most recent album, *Debranche.*

KANPECH (Haiti)
See 707

KASSAV' (French Antilles/France)
See also 152, 156, 159, 167, 244, 250, 702

910. Berrian, Brenda F. "'An-ba-chen'n-la' (Chained together): the landscape of Kassav's zouk." In *Language, rhythm, & sound,* eds. Joseph K. Adjaye and Adrianne R. Andrews. Pittsburgh, PA: University of Pittsburgh Press, 1997, pp. 203–220.

911. ———. "Piggyback exchange: Kassav' and black musicians in Paris." In *Music, writing, and cultural unity in the Caribbean,* ed. Timothy J. Reiss. Trenton, NJ: Africa World Press, 2005, pp. 391–405.

912. Conrath, Philippe. *Kassav'.* Paris: Le Club des Stars, etc., 1987. 190 p.: ill. Discography: p. 186–188. Portrait of the zouk supergroup from its genesis in Martinique and Guadeloupe to its breakout success as the king of French Antillean pop. Includes sketches of each of the band's members—Jocelyne Beroard, Georges and Pierre-Edouard Decimus, Jacob Desvarieux, Jean-Philippe Marthely, Jean-Claude Naimro, Patrick Saint-Eloi and Claude Vamur, along with an extensive selection of the group's song texts (p. [133]–184).

*913. Nossant, Francois. *Zoukassav'.* Paris: Messidor, 1990. 116 p.: ill. Biographical portrait. [Copies are held by several libraries in Quebec, Martinique, and France]

914. Winders, James A. "'Le Francais dans la rue': Caribbean music, language, and the African diaspora." In *Musical migrations,* eds. Frances R. Aparicio, et al. New York: Palgrave Macmillan, 2003, v. 1. On the music of Kassav.

Articles

915. Ahonto, Lucien. "Kassav (groupe afro-antillais): musique a 'bomber.'" *Ivoire Dimanche,* No. 755 (juil. 28 1985): 4–7. Feature on Kassav followed by an interview with the group's founder and leader, Jacob Desvarieux (p. 8–11).

916. Delsham, Tony. "Kassav: la fausse note cocaine." *Antilla*, No. 381 (mai 3–9 1990): 12–15. Feature on a visit by Kassav to Martinique and their response to rumors of drug use by the group.

917. Eyre, Banning. "Kassav' medicine: magic multinational." *Rhythm Music Magazine*, Vol. 3, No. 6 (1994): 14–17, 52. Conversation with Jocelyne Beroard about the group and its history.

918. Laurencine, Ronald. "Kassav': zouk machine?; Pierre-Edouard Decimus repond." *Antilla*, No. 161 (juil.–aout 1985): 15–19. Interview with Kassav's leader about the group and its zouk competitors.

919. Lucas, Rafael. "Les revolutions Kassav." *Afiavi*, No. 27 (dec. 2001–jan. 2002): 14–15. Profile.

920. Lund, Lotte. "Zouk!" *MM* (Copenhagen), Vol. 21, No. 6–7 (June–August 1988): 36. In Danish. Conversation with Kassav's vocalist and spokesperson, Jocelyne Beroard.

921. Nash, Phil. "Kassav': le zouk d'abord." *Afrique Elite*, No. 3 (avril 1986): 14–19. Feature.

922. Nja Kwa, Samy. "Musique: 'Le meilleur, c'est nous-memes!' Entretien avec Jocelyne Beroard (Kassav)." *Africultures*, No. 30 (septembre 2000): 57–60. Interview with Beroard about Kassav and their new recording *Nou la*.

923. O'Connor, Lorraine. "Doctor Zouk." *BWee Caribbean Beat*, No. 8 (Winter 1993). Also available online: http://www.meppublishers. com/online/caribbean-beat/archive/index.php?pid=6001. Chronicle of Kassav's history as a group.

924. Scaramuzzo, Gene. "Is America finally ready for ... Kassav'?" *The Beat*, Vol. 13, No. 6 (1994): 50–53. Feature outlining the group's history and potential for crossover success.

925. ———. "Kassav': *Majestik Zouk*." *The Beat*, Vol. 8, No. 5 (1989): 49–51. Long review of Kassav's second American release providing background on the group and its efforts at breaking into the U.S. market.

926. ———. "Kassav' takes Manhattan." *The Reggae & African Beat*, Vol. 7, No. 4 (1988): 30–31. Interview with Kassav's lead singer, Jocelyne Beroard, about the group's current activities and future plans.

927. Sergio, Paulo. "Kassav, em Maputo: musica, emocao e ... campanha." *Tempo* (Maputo), No. 1128 (julho 3 1994): 4–9. Feature on a concert appearance by Kassav in Maputo, Mozambique.

928. Sinker, Mark. "A little Latin Guadeloupe." *New Musical Express* (April 18 1987): 21. Feature.

929. Stapleton, Chris. "Who's zouking who?" *Blues & Soul* (London), No. 481 (April 14–27 1987): 32–33. Discusses Kassav's impact on recent African popular music.

930. Tenaille, Frank. "Kassav'." *Paroles et Musique*, No. 70 (mai 1987): 20–22, 24. Interview with Pierre-Edouard Decimus and Jocelyne Beroard.

Newspaper Articles

931. Dibbell, Julian. "Kassav': zouk is the world." *Village Voice* (June 14 1988): 81–82. Introduction to the group and its music.

932. Johnson, Martin. "Zouk: a Paris stew." *New York Newsday* (November 17 1988): Pt. 2, p. 8. Feature.

933. Palmer, Robert. "Zouk, new musical amalgam, a hit." *New York Times* (November 12 1986): C20. Brief introduction to the idiom focusing mainly on Kassav, its best known exponent.

934. Pareles, Jon. "Kassav' plays zouk, sound of Caribbean." *New York Times* (May 31 1988): C20. Review of a concert performance at The Ritz nightclub in New York.

935. ———. "Zouk, a distinctive, infectious dance music; the French-speaking group named Kassav' combines African and Caribbean influences in Paris studios." *New York Times* (May 29 1988): Sec. 2, p. 23. Profile of Kassav and its recorded work.

936. Zwerin, Mike. "A zouk band in the African 'swap shop.'" *International Herald Tribune* (January 28 1988): 16.

Media Materials

*937. *Kassav' [videorecording]: le zouk, un sacre medicament* / Jose Reynes, realisateur. [Paris]: Films du Village: [distributor] Harmattan, [2006], c1997. 1 DVD. 52 min. Documentary.

KATEL (Guadeloupe)

938. "Esnard Boisdur et Katel: sa ki taw, se taw!" *Son!* (Abymes), No. 1 (1983): 17–19. Kreyol-language interview with Esnard Boisdur, leader of the Guadeloupean gwo ka ensemble Katel.

KING KINO [Pierre Raymond Divers] (Haiti/US)
See also **PHANTOMS**

939. "Kino Kajou: une nouvelle etoile." *Haiti Culture*, Vol. 5, No. 3 (dec. 1988): 6–7, 28. Interview with a leading Nouvel Generasyon singer from Haiti.

KONKET, GUY [Guy Conquet] (Guadeloupe/France)
See also 349

940. P.I., Alexandre. "La Guyane: Le triomphe de Guy Conquete." *Antilla*, No. 160 (juillet 19–26 1985): 19–22. Feature on a visit to French Guiana by gwo ka musician and bandleader Guy Konket.

KWAK (Martinique)
See 152

LAGIER, JEAN JOSE (1944–) (Martinique)
See **MALAVOI**

LAGUERRE, FEDIA (Haiti)
See also 713

941. "Dernier temoignage de Fedia sur la chanson." *Haiti Culture*, Vol. 2, No. 4 (aout 1985): 4–5, 13. Interview with Haitian popular singer Fedia Laguerre.

942. "Fedia Laguerre fustige le general." *Haiti Culture*, Vol. 4, No. 7 (dec. 1987): 16. Conversation with Laguerre about her new album *Rache Manyok ou yo*.

943. "Fedia, la voix d'or d'Haiti." *Haiti Culture* (juin 1984): 2; Vol. 1, No. 3 (juillet 1984): 2. Two-part interview.

944. [Laguerre], Fedia. "Mise au point de Fedia Laguere." *Haiti Culture*, Vol. 3, No. 11 (mars 1987): 14, 16. Laguerre defends herself against charges made in a recent interview with composer Wawa (see 1137) and elsewhere that she has failed to follow through on several business commitments.

945. "Qui a tort et qui a raison??" *Haiti Culture*, Vol. 3, No. 9 (janvier 1987): 3, 5. Interview with Laguerre about a financial dispute with her longtime collaborator, lyricist Wawa [Jacques Fortere].

LAHENS, LOUIS (1926–1986) (Cuba/Haiti)
See 704

LALANNE, WAGNER (Haiti/US)
See 690, 704

LAMOTHE, CHARLY
See **CHOMEREAU-LAMOTHE, CHARLY**

LAROSE, DIEUDONNE (Haiti/US)

946. Larose, Dieudonne. *Je chante pour l'humanite: entretiens avec Eric Sauray et Ketty Sauray*. Paris: Dauphin noir, 2005. 156 p.: ill. Discography: p. 139–141. Interviews with Larose, the popular compas singer from Haiti.

LATAYE (Haiti)
See **BEAUBRUN, DANIEL**

LA VINY, GERARD (1933–) (Guadeloupe)
See 158

LEARDEE, ERNEST (1896–1988) (Martinique)
See also 158

947. Confiant, Raphael. "Ernest Leardee: le roman de la biguine." *Antilla*, No. 367 (janv 25–31 1990): 37–39. Review of Leardee's autobiography (950).

948. "En memoire: La mort d'un grand musicien." *Antilla*, No. 285 (avril 28–mai 4 1988): 29. Brief obituary for the veteran biguine bandleader from Martinique.

949. Juraver, Jean. "Quelques questions a Christiane Succab-Goldman." *Echo Jeunesse*, No. 21 (Dec. 1988–Jan. 1989): 9. Filmmaker Succab-Goldman discusses her 1988 documentary *Ernest Leardee ou le roman de la biguine* on the Martinican bandleader.

950. Leardee, Ernest. *La biguine de l'Oncle Ben's: Ernest Leardee raconte* / Jean-Pierre Meunier, Brigitte Leardee. Paris: Editions Caribeennes, 1989. 323 p.: ill. Discography: p. 284–288. Includes a list of Leardee's compositions (p. 289–317). An as-told-to memoir

recounting Leardee's career as a dance band leader in Martinique from the 1930s on.

LEDAN, JEAN ["Nadej Naej"] (Haiti)
See 704

LEFEL, EDITH (1963–2003) (French Guiana/France)
See also 152, 719

951. Cadet-Petit, Alexandre. "Musique: Edith Lefel, en route vers le succes." *Fouyaya*, No. 56 (juin 1987): 42. Feature.

952. "Hommage a Edith Lefel." *Divas* (Paris), No. 36 (fevrier 2003): 16–23. Photo-feature paying tribute to the recently deceased popular singer from the French Antilles. Includes details about and photos from her large Paris funeral.

953. Scaramuzzo, Gene. "Passings: Edith Lefel, 1964–2003." *The Beat*, Vol. 22, No. 2 (2003): 67–68. Obituary.

954. Shepherd, Kenneth R. "Edith Lefel." In *Contemporary Black biography*. Detroit: Gale, 2004, v. 41, pp. 126–128.

LEGITIMUS, GESIP [Victor-Hegessipe Legitimus] (1930–2000) (France)
See 159

LINDOR, GASTON (1929–) (French Guiana/France)
See 158

LIRVAT, AL (1916–2007) (Guadeloupe/France)
See also 158, 349

*955. Pagesy, Hugues, and Osin Nagma. *Al Lirvat, trombone et wabap: Mi bel jounen.* [Paris]: New Legend, 2003. 185 p.: ill.

LISIMA, JEAN-MICHEL (Martinique)

956. Restog, Serge. "Jean-Michel Lisima, mizisyen, tanbouye, pent anle ve." *Antilla Kreyol*, No. 14 (janvier 1990): 39–40. In Kreyol. Interview with Martinican percussionist Jean-Michel Lisima.

LOCKEL, GERARD (Guadeloupe)
See 405

LOUINIS, LOUINES (Haiti/US)
See 686

LOUIS, DAMAS "FANFAN" (ca. 1967–) (Haiti/US)

957. Zwack, Michael. "Music: Damas 'Fanfan' Louis." *Bomb* (New York), No. 90 (Winter 2004–05): 42–47. Interview with the Haitian master drummer and Vodou priest.

LOUISAR, CURTIS (Guadeloupe)

958. Seraline, Yves Marie. "Curtis koze." *Antilla Kreyol*, No. 5 (octobre 1985): 4–5. In Kreyol. Interview with a French Antillean pop singer.

LOUISON, BIBI [Louis Louison] (1946–) (Martinique/France)
See 718

LOUISSAINT, YVON (1955–1993) (Haiti/US)

959. "Yvon Louissaint: est-il un martyr de la musique?" *Haiti Culture*, Vol. 2, No. 10 (fev. 1986): 3, 11. Interview with a Haitian dance band veteran.

960. "Yvon Louissaint resiste a la mort." *Haiti Culture*, Vol. 5, No. 10 (nov. 1989): 12–13, 26. Interview with Louissaint following his involvement in a near fatal car accident.

LYNCH, MELTHON (Haiti)
See **OLICHA**

MAGNUM BAND (Haiti/US)
See also 706, 709

961. "9e anniversaire du Magnum Band...mwen ce gro neg o." *Haiti Culture*, Vol. 2, No. 3 (juillet 1985): 8–9. Conversation with the band. Includes several portraits.

962. Comeau, Rene. "Ou est l'avenir de l'artiste haitien?" *Haiti Culture*, Vol. 1, No. 7 (novembre 1984): 3, 12. Interview with Dadou Pasquet, lead singer with the Magnum Band, about the group and its musical direction.

963. "Paka pala." *Haiti Culture*, Vol. 3, No. 11 (mars 1987): 2, 4. Interview with Magnum Band drummer Ticot Pasquet about the group's history, current activities and new recording.

MAJUMBE (Martinique)

964. Aribo, Tony. "Le groupe Majumbe: une priorite, la formation, leur choix, c'est la qualite." *Antilla*, No. 252 (aout 3 1987): 16. Short profile of a Martinican dance band.

MALAVOI (Martinique)
See also 152, 156, 159, 167, 719, 1039–1040

965. Cadet-Petit, Alexandre. "Malavoi: La Case a Lucie, album photos." *Fouyaya*, No. 54 (fevrier 1987): 23–27, 30–34. Photo-feature on the popular music group Malavoi including biographical sketches for some of its members—Philippe Porry, Christian De Negri, Denis Dantin, Jean Jose Lagier, J.M. Albicy and Nicol Bernard.

966. Elongui, Luigi. "Les Malavoi, pionniers de l'identite creole martiniquaise." *Africultures*, No. 8 (mai 1998): 16–20. Sketch of the group's early years.

967. Epaminondas, Guy. "Avec les Malavoi sur le plateau du Grand Echiquier." *Antilla*, No. 226 (janv. 30–fev. 5 1987): 30–31. Report on a Paris visit by Malavoi.

968. Erwan, Jacques. "Malavoi … a la conquete du monde!" *Paroles & Musique*, No. 69 (avril 1987): 18–21. Interview.

969. Laurencine, Ronald. "Les Malavoi: de la creation a la production." *Antilla*, No. 220 (dec. 10–17 1986): 19–20. Short transcript of a press conference with the group.

970. "Malavoi." *Fouyaya*, No. 37 (mai 1985): 20–22. Portraits of each member of Malavoi at a rehearsal in Strasbourg, France.

971. Martin, Denis-Constant. "Malavoi: le punch de la Martinique." *Jazz Magazine* (Paris), No. 359 (mars 1987): 29. Interview with the group's frontman, Paulo Rosine.

972. "Musique: Les 'divins' Malavoi." *Antilla Magazine*, No. 5 (juin 1984): 41–44. French and Creole text. Round-table discussion of the Michel Traore film *Viva Malavoi* by the Collectif Antilla Emigration.

973. Pinalie-Dracius, Pierre. "Le Zenith de Malavoi." *Antilla*, No. 238 (avril 23–30 1987): 28–29. Report on Malavoi's successful appearance at Zenith, the Paris concert hall.

974. "Retour des Malavoi." *Antilla*, No. 34 (decembre 20 1982): 32–34. Photo-feature on the group and its return to the music scene after a hiatus.

975. Scaramuzzo, Gene. "The other Caribbean: Two sides of the coin." *The Beat*, Vol. 14, No. 2 (1995): 30, 82. Column discussing the Malavoi recording *An Maniman* (Declic).

MAMBO LUCIENNE [Simone Lucienne Pierre] (Haiti/US)

976. "Mambo Lucienne." *Haiti Culture*, Vol. 4, No. 11 (mai 1988): 14–15. Interview with the Haitian folk singer.

MANGA, CELIA [Sandra Hubert] (Martinique/France)
See **MILLENIUM**

MANGA, SEKOU (Martinique/France)
See **MILLENIUM**

MARCE [Bernard Pago] (1949–) (Martinique)
See 152, 658

MARCELIN, ERNST CREPSAC (1951–1990) (Haiti/US)

977. "En memoire de Ernest Marcelin." *Haiti Culture*, Vol. 6, No. 1 (avril 1990): 19. Brief obituary.

978. McLane, Daisann. "Ernst Crepsac Marcelin, 1951–90." *Village Voice* (April 10 1990): 83. Obituary for the Tabou Combo pianist killed following a concert in Brooklyn, NY.

MARK, ROBERTT (St. Lucia)

979. Faria, Norman. "The banjo maker." *Caricom Perspective*, No. 52–53 (July–December 1991): 31, 81. Feature on the St. Lucian musician and banjo maker Robertt Mark.

MARTHELY, JEAN-PHILLIPE (1958–) (Martinique)
See also **KASSAV**

980. "Star: Jean-Philippe Marthely." *Fouyaya*, No. 40 (aout 1985): 27–28. Interview with the Martinican singer best known for his work with zouk supergroup Kassav.

MARTINO, REYNALDO (1978–) (Haiti/US)
See **T-VICE**

MARTINO, ROBERTO (1975–) (Haiti/US)
See 690, 1118–1119

MASS, JOSY (French Guiana/France)

981. Boukman, Daniel. "Josy Mass chante la Guyane." *Antilla*, No. 94 (mars 16–23 1984): 13–16. Interview with a French Guianese singer based in France.

MASTER DJI [George Lys Herard] (1961–1994) (Haiti/US)
See 204

MATHEUS, MARIANN (Guadeloupe)

982. Bourguignon, Line F. "Mariann Matheus, chanteuse et comedienne guadeloupeenne." *Jakata Magazine*, No. 5 (octobre 1986): 4–5. Interview with an up-and-coming singer and actress from Guadeloupe.

MATHON-BLANCHET, LINA
See **BLANCHET, LINA MATHON**

MAURINIER, CHARLES (Guadeloupe)

983. Epaminondas, Guy. "Musique: Un entretien avec Charles Maurinier." *Antilla*, No. 257 (oct. 8–14 1987): 26–27. Interview with a popular singer from Guadeloupe.

MAVOUNZY, ROBERT (1917–1974) (Panama/Guadeloupe/France)

984. Lotz, Rainer E. "Robert Mavounzy." In *The new Grove dictionary of jazz*. 2nd ed. New York, 2002, v. 2. Profile of the French Antillean dance band musician.

MELIANO, LEWIS [Meliano Jean-Louis] (Guadeloupe)

985. "Musique: Plus loin avec la chanteuse guadeloupeenne Lewis Meliano." *Amina*, No. 103 (janvier 1981): 42–44. Interview with a popular songstress from Guadeloupe.

MELTHON-LYNCH, MICHEL
See **OLICHA**

MERCERON, GERALD (Haiti)
See 701

METAL SOUND (Martinique)
See 204

†MEUNIER, JEAN-PIERRE (France)
See 159

MICHEL, EMELINE (Haiti/US)
See also 476, 706–707, 712

986. Wald, Elijah. *Global minstrels: voices of world music.* New York: Routledge, 2007, pp. 59–63. Profile of the singer.

Articles

987. Amoruso, Carol. "Emeline Michel is a woman on a mission." *Global Rhythm*, Vol. 12, No. 12 (December 2004): 26–27. Short feature.

988. Dring, Brian. "Emeline Michel: body and soul." *The Beat*, Vol. 19, No. 2 (2000): 40–43, 73. Interview.

989. ———. "The other Caribbean: interview with Emeline Michel." *The Beat*, Vol. 23, No. 6 (2004): 23. Conversation with Michel about her new recording *Rasin Kreyol.*

990. "Emeline Michel, une super star qui brille!" *Haiti Culture*, Vol. 6, No. 2 (juillet 1990): 14–15. Interview.

991. Sisario, Ben. "A diplomat of music, longing for her homeland." *New York Times* (Nov. 19 2004): E3. Feature on the Haitian singer and her new recording, *Rasin Kreyol,* on Times Square Records.

MIDNIGHT GROOVERS (Dominica)
See 716

MIDONET, GRATIEN (ca. 1951–) (Martinique)
See 158

MIEL (Haiti/US)

992. Dring, Brian. "The other Caribbean: Sweet like honey." *The Beat*, Vol. 22, No. 1 (2003): 48. Short interview with Stephane 'Stef' Alexandre, leader of the recently formed dance band, Miel.

MILIEN, RODRIGUE (Haiti)
See 701, 710

MILLENIUM (French Antilles)

993. Mana, Felicien. "Problemes des musiciens antillais en France." *Antilla*, No. 366 (janv. 18–24 1990): 31–35. Conversation with

Celia and Sekou Manga of Millenium, a popular Paris-based music group, about their experiences on the Antillean music scene in France.

MINI ALL STARS (Haiti)
See 701

MOISE, ALFRED (d.1986) (Haiti)

994. "Alfred Moise est mort." *Haiti Culture*, Vol. 3, No. 9 (janvier 1987): 7. Short obit for one of the founding members of Haiti's Orchestre Septentrional.

MOISE, THONY (Haiti)
See 704

MOLIN, ROBERT (Haiti)
See 704

MONA, EUGENE [Georges Venus Nilecame] (1943–1991) (Martinique)
See also 152, 159, 627

995. Berrian, Brenda F. "Eugene Mona: the Martinican performer of angage songs." In *Caribe 2000: definiciones, identidades y culturas regionales y/o nacionales*, eds. Lowell Fiet and Janette Becerra. San Juan: Caribe 2000, Universidad de Puerto Rico, Facultad de Humanidades, 1998, pp. 59–73.

996. Cyrille, Dominique. *Mona* / avec une preface de Victor Lina. Fort-de-France [Martinique]: Sim'LN, [1999]. 118 p.: ill., music. (Collection Sim'Ekol). Discography: p. [71]–78. Bio-critical portrait. Includes a biographical sketch, discography, and transcriptions of several Mona compositions (p. [79]–118).

Articles

997. Cauver, J.G. "Antilla culture: Eugene Mona." *Antilla*, No. 326 (mars 27–avril 2 1989): 24–25. Interview with Mona about his return to the Martinican scene following a lengthy absence.

998. Corbin, Henri. "Tombeau d'Eugene Mona." *Antilla*, No. 454 (oct 4–10 1991): 28. Poetic tribute.

999. Cyrille, Dominique. "Imagining an Afro-Creole nation: Eugene Mona's music in Martinique of the 1980s." *Latin American Music Review*, Vol. 27, No. 2 (Fall–Winter 2006): 148–170.

1000. ———. "Popular music and the Martinican-Creole identity."
Black Music Research Journal, Vol. 22, No. 1 (Spring 2002): 65–
83. Examines the music and careers of Martinican musicians
Francisco and Eugene Mona.

1001. "Mona est mort." *Antilla*, No. 453 (sept. 27–oct. 3 1991): 3–10.
Two elegies for Mona by Lisa David and journalist Tony
Delsham accompanied by photos of Mona's funeral cortege.

1002. Ponnamah, Michel. "Mona mystique." *Antilla*, No. 36 (janvier 13
1983): 37. Review of a Christmas eve broadcast of a Mona
concert aired on Martinican television.

1003. Rivel, Moune de. "La flute magique d'Eugene Mona." *Bingo*
(Paris), No. 355 (aout 1982): 47. Interview.

1004. Scaramuzzo, Gene. "The other Caribbean: Mourning Mona." *The
Beat*, Vol. 11, No. 1 (1992): 26. Obituary.

MONTOUT, LUCIEN FABIEN (1932–1991) (Martinique/France)
See 159

MONTREDON, JEAN-CLAUDE (1949–) (Martinique/France)

1005. Mandibele. "J.C. Montredon: je suis un musicien." *Antilla*, No.
356 (nov 2–8 1989): 35–36. Interview with the Martinican
percussionist.

MORSE, RICHARD (1957–) (US/Haiti)
See also **RAM**

1006. Shacochis, Bob. "The day you see me fall is not the day I die:
Voudou rhythms." In *The archipelago: new writing from and
about the Caribbean*, eds. Robert Antoni and Bradford Morrow.
Annandale-on-Hudson, NY: Bard College, 1996, pp. 167–192.
Profile of the Haitian-American leader of Ram, a roots-rock
ensemble based in Port-au-Prince, Haiti.

MOUNE DE RIVEL
See **RIVEL, MOUNE DE**

MURRAY, DAVID (1955–) (US/France)

1007. Denis, Jacques. "Le ka cogne!; Depuis dix ans, le saxophoniste
David Murray mene le Creole Project, une aventure qui remit a
sa juste place la tradition guadeloupeenne du gwo ka, musique
rebelle que se connecte avec le jazz et le hip hop." *Vibrations*

(Lausanne), No. 65 (juillet–aout 2004): 50–53. Feature on Murray, the African American saxophonist, and his Paris-based Creole Project, a collaborative effort fusing his jazz-rooted style with gwo ka drumming from Guadeloupe.

1008.   Giddins, Gary. "Weatherbird: Aqui se habla espanol; David Murray makes a Cuban connection." *Village Voice* (Feb 19–25 2003): 64. Recap of Murray's career from his arrival in New York in 1975 to his most recent forays into music from Senegal, Guadeloupe and Cuba.

1009.   Mandel, Howard. "The world according to David; David Murray's musical quests from Guadaloupe [sic], Cuba, Paris, New York and beyond." *Down Beat* (May 2003): 42–46. Conversation with the American saxophonist about his recent collaborations with musicians from Guadeloupe, Cuba, West Africa, and beyond.

1010.   Palmer, Don. "David Murray, Afro-Caribbean connections." *Rhythm* (New York), Vol. 8, No. 4 (April 1999): 34–35. Feature on Murray's recent collaborations with West African and French Antillean musicians based in Paris.

NAIMRO, JEAN-CLAUDE (1951–) (Martinique)
See **KASSAV**

NANKIN, JOEL (Guadeloupe)

1011.   Nuissier, Tony. "Joel Nankin, musicien guadeloupeen en prison." *Antilla*, No. 117 (sept 21–28 1984): 25–27. Report on the imprisonment of a veteran Guadeloupean folk musician.

NARDAL, PAULETTE (1896–1985) (Martinique)
See 236

NEGRI, CHRISTIAN DE (1946–) (Martinique)
See **MALAVOI**

NUMBER ONE (Haiti)

1012.   Coradin, Leslie. "Divertissements: 'Number One' un nouvel orchestre." *Haiti New York Magazine*, Vol. 1, No. 1 (dec. 1980): 24–25, 27. Interview with the group's leader, Loubert Chancy.

OBAS, BEETHOVA (1964–) (Haiti)

1013. Amoruso, Carol. "Beethova Obas: creole cosmopolitan." *Rhythm* (New York), Vol. 9, No. 5 (May 2000): 30–31. Feature on the popular Haitian balladeer.

1014. Averill, Gage. "Haitian fascination: *Debode*—breaking out." *The Beat*, Vol. 14, No. 1 (1995): 26–27. Column discussing two recent recordings by Zshea (*Debode*) and Beethova Obas (*Si*).

OKAY (Cuba)

1015. Barcelo, Tomas. "Okay: la otra identidad." *Bohemia*, ano 83, no. 13 (marzo 29 1991): 12–14. Feature on the Cuban-Haitian folkloric group from Ciego de Avila province.

OLICHA [Michel Melthon-Lynch] (ca. 1969–1994) (Haiti)
See also **BOUKMAN EKSPERYANS**

1016. Averill, Gage. "Olicha (Michel Melthon-Lynch), Boukman Eksperyans bassist and percussionist." *The Beat*, Vol. 13, No. 4 (1994): 41. Report on Olicha's death in Haiti.

1017. "Michel-Melthon Lynch." *Rhythm Music Magazine*, Vol. 3, No. 7 (1994): 62. Obituary.

1018. "Michel-Melthon Lynch, 25, musician." *New York Times* (June 18 1994): 54. Obituary.

ORCHESTRE CITADELLE (Haiti)
See 704

ORCHESTRE SAIEH (Haiti)
See 474

ORCHESTRE SEPTENTRIONAL (Haiti)
See also 701, 994

1019. Averill, Gage. "The pride of the North: the other side of Haitian music." *The Beat*, Vol. 8, No. 5 (1989): 45, 56. Column on the venerable Haitian dance bands Orchestre Tropicana and Orchestra Septentrionale.

1020. Regan, Jane. "Haiti's ball of fire; Rooted in rhythms of the Northern countryside, this nation's oldest big band is threatened by the invasion of foreign music and a failing economy." *Americas*, Vol. 56, No. 2 (March–April 2004): 20–27. Feature on Cap Haitien's Septentrional and its storied history.

ORCHESTRE TROPICANA (Haiti)
See also 701, 706

1021. Averill, Gage. "The pride of the North: the other side of Haitian music." *The Beat*, Vol. 8, No. 5 (1989): 45, 56. Column on the venerable dance bands Orchestre Tropicana and Orchestra Septentrionale.

1022. Golden, Tim. "Haitian music from another era." *New York Times* (April 20 1991): 13–14. Feature on the veteran Cap Haitien big band and its continuing popularity with Haitian audiences based in Brooklyn, NY.

PAKATAK (Martinique)

1023. Chamoiseau, Patrick. "Pakatak: l'esprit creole." *Antilla*, No. 235 (avril 2–9 1987): 7, 11. Review essay on the music of Martinican chouval bwa group Pakatak and its leader, Krisyan Jesophe.

1024. Dynma. "Musique: Le retour de Pakatak." *Antilla*, No. 44 (mars 10 1983): 34–36. Interview with the chouval bwa group from Martinique.

PALAVIRE (Martinique)
See 152

PAPA JUBE [John Jube Altino] (Haiti/US)

1025. Averill, Gage. "Haitian fascination: Sifting through the wreckage." *The Beat*, Vol. 12, No. 5 (1993): 24. Column on the Papa Jube recording *Liberasyon*.

1026. Birnbaum, Larry. "World music: Post–crossover meltdown." *Pulse!* [West Sacramento] (February 1994): 57. Brief profile.

PASCAL, ALIX "TIT" (Haiti)
See also **AYIZAN**

1027. "La musique haitienne, grandeur et faiblesse." *Haiti Culture*, Vol. 2, No. 5 (sept. 1985): 3, 12. Interview with Haitian musician Tit Pascal.

PASQUET, DADOU [Alix Pasquet] (1953–) (Haiti/US)
See 690, 710

PAUL, FRED (Haiti/US)
See also 702

1028. Averill, Gage. "Haitian fascination: Three antidotes to a bleak outlook." *The Beat*, Vol. 11, No. 1 (1992): 25, 60. Conversation with record producer and Mini Records chief, Fred Paul, about his career in the Haitian record industry.

PEAN, PIERRE MICHEL ["Tonton Pe"] (d. 1994) (Haiti)
See 704

PHILIPPE, LUC (Haiti)
See 704

PIROGUE (Haiti)
See 701

PLASTIC SYSTEM BAND (Martinique)
See 132

POGLO [Eric Lugiery] (Martinique)
See 152

POLICARD, REGINALD (1953–) (Haiti)
See 706

†**PORRY, PHILIPPE** (Martinique)
See **MALAVOI**

PRESSOIR, MICHEL (1934–) (Haiti)
See 704

PYRONEAU, ELYSEE (Haiti)

1029. "Elysee Pyroneau, guitariste du Tabou." *Haiti Culture*, Vol. 1, No. 6 (octobre 1984): 5. Interview with the Tabou Combo guitarist.

RAM (Haiti)
See also 458, 712, 1006

1030. French, Howard W. "Movie is bridge to U.S. for Haitian pop group." *New York Times* (March 10 1994): C20. Interview with Ram's leader Richard Morse about his background and that of his group.

1031. Lusk, Jon. "Root salad: Ram." *Folk Roots*, No. 259–260 (Jan–Feb 2005): 25–26. Conversation with the group's leader, Richard Morse.

1032. Steward, Sue. "Ram dancehall; Despite the volatile politics and grinding poverty, the Vodou inspired musicians and artists of Haiti, like Ram, continue to create." *Straight, No Chaser*, Vol. 2, No. 17 (Autumn 2001): 50–51, 53. Feature on the Haitian roots rock group Ram and its leader, Richard Morse.

RANSAY, MAX (1942–) (Martinique)

1033. Delsham, Tony. "Max Ransay: Monsieur Tete lang mwen." *Antilla*, No. 343 (juillet 24–30 1989): 34–35. Short interview with a veteran popular musician from Martinique.

RAPON, JACKY (Martinique)
See 717

RARA MACHINE (Haiti)
See also 458, 480, 702, 711

1034. Averill, Gage. "Haitian fascination: Rara to go." *The Beat*, Vol. 13, No. 4 (1994): 40–41. Detailed review of the Rara Machine recording *Voudou Nou* (Shanachie).

REMION, SERGE
See 248

RISKE (Haiti/US)
See 713

RIVEL, MOUNE DE [Cecile Jean-Louis Baghio'o] (1918–) (France/Guadeloupe)
See also 159

1035. Alphonse, Jean. "Une ambassadrice du folklore antillais: Moune de Rivel." *Revue Guadeloupeenne*, No. 48 (1962): 23–25. Profile.

1036. Diakhate, Lydie. "Moune de Rivel: la memoire du folklore creole." *Divas* (Paris), No. 13 (decembre 2000): 56–59. Feature on the legendary French Antillean singer and her nearly six decade career as an entertainer.

RODRIGUE, JOHNNY [Jean Rodrigue] (1959–1985) (Haiti)

1037. "Johnny n'est plus." *Haiti Culture*, Vol. 2, No. 8 (dec. 1985): 6, 11. Obituary followed by a posthumously published interview with the popular Haitian singer.

RODRIGUEZ, GEORGES (Haiti/Canada)

1038. Fleury, Bergman. "Entrevue avec Georges Rodriguez." *Mapou* (Ottawa), Vol. 1, No. 3 (printemps 1978): 16–23. Interview with the Haitian percussionist currently based in Montreal.

ROSENTHAL, SERGE (Haiti)
See 704

ROSINE, PAULO (1948–1993) (Martinique)
See also 159, 965–975, 1138

1039. Menil, Rene. "Musique: 'Paulo Rosine, l'invention de la musique.'" *Antilla*, No. 524 (fevrier 19–25 1993): 27. Memorial tribute.

1040. Scaramuzzo, Gene. "Passings: Paulo Rosine 1948–1993." *The Beat*, Vol. 12, No. 2 (1993): 66. Obituary for the Martinican pianist and founder of Malavoi.

ROTIN, JEAN-MICHEL (1970–) (Guadeloupe)
See 717

RUBINEL, RONALD (1963–) (Martinique)

1041. Cadet-Petit, Alexandre. "Musique: Ronald Rubinel, le zoulou de la paix." *Fouyaya*, No. 56 (juin 1987): 43–44. Profile.

†**SAIEH, ISSA EL** (1919–2005) (Haiti)
See 474, 704

ST AUDE, RENE (1909–1995) (Haiti)
See also 891–892, 1116

1042. Averill, Gage. "Passings: Rene St. Aude, Haitian roots pioneer." *The Beat*, Vol. 14, No. 3 (1995): 90–91. Obituary for the founder of Haiti's iconic dance band Jazz des Jeunes.

SAINT-CYREL, FELIX (Guadeloupe)

1043. "Felix Saint-Cyrel: 'j'aime la musique qui est libre....'" *Grin Fos*, No. 2 (oct–nov 1987): 9–12. Interview with Guadeloupean jazz musician Felix Saint-Cyrel.

SAINT-ELOI, PATRICK (1958–) (Guadeloupe)
See **KASSAV**

ST. LOT, PAULETTE (Haiti/US)
See 686

SAINT-PRIX, DEDE (1953–) (Martinique/France)
See also 152, 1023–1024

1044. Baehler, Jean-Marc. "Tropical." *Vibrations* (Lausanne), n.s. No. 15 (dec 1996–fev 1997): 40. Interview.

1045. Cadet-Petit, Alexandre. "Musique et sponsor: les Rhums en tete." *Fouyaya*, No. 58 (sept. 1987): 5. Conversation with Saint-Prix about the differences between the music industry and its operation in Martinique and France.

1046. Cauver, J.G. "Musique: Dede Saint-Prix et Avan Van." *Antilla*, No. 320 (fevrier 13–19 1989): 6–10. Conversation with Saint-Prix about the differences between the professional music scenes in Martinique and France, his group, Avan Van, and more.

1047. Chamoiseau, Patrick. "Saint-Prix, le nouveau Dede." *Antilla*, No. 232 (mars 12–19 1987): 7, 11. Critique of a new Dede Saint-Prix recording.

1048. Elongui, Luigi. "Dede Saint-Prix: 'le chouval bwa est une maniere de vivre et de parler.'" *La Lettre des Musiques et des Arts Africains*, No. 31 (juin 5 1996): 2–4. Interview.

1049. ———. "Entretien avec Dede Saint-Prix." *Africultures*, No. 8 (mai 1998): 12–13, 15–16. Excerpts from the previous entry.

1050. Galland, Stephane. "Dede Saint Prix: mon manege a moi, c'est chouval bwa." *Afiavi*, No. 26 (avril–mai 2001): 8–9. Interview.

1051. Souza, Nicolas-Raphael de. "Dede Saint-Prix, Martinique." *Revue Noire*, No. 21 (juin–aout 1996): 92. Interview.

SAINT-VAL, TANYA (1965–) (Guadeloupe)
See also 152, 715

1052. Cadet-Petit, Alexandre. "Musique: Tania St-Val." *Fouyaya*, No. 56 (juin 1987): 46. Short profile.

1053. Fundere, Thierry. "Tanya Saint-Val: itineraire d'une chanteuse d'exception." *Divas* (Paris), No. 3 (oct–nov 1999): 116. Profile of the popular zouk love singer currently based in France.

SAKAD (Haiti/US)

1054. "Sakad." *Haiti Culture*, Vol. 5, No. 8 (aout 1989): 10–11, 24. Interview with the group's spokesman, Nikol Levy, about recent changes in Sakad's lineup.

SAKAJ (Haiti/US)
See 708

SALVADOR, HENRI (1917–2008) (French Guiana/France)

1055. Delannoy, Luc. *Sacre Henri!* Montreal: Lemeac, 2002. 99 p. Informal portrait of the Paris-based jazz singer and guitarist.

1056. Denis, Jacques. "Henri Salvador, un jeune homme pas presse." In *Histoires de musiciens*, ed. Pierre-Jean Crittin. Gollion: Infolio, 2006, pp. 205–216. Reprint of 1060.

1057. Manheim, James M. "Henri Salvador." In *Contemporary musicians*. Detroit: Gale Research, 2004, v. 48, pp. 150–151.

1058. Miquel, Olivier. *Henri Salvador, le rire du destin*. Paris: Moment, 2007. 275 p.: ports. Biography.

1059. Salvador, Henri. *Attention ma vie*. [France]: J.-C. Lattes, 1994. 314 p.: ill. Memoir.

Articles

1060. Denis, Jacques. "Sans se presser." *Vibrations* (Lausanne), No. 28 (octobre 2000): 26–30, 33. Interview with the popular balladeer and guitarist. Reprinted in 1056.

1061. Harris, Craig. "Henri Salvador: songs from a lazy man." *Global Rhythm*, Vol. 11, No. 8 (August 2002): 22–25. Feature on Salvador and his new recording *Chambre Avec Vu*.

1062. "Henri Salvador, 90, singer; Helped bring rock to France." *New York Times* (Feb. 14 2008): C12. Obituary.

1063. "Henri Salvador, the French atomic bomb; With rapid fire songs, dances and comedy, he keeps audiences howling." *Our World*, Vol. 10, No. 11 (November 1955): 9–11. Photo-feature.

1064. Jackson, Tom. "Henri Salvador takes a final curtain call with Reverence." *Global Rhythm*, Vol. 16, No. 7 (July 2007): 18–19. Profile of the 89-year-old Salvador as he prepares to finally retire from the music scene.

1065. Vian, Boris. "Henri Salvador: le jazzman, le crooner et le clown." *Jazz Hot*, No. 425 (octobre 1985): 14–18. Interview.

SANBA-YO (Haiti)
See 711

SARDABY, MICHEL (1935–) (Martinique)

1066. "Silhouette: Michel Sardaby, pianiste de jazz." *Paralleles*, No. 1 (novembre 1964): 24. Profile.

SARTANA (Guadeloupe)
See 719

SASAYESA (Martinique)
See 132

SAUSS, LA (Martinique
See 414

SAXE [Franck Saxemard] (1965?–2003) (Martinique)
See 717

SCHWARZ-BART, JACQUES (1962–) (Guadeloupe/US)

1067. Murph, John. "Jacques Schwarz-Bart: gwoka bridge." *Down Beat* (Dec. 2007): 28–29. Short feature.

1068. Tamarkin, Jeff. "Jacques Schwarz-Bart lets the drums resound." *Global Rhythm*, Vol. 16, No. 10 (Oct. 2007): 22–23. Feature.

SCORPIO (Haiti)
See 701

SEININ, GERTRUDE (Martinique)

1069. Cadet-Petit, Alexandre. "Gertrude Seinin." *Fouyaya*, No. 44 (dec. 1985): 22. Tribute to the singing talents of Martinican vocalist Gertrude Seinin.

1070. "Chanson: Gertrude Seinin." *Antilla*, No. 367 (janv 25–31 1990): 35. Short feature.

SENEY, EVENS (Haiti)
See **BOUKAN GINEN**

SENEY, GARY (Haiti)
See **BOUKMAN EKSPERYANS**

SHLEU SHLEU (Haiti)
See also 701, 704

1071. Averill, Gage. "Haitian fascination: Schleu Schleu over you." *The Beat*, Vol. 10, No. 6 (1991): 28–29. Profile of a leading Haitian compas band.

1072. "La renaissance des Shleu Shleu." *Haiti Culture*, Vol. 2, No. 8 (dec. 1985): 5, 11. Interview with the group's leader, Tony Moise.

SHOUBOU [Roger M. Eugene] (1947–) (Haiti/US)

1073. Dring, Brian. "The other Caribbean: Sweet like honey." *The Beat*, Vol. 22, No. 1 (2003): 49. Brief interview with the Tabou Combo stalwart about his first recording as a leader, *Shou...Badou* (Antilles Mizik).

1074. Shoubou raconte sa vie au sein du Tabou-Combo." *Haiti Culture*, Vol. 3, No. 3 (juillet 1986): 3, 9, 16. Interview.

SIAR, CLAUDY (France)
See 159

SICOT, WEBER (1930–1985) (Haiti)
See also 474, 509, 701, 704

1075. "Sicot et la verite." *Haiti Culture*, Vol. 1, No. 11 (mars 1985): 3, 9, 16. Interview with singer Andre Dorismond about the pioneering Haitian bandleader and saxophonist Weber Sicot.

SKAH SHAH (Haiti/US)
See also 701, 706, 784

1076. "Les 14 ans de Skah Shah." *Haiti Culture*, Vol. 4, No. 12 (juillet 1988): 6–7, 26. Interview with lead singer Zou Zoul about Skah Shah, the popular Haitian dance band, and its history.

SKANDAL (Haiti/US)
See 708

SOIME, JEAN-PAUL (1950–2007) (Martinique)
See **MALAVOI**

SON LAWO (Martinique)

1077. Rome, Emmanuel. "Musique: Son Lawo." *Antilla*, No. 13 (fevrier 20 1982): 47. Concert review.

STELLIO, ALEXANDRE [Alexandre Fructueux] (1885–1939) (Martinique/France)
See 151, 179, 215

SURIN, WILLIAM (Haiti)

1078. "William Surin." *Haiti Culture*, Vol. 2, No. 8 (dec. 1985): 7, 13. Interview with the popular Haitian singer.

SWEET MICKY [Michel Martelly] (1961–) (Haiti/US)

1079. Ackerman, Elise. "His music rules in Haiti; Sweet Micky's provocative music moves Haitians with an infectious beat and political overtones." *Miami New Times* (May 29 1997). Also available online: http://www.miaminewtimes.com. Feature highlighting the volatile mix of music, race, and politics in contemporary Haiti and Sweet Micky's place in it.

1080. Amoruso, Carol. "Naughty but nice: Sweet Micky/Michel Martelly." *Rhythm* (New York), Vol. 9, No. 3 (March 2000): 30. Feature on the popular compas star and his dueling personas.

1081. Daniel, Trenton. "I don't care: a conversation with Michel 'Sweet Micky' Martelly." *Transition* (Kampala), No. 91 (2002): 88–104. Interview.

1082. ———. "'Sweet Micky' turns down volume." *Miami Herald* (Mar. 1 2007): A1, A18. Feature on the compas star and his decision, at age 46, to go into semi-retirement.

SYLVAIN, CLIFFORD (Haiti/US)
See also 702

1083. "Clifford Sylvain ex-musicien de Kajou, vieux baroudeur des mini-jazz, prend la route en solo." *Haiti Culture*, Vol. 5, No. 11 (dec. 1989): 14–15, 18. Interview.

SYSTEM BAND (Haiti)
See 701, 706

TABOU COMBO (Haiti/US)
See also 468, 701, 707, 1029, 1074

1084. Averill, Gage. "Moving the Big Apple: Tabou Combo's diasporic dreams." In *Island sounds in the global city: Caribbean popular music and identity in New York*, eds. Ray Allen and Lois Wilcken. New York: New York Folklore Society, etc., 1998, pp. 138–161.

1085. Laroche, Maximilien. "Dyaz, rap, mereng: creativite dans la musique et dans la langue haitienne." In *La decouverte de l'Amerique par les Americains*. Sainte-Foy, Quebec: GRELCA, Universite Laval, 1989, pp. 243–252. Literary analysis of two versions of a Tabou Combo song—"Bolero jouc li jou" (1981) and "Bolero rap" (1983). Revised version of 1092.

1086. Wald, Elijah. *Global minstrels: voices of world music*. New York: Routledge, 2007, pp. 55–58. Profile of Tabou Combo.

Articles

1087. Averill, Gage. "Haitian fascination: Old grooves, new directions." *The Beat*, Vol. 8, No. 2 (1989): 20–21. Review of the Tabou Combo recording *Aux Antilles*.

1088. ———. "Tabou Combo: Brooklyn's bridge to the Caribbean." *The Beat*, Vol. 9, No. 4 (1990): 27–31, 39, 62. Feature on the group and its recorded history from 1967 to 1990.

1089. Ferguson, Eve M. "Haitian homecoming; on the road in Haiti with Tabou Combo—gaping potholes, political pitfalls and roaring fans around every corner." *Rhythm Music*, Vol. 5, No. 1–2 (1996): 10–11. Reports on a Haitian tour by the veteran dance band Tabou Combo.

1090. Fuller, Charles. "Tabou Combo: 30 years of kompas music and still going strong." *Reggae Report*, Vol. 16, No. 2 (1998): 10–11. Feature.

1091. Kramer, Stella. "Tabou Combo: ambassadors of Haitian music." *Class* (New York), Vol. 6, No. 9 (September 1985): 12–13. Short feature.

1092. Laroche, Maximilien. "Le 'rap' et Tabou Combo." *Carbet* (Fort-de-France), No. 2 (juin 1984): 74–79. Published in revised form as 1085.

1093. McLane, Daisann. "Tabou Combo: compas rock." *Village Voice* (August 25 1987): 72, 75. Appreciation of the group and its music.

1094. Pareles, Jon. "Syncopations with flavor from Haiti." *New York Times* (September 19 1986): C26. Feature on Tabou Combo, the compas veterans from Petion-Ville.

TANBOU BO KANNAL (Martinique)
See 132

TAXIKREOL (Martinique)
See 152

THAMAD BAND (Haiti)

1095. "Thamad Band." *Haiti Culture*, Vol. 2, No. 9 (janv. 1986): 12. Interview with the group's leader, Smith Jn Baptiste.

1096. "Thamad Band." *Haiti Culture*, Vol. 4, No. 9 (fevrier 1988): 16–18. Conversation with the group's leader, drummer Smith Jn Baptiste.

THAMAR, RALPH (1952–) (Martinique)
See also 719

1097. Cadet-Petit, Alexandre. "Star: Ralph Thamar." *Fouyaya*, No. 41 (sept. 1985): 41. Feature.

1098. Mandibele. "Ralph Thamar: j'ai beaucoup d'admiration pour Ti-Ayoul Grivallier." *Antilla*, No. 277 (mars 3–9 1988): 6–7. Interview with the popular singer from Martinique.

THIFAULT, GERARD (Haiti)

1099. Lucas, Mario. "Still more Ay-bo-le." *Ballroom Dance Magazine*, Vol. 4, No. 5 (May 1963): 19–20. *See also* Jim Smith's "More Ay-bo-le" in this same issue (p. 18).

1100. Peri, Franc. "Ay-bo-le! The new Haitian rhythm." *Ballroom Dance Magazine*, Vol. 4, No. 3 (March 1963): 4–5. Discusses the dance craze associated with Gerard Thifault's song of the same name. Includes diagrams for the dance's basic steps.

1101. Smith, Jim. *Ay-bo-le! The exciting new dance from Haiti.* [Waldwick, NJ: Dance Records, Inc., 1963]. 10 p.: ill. Instructions on how to perform the popular dance created by Montreal-based bandleader Gerard Thifault.

TI EMILE [Emmanuel Caserus] (1924–1992) (Martinique)
See also 159, 627

1103. Chamoiseau, Patrick. "Hommage: La voix de Ti Emile." *Antilla*, No. 477 (mars 22–28 1992): 3. Tribute to the recently deceased *bele* musician from Martinique.

1104. "Hommage a Ti-Emile et Vava Grivalliers." *Antilla*, No. 285 (avril 28–mai 4 1988): 6–7. Biographical sketches for two veteran Martinican folk musicians/dancers.

1105. Scaramuzzo, Gene. "Passings: 'Ti Emile' Caserius [sic] 1925–1992." *The Beat*, Vol. 12, No. 5 (1993): 75. Obituary.

TI MANNO [Antoine Rossini Jean-Baptiste] (1953–1985) (Haiti)
See also 710

1106. Camille, Jacques. "Hommage a Ti Manno." *Haiti Culture*, Vol. 4, No. 12 (juillet 1988): 23, 30. Appreciation.

1107. Glick-Schiller, Nina, and Georges Fouron. "'Everywhere we go, we are in danger': Ti Manno and the emergence of a Haitian transnational identity." *American Anthropologist*, Vol. 17, No. 2 (May 1990): 329–347. Discusses the role of twoubadou singer Ti Manno in helping diasporic Haitians define their dual identities as Haitians and immigrants.

1108. "Musique: Interview exclusive avec Ti Manno." *Demain-Haiti*, Vol. 1, No. 11 (1984?): 34. Interview with the Haitian angage singer.

1109. Prudent, Lambert-Felix. "Antiya-Mizik: La tendre fureur et la colere: Negre de Ti Manno, haitien emigre et chanteur de talent." *Antilla*, No. 52 (mai 5–12, 1983): 38–39. Reviews two Ti Manno recordings, one with the Gemini All Stars and another with Atis Independan.

TI MARCEL [Marcel Jean] (Haiti)
See 1116

TI MARCEL [Marcel Louis-Joseph] (1929–) (Guadeloupe)
See 349

TI MOI [Maurice Marie-Louise] (Martinique)

1110. "Actualites: Ti Moi est de retour." *Antilla*, No. 298 (aout 1988): 31. Profile of Martinican popular musician Ti Moi.

TI PARIS [Achille Paris] (Haiti)
See 709

TI PIERRE (Haiti)

1111. "La tragedie de Ti Pierre: un artiste dechouke." *Haiti Culture*, Vol. 6, No. 4 (fevrier 1991): 6. Remembrance of the recently murdered musician by singer Ti Plume.

TI PLUME [Ricardo Franck] (Haiti)

1112. Averill, Gage. "Haitian fascination: Another feather in his cap." *The Beat*, Vol. 12, No. 4 (1993): 30–32. Interview with musician Ti Plume about his music and career.

TI RAOUL [Raoul Grivalliers] (1934–) (Martinique)

1102. Cauver, J.G. "Ti-Ayul, chanteur de bel-aire." *Antilla*, No. 283 (avril 14–20 1988): 6–7. Short interview with the veteran *bele* singer about a recent recording.

TI RORO [Raymond Ballergeau] (1920–1980) (Haiti)
See also 1116

1113. *Spotlight Illustrated*, Vol. 2, No. 2–3 (1955): 10. Portrait of Haitian folkloric drummer Ti Roro.

TOP VICE (Haiti/US)

1114. "Le miracle du Top Vice." *Haiti Culture*, Vol. 5, No. 10 (novembre 1989): 20–21. Interview with group members Robert Charlot, Robert Martino, and Freddy.

TREBEAU, SUZY (Martinique)
See 152

TROUILLOT, JOE [Joseph Francois Andre] (1922–) (Haiti/Canada)

*1115. Rubrini, Nathalie. *Joe Trouillot, d'hier a aujourd'hui*. [Montreal-Nord]: Editions Caraibes, [1999]. 192 p.: music, port. Discography: p. [165]–174. Biography of the Haitian popular singer. [Held by the National Library of Quebec]

TROUPE FOLKLORIQUE NATIONALE (Haiti)

1116. Sarteur, Ramiro. "Embajada de arte popular haitiano." *Carteles*, ano 32, no. 11 (marzo 18 1951): 51. Illustrated feature on a visit to Cuba by Haiti's national folkloric troupe led by music director Rene St. Aude and featuring master drummers Ti Roro and Ti Marcel.

TROUPE MAKANDAL, LA (Haiti/US)
See also 686, 729–733

1117. Wilcken, Lois. "Rising sun: Gede's drama of death and rebirth in Brooklyn, New York." *Journal of Haitian Studies*, Vol. 10, No. 2 (Fall 2004): 156–161. Describes the genesis and evolution of 'Rising Sun: a Vodou drama of death and rebirth in three parts.' The music-drama is a creation of the New York ensemble La Troupe Makandal led by drummer Frisner Augustin.

T-VICE (Haiti/US)

1118. Darling, Cary. "Miami T-Vice; Brothers Roberto and Reynaldo Martino, the duo known as T-Vice, are helping to make the local Haitian music scene America's best. Conquering the mainstream may prove tougher." *Miami Herald* (May 21 2000): 5M, 7M. Long feature on the popular Miami-based compas group.

1119. Fraser Delgado, Celeste. "Got milk?; Reynaldo and Roberto Martino are T-Vice." *Miami New Times* (April 20 2000). Also available online: http://www.miaminewtimes.com. Feature on T-Vice's leaders.

ULTRA-MARINE (Martinique)
See **CANONGE, MARIO**

URSULL, JOELLE (1960–) (Martinique/France)
See 152

VADELEUX, GUY (1952–) (Martinique)
See 248

VALLOT, PASCAL (Guadeloupe)
See 719

VALVERT, FELIX (1905–1995) (Guadeloupe/France)

*1120. Valvert, Felix. *Felix Valvert, le roi de la rumba: memoires /* recueillis par sa fille— Isabelle de Valvert. Paris: New Legend, 2001. 177 p.: ill. (Collection Loseyando)

VAMUR, CLAUDE (1950–) (Guadeloupe)
See 152, 912

VAN LEVE (Guadeloupe)

1121. "Van Leve: 'nous sommes sideres de voir les jeunes danser.'"
Moun (Pointe-a-Pitre), No. 2 (juillet–sept. 1986): 19. Short
interview with Van Leve's leader Jean-Claude Antoinette about
the group and its history.

VARASSE, ROSY (Martinique/France)

1122. Cauver, J.G. "Spectacles: Rosy Varasse au CMAC." *Antilla*, No.
232 (mars 12–19 1987): 17–18. Interview.

VELO [Marcel Lollia] (1931–1984) (Guadeloupe)
See also 152

1123. Boulogne, Edouard. "La mort de Velo: une recuperation
sacrilege." *Guadeloupe 2000 Magazine*, No. 98 (mai–juin 1984):
3–4, 6–7. Report/commentary on Velo's funeral which Boulogne
claims was hijacked by partisans of Guadeloupe's Independence
movement.

1124. "Gwadloup jodijou: Trois hommages a Velo." *Antilla*, No. 107
(juin 15–22 1984): 22–25, 28. Three tributes to Velo, the recently
deceased gwo ka master drummer from Guadeloupe.

1125. Kafe. "Velo: Kafe temoigne." *Moun* (Pointe-a-Pitre), No. 1 (aout–
octobre 1985): 22–24. Memories of Velo from fellow gwo ka
drummer and friend, Kafe.

1126. Pepin, Ernest. "La felure d'un silence de 'domine': la mort de
Velo." *Carbet* (Fort-de-France), No. 3 (mai 1985): 26–29. Elegy
for the late drum master from Guadeloupe.

VENET DANGER, CONSUELO ["Tecla"] (1896–1990) (Cuba)

1127. Rivero, Angel. "La reina cantadora: 'Yo canto el recuerdo que me
dejaron mis antepasados' decir Tecla Benet Danger es hablar de
la tumba francesa de Santiago de Cuba." *Revolucion y Cultura*,
No. 90 (febrero 1980): 26–28. Conversation with a matriarch of
the Haitian-Cuban tumba francesa tradition.

VENET DANGER, GAUDIOSA ["Yoya"] (1917–1997) (Cuba)

1128. Cruz Diaz, Laura. "Voz de la historia: Gaudiosa Venet Danger:
'No quiero morir y pensar que no exista la tumba francesa.'" *Del
Caribe*, No. 27 (1997): 108–111. A final interview with master
dancer Gaudiosa Venet Danger about the Haitian-derived tumba
francesa drum-dance tradition from eastern Cuba.

1129. Pino, Pompeyo. "Yoya: el baile en la sangre." *Bohemia*, ano 74, no. 33 (agosto 13 1982): 22. Interview.

VICTOR, EMMANUELLE (1953–) (Haiti)

1130. O'Brien, Martha Estep. "A feminine voice in contemporary Haitian Roman Catholic religious music: the songs of Petite Soeur Emmanuelle Victor, P.S.I." *Journal of Haitian Studies*, Vol. 10, No. 2 (Fall 2004): 58–67. Examines the work of a liturgical music composer.

VILLEVALEIX, LECONTE (Haiti)
See 704

VINCENT, FRANCKY [Vincent Franck] (1956–) (Guadeloupe)
See also 159

1131. Migow, Erwan. "Franky le saint Vincent du zouk." *Divas* (Paris), No. 6 (avril–mai 2000): 108. Feature.

VIRGAL, ERIC (1952–) (Martinique)

1132. Amoruso, Carol. "Eric Virgal: love Martinican style." *Rhythm* (New York), Vol. 9, No. 6 (June 2000): 30. Profile of the zouk love singer from Martinique.

1133. Cadet-Petit, Alexandre. "Eric Virgal: les recettes du succes." *Fouyaya*, No. 58 (sept. 1987): 18–19. Interview.

1134. Mandibele. "Varietes: Eric Virgal, le charme des vacances." *Antilla*, No. 347 (aout 28–sept 5 1989): 20–21. Interview.

VODU 155 (US)
See 464

VOLCY, MARIO DE (Haiti)

1135. "Mario de Volcy." *Haiti Culture*, Vol. 4, No. 10 (avril 1988): 16–17, 24. Interview with the Haitian dance band musician.

VOLEL, EMILE (d. 1999) (Haiti)
See 704

VOLO-VOLO DE BOSTON (Haiti)
See 701

VOLT FACE (Guadeloupe)
See 152

WAILING ROOTS (French Guiana)
See 204, 355, 364

WAINWRIGHT, JEFF
See 689

WAPA (French Guiana)
See also 627

1136. Weimert, Alex. "Guyane actualites: Annou danse lerol!" *Antilla*,
No. 85 (jan. 13–20 1984): 28–29. Review of a recording by Wapa,
the folkloric music and dance ensemble from French Guiana.
Includes a discussion of the group's history.

WAWA [Jacques Fortere] (Haiti/US)
See also 944–945

1137. "Rebondissement de l'affaire Fedia-Wawa." *Haiti Culture*, Vol. 3,
No. 10 (fevrier 1987): 7–8. Interview with Fortere about his
falling out with singer Fedia Laguerre following a business
dispute over his compositions.

WCK (Dominica)
See 716

WEST INDIES JAZZ BAND (French Antilles)

1138. Cauver, J.G. "Tout sur West Indies Jazz Band." *Antilla*, No. 265
(dec. 3–9 1987): 10–14. Interviews with three members of the
WIJB—Jacky Bernard, Luther Francois, and Paulo Rosine,
looking at the group and its collaborative process.

WEY NOV-JONCTION (French Guiana)

1139. Lucenay, Emmanuel. "Le nouveau 'son' guyanais: 'Wey-Nov'
Jonction." *Antilla*, No. 179 (janvier 10–17 1986): 14–15. Profile of
a new group from French Guiana.

WILLIAMS, LAVINIA (1916–1989) (US)
See 686

ZEKLE (Haiti)
See also 476, 701

1140. Averill, Gage. "Haitian fascination: Mixed blood." *The Beat*, Vol.
13, No. 3 (1994): 42–43. Detailed review of the Zekle recording,
San Mele.

ZIN (US)

1141. "Zin." *Haiti Culture*, Vol. 5, No. 7 (juin 1989): 18–19, 30. Interview with the Nouvel Jenerasyon dance band.

ZINGLIN (Haiti)
See 706

ZOUK ALLSTARS (French Antilles)
See 248

ZOUK MACHINE (Guadeloupe)
See also 159, 715, 719, 861

1142. Faraux, Francois. "Zouk Machine." *Echo Jeunesse*, No. 22 (fevrier–mars 1989): 17–19. Interview.

ZOU ZOUL [Jn Michel St Victor] (Haiti/US)
See **SKAH SHAH**

ZSHEA [Florence Caze] (Haiti/US)
See also 709

1143. Averill, Gage. "Haitian fascination: *Debode*—breaking out." *The Beat*, Vol. 14, No. 1 (1995): 26–27. Column discussing two recent recordings by Zshea (*Debode*) and Beethova Obas (*Si*).

Sources Consulted

A. Electronic Resources

1144. *ArticleFirst [electronic resource]*. Dublin, OH: OCLC Online
 Computer Library Center, Inc. Began 1990s? Accessible via
 WorldCat (www.worldcat.org). Choose Advanced Search and
 limit material type to Articles. Contains citations for articles
 listed in the tables of contents of more than 13,000 journals in
 the social sciences, humanities, popular culture, business,
 science, and more.

1145. *Digital Library of the Caribbean [electronic resource]*.
 [Gainesville, FL]: Digital Library of the Caribbean, c2005–.
 http://www.dloc.com. The DLOC is a cooperative digital library
 for resources from and about the Caribbean and circum-
 Caribbean. It provides access to digitized versions of Caribbean
 cultural, historical and research materials currently held in
 archives, libraries, and private collections.

1146. *IngentaConnect [electronic resource]*. Bath, UK: Ingenta, 2004–.
 http://www.ingentaconnect.com. Free database of citations, often
 with abstracts, to the literature of thousands of scholarly books
 and journals. Especially useful for identifying recently published
 articles.

1147. *MLA international bibliography [electronic resource]*. New York:
 Modern Language Association of America. Database of citations
 to scholarly publications relating to literature, popular culture,
 folklore, ethnomusicology, drama, film, etc., published since

1963. Access restricted to users affiliated with licensed institutions, e.g. university libraries.

1148. *ProQuest digital dissertations [electronic resource].* [Ann Arbor, MI]: UMI Company. Database offering abstracts, tables of contents, 24–page summaries, and full-text PDF versions of North American Ph.D. theses ranging from 1861 to the present. Access is limited to users of subscribing institutions, e.g. university libraries. A free version of the database, limited to citations only, is available online at: http://www.umi.com.

1149. *RILM abstracts of music literature [electronic resource].* Baltimore: National Information Services Corporation. International database of citations to scholarly literature on music covering books, conference proceedings, theses, periodicals, and more. Covers the period 1967–present.

1150. *WorldCat [electronic resource].* Dublin, OH: OCLC, 1979–. http://www.worldcat.org. Database covering the holdings of a large portion of North American libraries as well as an increasing number of national and large university libraries in Europe, the English-speaking Caribbean and Brazil. An extraordinarily rich bibliographic resource.

B. Print Sources

Encyclopedias and Biographical Dictionaries

1151. *Contemporary musicians.* Detroit, MI: Gale Research, 1989–2007. Vol. 1–61.

1152. *Dictionnaire encyclopedique Desormeaux* / sous la direction du professeur Jack Corzani. Fort-de-France: Ed. Desormeaux, 1992. 7 v.: ill.

1153. *International dictionary of Black composers* / editor Samuel A. Floyd Jr. Chicago: Fitzroy Dearborn, 1999. 2 v.

1154. *The new Grove dictionary of music and musicians* / edited by Stanley Sadie; executive editor, John Tyrrell. 2nd ed. New York: Grove's Dictionaries, 2001. 29 v.: ill.

1155. *The new Grove dictionary of music and musicians* / edited by Stanley Sadie. London: Macmillan Publishers, 1980. 20 v.: ill.

*1156. *Oxford music online [electronic resource].* [Oxford, New York]: Oxford University Press, [1999?–]. Includes online versions, with ongoing updates, of *The new Grove dictionary of music and musicians* (2nd ed., 2001) and *The new Grove dictionary of jazz* (2nd ed., 2002).

1157. Southern, Eileen. *Biographical dictionary of Afro-American and African musicians.* Westport, CT: Greenwood Press, 1982. 478 p.

Bibliographies and Discographies

1158. Bloomfield, Valerie. "Caribbean recordings: notes on sources with a select discography." *Journal of Librarianship*, Vol. 8, No. 1 (January 1976): 47–72. Overview of recorded sound materials from the non-Hispanic Caribbean available to researchers ca. the mid-1970s. Includes sections on institutional collections in the U.S., Caribbean and Europe; literature on the music; musical styles; record companies and catalogs; and a selected discography and bibliography.

1159. De Lerma, Dominique-Rene. *Bibliography of black music.* Westport, CT: Greenwood Press, 1981–1984. 4 v. See in particular: v. 3 (The Caribbean, p. 127–163).

1160. *Ethnomusicology.* Examined all "Americas" sections of the journal's "Current Bibliography" and "Dissertations and Theses" sections from 1958 to 2005.

1161. *Ethnomusicology Newsletter*, No. 1–11 (Dec 1953–Sept. 1957). Examined the "America" and "Europe" segments of all "Current Bibliographies" published in the newsletter.

1162. Manigat, Max. *Haitiana 1991–1995: bibliographie haitienne.* [Montreal]: Editions du CIDIHCA, [1997]. 185 p.

1163. ———. *Haitiana, 1996–2000: bibliographie haitienne.* [Haiti]: Editions SANBA, 2003. 238 p.

1164. Stevenson, Robert Murrell. "Caribbean music history: a selective annotated bibliography with musical supplement." *Inter-American Music Review*, Vol. 4, No. 1 (Fall 1981). 112 p. A valuable resource on art and church musics, as well as folkloric and popular traditions of European, African and Amerindian origin. Most items cited include extremely detailed annotations, often with lengthy extracts from the works themselves.

1165. ———. *A guide to Caribbean music history: bibliographic supplement to a paper read at the 1975 annual meeting of the Music Library Association in San Juan, Puerto Rico.* Lima: Ediciones Cultura, 1975. 101 p. Extensively annotated bibliography of literature on art and folkloric musics from the Caribbean published before 1900. Includes citations for 222 items.

Dissertation and Theses Indexes

1166. *Dissertation Abstracts International. A: The humanities and social sciences.* Viewed all "Music" and "Cultural Anthropology" sections of print volumes from 1990–2006.

1167. Gillis, Frank J. "An annotated bibliography of theses and dissertations in ethnomusicology and folk music accepted at American and foreign universities. Supplement 1." *Ethnomusicology*, Vol. 6, No. 3 (September 1962): 191–214. Update of 1169.

1168. Lucas, Maria Elizabeth. "Directory of Latin American and Caribbean music theses and dissertations, 1984–1988." *Latin American Music Review*, Vol. 10, No. 1 (Spring–Summer 1989): 148–176. Annotated list with author abstracts.

1169. Merriam, Alan P. "An annotated bibliography of theses and dissertations in ethno-musicology and folk music accepted at American universities." *Ethnomusicology*, Vol. 4, No. 1 (January 1960): 21–39.

1170. Moore, Robin. "Directory of Latin American and Caribbean music theses and dissertations since 1988." *Latin American Music Review*, Vol. 14, No. 1 (Spring–Summer 1993): 145–171. Includes author abstracts.

1171. Thompson, Donald. "Music, theater and dance in Central America and the Caribbean: an annotated bibliography of dissertations and theses." *Revista/Review Interamericana* (Spring 1979): 113–140.

1172. Wong, Ketty. "Directory of Latin American and Caribbean music theses and dissertations, 1992–1998." *Latin American Music Review*, Vol. 20, No. 2 (Fall–Winter 1999): 253–309.

Journals and Newspapers Indexed

1173. *Afiavi Magazine*, No. 17; 24–28; 1–2 (1997?–May 2007)

1174. *Africultures*, No. 1–71 (1997–Nov. 2007)

1175. *Americas* [English ed.], Vol. 1–58 (1949–2006)

1176. *Antilia*, No. 1–3 (1984)

1177. *Antilla*, No. 1–535 (fev. 1981–mai 13 1993)

1178. *Antilla Kreyol*, No. 1–15 (juillet 1984–juin 1990)

1179. *Antilla Magazine*, No. 1–12 (juin 1983–dec. 1986)

1180. *Antilla Special*, No. 1–4; 7; 9 (dec. 1983–juil. 1987)

1181. *Aya Bombe!*, Vol. 1–2 (Oct. 1946–Feb. 1948)

1182. *The Beat* [Los Angeles], v. 7, no. 5–v. 26 (1988–2007)

1183. *Bohemia* [La Habana], ano 16–97 (1925–2005)

1184. *Bulletin du Bureau d'Ethnologie*, Ser. 2–4, No. 2–3; 5; 12–13; 15–32 (1946–oct. 1974)

1185. *Bulletin du Bureau National d'Ethnologie* (1984–1986; 1995–97)

1186. *Bulletin* [Folk Research Centre], v. 1–3 (1990–1992)

1187. *C.A.C.G.: le magazine*, No. 2 (avril–juin 1988)

1188. *Cahiers de l'INAGHEI*, Vol. 1–2 (1982)

1189. *Cahiers d'Haiti*, Vol. 1–3 (Aug. 1943–Dec. 1945)

1190. *Carbet*, No. 1–11 (nov. 1982–1991)

1191. *CARE* (Series) [Paris], No. 8–9; 11; 13 (1981–1988)

1192. *Carib* [Basse Terre], No. 1–8 (1982–1984)

1193. *Carteles* [La Habana] (1925–June 26 1960)

1194. *Chemins Critiques*, Vol. 1–5 (1989–2001)

1195. *Conjonction*, No. 1–95; 102–214 (1946–2006)

1196. *Demain-Haiti*, No. 1–4; 6–9; 11; 15 (1982–1986)

1197. *Divas* [Paris], No. 1–55 (juin 1999–oct. 2005)

1198. *Echo Jeunesse* [Abymes], No. 3–24 (1983–1989)

1199. *Espace Caraibe*, No. 1–4 (1993–1996)

1200. *Ethnomusicology*, Vol. 2–51 (1958–2007)

1201. *Etudes Creoles*, Vol. 1–6; 8–24; 26–29 (1978–83; 1985–2001; 2003–2006)

1202. *Etudes Guadeloupeennes*, No. 2–5 (avr. 1990–fev. 1992)

1203. *Fil d'Ariane*, No. 3–8 (mai 1978–mai 1979)

1204. *Fouyaya*, No. 22–58 (janv. 1984–sept. 1987)

1205. *Gaceta de Cuba* (1962–1979; 1986–Aug. 1990; 1992–2007)

1206. *Global Rhythm*, Vol. 11, No. 7 (July 2002)–Vol. 16 (2007)

1207. *Grin Fos*, No. 1–2 (aout–nov. 1987)

1208. *Les Griots* [Port-au-Prince], Vol. 1–3 (1938–1940)

1209. *Guadeloupe 2000 Magazine*, No. 71–165 (mars 1981–avril 1993)

1210. *Haiti Culture*, Vol. 1–6 (juin 1984–juil. 1991)

1211. *Haiti New York Magazine*, Vol. 1, No. 1 (dec. 1980)

1212. *Horizons Caraibes*, No. 4; 6–9; 11–18; 22–27 (1953–1955)

1213. *Interview* [Abymes], No. 2–3 (1984)

1214. *Jakata Magazine*, No. 3–7 (mars 1986–sept. 1987)

1215. *Jougwa*, No. 4; 9; 12?–14 (1982–1986)

1216. *Journal of Haitian Studies*, Vol. 1–12 (1995–2006)

1217. *Kreyol Connection*, v. 2–4, no. 4–16 (1996–1998)

1218. *Lakansiel*, No. 2–3 (1975)

1219. *Magazine Guadeloupeen*, No. 1–6; 10 (nov. 1981–juin 1982; janv. 1983)

1220. *Magwa*, No. 12; 14–18 (1984–1989)

1221. *Mapou* [Ottawa], Vol. 1, No. 1–4 (1977–1978)

1222. *Martinique* [Fort-de-France] (1944–1946)

1223. *Moun: mes e labitid*, No. 1–2 (Aug. 1985–Sept. 1986)

1224. *Le Naif*, No. 319; 340; 384–387; 466–470 (1981–1984)

1225. *Le Naif*, No. 3–37 (mai 1989–avril 1993)

1226. *Negritud*, No. 1–2 (1977–1978)

1227. *Nouvelle Optique*, No. 1–2; 4–6; 8–9 (1971–1973)

1228. *Nouvelle Revue des Antilles*, No. 1–3 (1988–1990)

1229. *Optique*, No. 1–36 (mars 1954–juin 1957)

1230. *Paralleles*, No. 1–40 (1964–Nov. 1971)

1231. *Pour Haiti*, No. 4–5; 7; 9–10 (1989–90)

1232. *Presence Haitienne*, No. 1–4 (Aug.–Dec. 1975)

1233. *Publication du Bureau National d'Ethnologie*, No. 1–2 (1998)

1234. *Regard*, No. 4–49 (May 26 1979–Nov. 29 1980)

1235. *Revolucion y Cultura* (1972–June 2007)

1236. *Revue de la Faculte d'Ethnologie et du Centre de Recherches en Sciences Humaines et Sociales d'Haiti*, No. 1; 4–6; 8; 10–13; 16; 19; 23–25; 27; 30–31; 33; 36–37; 39–40; 43

1237. *Revue du CERC*, No. 1–3 (1984–1986)

1238. *La Revue du Monde Noir* [Paris], No. 1–6 (1931–1932)

1239. *Revue Guadeloupeenne*, No. 35, 39, 43–48 (1959–1962)

1240. *Rhythm: global sounds and ideas*, v. 8 (1999)-v. 11, No. 6 (June 2002)

1241. *Rhythm Music Magazine*, Vol. 2, No. 9 (Sept. 1993)–Vol. 5, No. 9 (Sept. 1996); Aug. 1997–Aug. 1998

1242. *Rhythm Music Monthly*, Vol. 1, No. 3 (Oct. 1992)–Vol. 2, No. 8 (Aug. 1993)

1243. *Son!* [Abymes], No. 1; 3; 5 (1983–1985)

LIBRARIES AND ARCHIVES

A. Latin America, The Caribbean and Europe

See also 1158

1244. Dower, Catherine A. "Libraries with music collections in the Caribbean islands." *Notes* (Music Library Association), Vol. 34, No. 1 (September 1977): 27–38. Includes descriptions for collections in Aruba, Barbados, Bermuda, Cuba, Curacao, Haiti, Jamaica, Martinique, Puerto Rico, Trinidad, and the Virgin Islands.

1245. Moreno Cha, Ercilia. "Bibliografia, centros de investigacion y archivos sonoros de musica tradicional en Latinoamerica." *Latin American Music Review*, Vol. 12, No. 1 (Spring–Summer 1991): 42–64. Annotated list of specialist research centers and sound archives in Latin America.

CUBA

1246. Delgado Miranda, Rolando. "The Cuban experience in creating music information services." *Crescendo: bulletin of the International Association of Music Libraries (New Zealand Branch)*, No. 59 (August 2001): 18–20. Description of Cuba's network of provincial music archives and their holdings. Includes addresses and contact information for each.

1247. BIBLIOTECA NACIONAL "JOSE MARTI" (Ave. Independencia y 20 de Mayo, Plaza de la Revolucion, Apartado Postal 6670, La Habana, Cuba). Website: www.bnjm.cu.

1248. Lapique Becali, Zoila. *Catalogacion y clasificacion de la musica cubana*. La Habana: Biblioteca Nacional "Jose Marti," 1963. 104

p.: music. (Biblioteca Nacional (Cuba). Coleccion Manuales tecnicos; no. 4)). Manual for the cataloging and classification of Cuban music written by a cataloger at the Cuban national library. Includes details on Afro-Cuban idioms with examples of how they are addressed in the Cuban cataloging system.

1249. CIDMUC [Centro de Investigacion y Desarollo de Musica Cubana] (Calle G No. 505 e/21 y 23, Vedado, Habana 4, Ciudad de La Habana, Cuba).

1250. Alen Rodriguez, Olavo. "Centro de Investigacion y Desarrollo de la Musica Cubana (CIDMUC)." *The World of Music*, Vol. 35, No. 2 (1993): 139–141. Description of the Center, its holdings and activities.

1251. ———. "Forschungszentrum in Habana." *Beitrage zur Musikwissenschaft*, Jahrg. 28, Hft. 3 (1986): 214–216. Description of the Havana music archive and research center.

1252. ———. "The music archives at the CIDMUC and their influence on the musical culture of Cuba." In *Archives for the future: global perspectives on audiovisual archives in the 21st century*, eds. Anthony Seeger and Shubha Chaudhuri. Calcutta: Seagull Books, 2004, pp. 130–142. Paper on the aims, goals and activities of CIDMUC, one of Cuba's leading music archives. The Center is a major source of materials (field research and recordings) related to Afro-Cuban musical traditions.

1253. MUSEO NACIONAL DE LA MUSICA (Capdevila #1, Habana y Aguiar, La Habana Vieja, Cuba).

*1254. Delgado Miranda, Rolando. "Centro de Informacion y Documentacion Musical 'Odilio Urfe' y la documentacion musical en Cuba." *AEDOM: Boletin de la Asociacion Espanola de Documentacion Musical* (Madrid), ano 4, no. 2 (julio–dic. 1997): 108–118.

1255. ———. "Fifty years at the service of Cuban music." *IASA Journal*, No. 14 (December 1999): 53–56. Describes the holdings of the Museo's Centro de Informacion y Documentacion Musical "Odilio Urfe."

1256. Morales, Pedro. "Cultura: De tambores, laudes y pianolas." *Cuba Internacional*, No. 208 (abril 1987): 42–47. Feature on the Museo Nacional de la Musica which is home to Fernando Ortiz's collection of Afro-Cuban musical instruments.

1257. Robinson Calvet, Nancy. "Museo Nacional de la Musica: cofre abierto de sonoridades." *Tropicana Internacional*, No. 15 (2003): 9–12. Conversation with the Museum's director about some of the highlights of its collection.

1258. Rodriguez, Lucia. "Tres lustros de un museo." *Clave* (Havana), No. 3 (1986): 18–21. Feature on Cuba's national music museum and its director, Maria Teresa Linares.

1259. Valdes, Daniela. "Museo Nacional de la Musica: casa embrujada por sus tesoros." *Prisma* (Havana), ano 28, no. 316 (marzo–abril 2003): 44–45. Introduction to the Museum and its collections.

FRANCE

1260. *Bibliotheque nationale de France [electronic resource]*. http://www.bnf.fr. Home page for France's national library, with links to its online catalogs—BN-Opale Plus, BN-Opaline, CCFR.

1261. *Systeme Universitaire de Documentation (SUDOC) [electronic resource]*. http://www.sudoc.abes.fr. Online catalog of resources held by some 2400 French academic libraries. Particularly useful for information on French doctoral theses not found in other databases.

FRENCH ANTILLES

1262. UNIVERSITE DES ANTILLES ET DE LA GUYANE. University system of the French Antilles consisting of three campuses located in Guadeloupe, Martinique, and French Guiana. The university's library catalog lists holdings for all three campuses at: http://kolibris.univ-ag.fr.

FRENCH GUIANA
See FRENCH ANTILLES

GERMANY

1263. BERLINER PHONOGRAMM-ARCHIV (Museum fur Volkerkunde, Staatliche Museen zu Berlin, Stiftung Preussischer Kulturbesitz, Amimallee 23–27, D-14195 Berlin, Germany). Email: phonoarch@smb.spk-berlin.de.

1264. *Das Berliner Phonogramm-Archiv 1900–2000: Sammlung der traditionellen Musik der Welt = The Berlin Phonogramm-Archiv, 1900–2000: collections of traditional music of the world* / Artur Simon (Hg./ed.). Berlin: Verlag fur Wissenschaft und Bildung,

2000. 264 p.: ill. Catalog and history of one of Europe's oldest and most extensive collections of ethnographic sound recordings.

1265. Reinhard, Kurt. "Das Berliner Phonogramm-Archiv." *Baessler-Archiv*, N.F., Bd. 9, Hft. 1 (1961): 83–94. Introduction to the Phonogramm-Archiv and its holdings.

1266. IBERO-AMERIKANISCHES INSTITUT PREUSSISCHER KULTURBESITZ (Potsdamer Str. 37, D-10785 Berlin). Website: www.iai.spk-berlin.de; OPAC: www.iaicat.de. One of Europe's largest archives focusing on the history and culture of Latin America, the Caribbean, Spain and Portugal.

GREAT BRITAIN

1267. BRITISH LIBRARY SOUND ARCHIVE – World and Traditional Music Section (96 Euston Road, London NW1 2DB). Website: www.bl.uk/collections/sound-archive; OPAC: http://cadensabl.uk. National sound archive. Has extensive holdings of folk and popular musics from around the globe.

1268. *COPAC Academic and National Library Catalogue [electronic resource].* http://copac.ac.uk. The Copac library catalogue gives free access to the merged online catalogues of major university and national libraries in the UK and Ireland, including the British Library (www.bl.uk).

GUADELOUPE
See also **FRENCH ANTILLES**

1269. LA MEDIATHEQUE CARAIBE (54, rue Amedee Fengarol, Basse-Terre, Guadeloupe). Website: www.lameca.org; Email: ecm@lameca.org. Caribbean-focused audio-visual archive.

MARTINIQUE
See **FRENCH ANTILLES**

THE NETHERLANDS

1270. KITLV/Royal Netherlands Institute of South Asian and Caribbean Studies (Reuvensplaats 2, 2311 BE Leiden, Netherlands). Website: www.kitlv.nl; Email: kitlv@kitlv.nl. Major archive founded in 1851. Has a large collection of materials relating to the Caribbean region in areas such as anthropology, linguistics, the social sciences and history. The KITLV library catalog is another rich resource including long abstracts for articles from a large number of Caribbeanist journals and collected works.

B. North America

CALIFORNIA

1271. UCLA ETHNOMUSICOLOGY ARCHIVE (1630 Schoenberg Music Bldg., Box 951657, Los Angeles, CA 90095–1657). Website: www.ethnomusic.ucla.edu/Archive; Email: archive@arts.ucla.edu. One of the largest archives of ethnographic recordings and visual materials in North America.

1272. "The Courlander Collection at UCLA." *Ethnomusicology at UCLA* (Spring–Summer 1986): 4. Description of the Harold Courlander Collection of West African and Haitian music (400 items).

DISTRICT OF COLUMBIA

1273. LIBRARY OF CONGRESS. AMERICAN FOLKLIFE CENTER (101 Independence Ave., SE, Washington, DC 20540–4610). Website: www.loc.gov/folklife; Email: folklife@loc.gov.

1274. LIBRARY OF CONGRESS. MUSIC DIVISION (101 Independence Ave., SE, James Madison Building, LM113, Performing Arts Reading Room, Washington, DC 20540–4710). Website: www.loc.gov/rr/perform.

1275. LIBRARY OF CONGRESS. MOTION PICTURE, BROADCASTING AND RECORDED SOUND DIVISION. RECORDED SOUND REFERENCE CENTER (101 Independence Ave., SE, James Madison Building, LM113, Performing Arts Reading Room, Washington, DC 20540–4690). Website: www.loc.gov/rr/record.

FLORIDA

1276. UNIVERSITY OF FLORIDA LIBRARIES – Latin American Collection (George A. Smathers Libraries, PO Box 117009, Gainesville, FL 32611–7009). Website: http://web.uflib.ufl.edu/lac. One of the preeminent collections of Caribbeana in the United States.

1277. UNIVERSITY OF MIAMI LIBRARIES – Caribbean Collection (Special Collections Division, Otto G. Richter Library); Cuban

Heritage Collection (1300 Memorial Dr., PO Box 248214, Coral Gables, FL 33124–0320). Website: www.library.miami.edu/chc; Email: chc@miami.edu.

ILLINOIS

1278. CENTER FOR BLACK MUSIC RESEARCH - COLUMBIA COLLEGE CHICAGO (600 S. Michigan Ave., Chicago, IL 60605–1996). Website: www.colum.edu/cbmr; Email: cbmrref@colum.edu.

1279. *CBMR Digest.* Vol. 1, no. 1 (Summer 1988)–. Chicago: Center for Black Music Research, Columbia College, 1988–. Semiannual. Free newsletter of the CBMR describing recent projects, developments and new acquisitions at the Center.

INDIANA

1280. INDIANA UNIVERSITY – ARCHIVES OF TRADITIONAL MUSIC (Morrison Hall 117 & 120, Bloomington, IN 47405). Website: www.indiana.edu/~libarchm; Email: atmusic@ indiana.edu. 'The largest university-based ethnographic sound archive in the United States' with extensive holdings of commercial and field recordings, videos, photographs and manuscripts, many relating to the black Americas. Of particular note are the many ethnographic field recording collections which have been donated by researchers documenting their Ph.D. work.

1281. *Catalog of Afroamerican music and oral data holdings* / [compiled by Philip M. Peek]. [Bloomington: Indiana University, Archives of Traditional Music], 1970. 28 p. Guide to sound recordings of the black Americas (North and South) held by the ATM as of March 1970.

1282. *Catalog of Latin American music and oral data holdings* / [compiled by Carol E. Robertson]. [Bloomington: Indiana University, Archives of Traditional Music], 1971. 17 p. "Sound recordings pertaining to Latin America (South America, the Caribbean, Central America, and Spanish speakers in the United States)."

1283. *A catalog of phonorecordings of music and oral data held by the Archives of Traditional Music.* Boston: G.K. Hall, 1975. 541 p. Reproduction of the Archive's card catalog for items cataloged through 1974.

1284. *Early field recordings: a catalogue of cylinder collections at the Indiana University Archives of Traditional Music* / edited by Anthony Seeger and Louise S. Spear. Bloomington: Indiana University Press, 1987. xviii, 198 p.

NEW YORK

1285. BLACK ARTS RESEARCH CENTER (30 Marion Street, Nyack, NY 10960). Website: www.barc0.tripod.com. Archival resource center dedicated to the documentation, preservation and dissemination of expressive culture from Africa and the African diaspora. Holdings include some 1400 recordings, cassettes and videotapes, 1000 books and journals, 500 clipping files and a 100,000+ entry database documenting the black presence in, and contributions to, the fields of music, dance, theatre, film, and traditional religion/healing.

1286. CARIBBEAN CULTURAL CENTER (408 W. 58th St., New York, NY 10019). Website: www.cccadi.org; Email: resource@cccadi.org; Tel. 212–307–7420 ext. 3009. Maintains a Resource Center devoted to books, photographs, and videos about expressive culture in the African diaspora. Of special interest are the many archival videos of Center-sponsored lectures and concert performances which feature a who's who of music and dance artists from the Caribbean and Latin America.

1287. CENTER FOR TRADITIONAL MUSIC AND DANCE (32 Broadway, Suite 1314, New York, NY 10004 (between Morris St. and Exchange Place)). Website: www.ctmd.org; Email: traditions@ctmd.org; Tel. 212–571–1555 ext. 26 (Archive). The CTMD's Archive documents and preserves the Center's research projects into folk, ethnic and immigrant performing arts traditions of cultural communities in New York City from the inception of the CTMD in 1968. Types of materials included are audio and videotapes, photographs and printed matter.

1288. CITY LORE (72 E. 1st Street, New York, NY 10003). Website: www.citylore.org; Email: citylore@citylore.org. Organization devoted to the urban folklore of New York City, including the music and dance traditions of its Caribbean enclaves.

1289. NEW YORK PUBLIC LIBRARY FOR THE PERFORMING ARTS (40 Lincoln Center Plaza, New York, NY 10023–7498). Website: www.nypl.org/research/lpa/lpa.html; Music Division:

Email: musicdiv@nypl.org; Tel. 212–870–1650 / Dance Division: Email: dance@nypl.org; Tel. 212–870–1657.

1290. NEW YORK PUBLIC LIBRARY – SCHWARZMAN BUILDING (Fifth Ave. at 42nd St., New York, NY 10018). Website: www.nypl.org/research/chss. Houses the humanities and social sciences collections of NYPL's Research Libraries.

1291. NEW YORK PUBLIC LIBRARY - SCHOMBURG CENTER FOR RESEARCH IN BLACK CULTURE (515 Malcolm X Blvd. (at 135th St.), New York, NY 10037). Website: www.nypl.org/ research/sc/sc.html. The holdings for all of the New York Public Library's collections may be found via their online catalog: http://catalog.nypl.org.

1292. NEW YORK UNIVERSITY –Elmer Holmes Bobst Library (70 Washington Square South, New York, NY 10012). The Bobst Library is now home to the Library for Caribbean Research, a major collection of Caribbeana formerly held by the Research Institute for the Study of Man. These materials have been integrated into the Library's general collections and may be found by searching its BobCat catalog (www.bobcat.nyu.edu).

1293. WORLD MUSIC INSTITUTE (49 W. 27th St., Ste. 930, New York, NY 10001). Website: www.worldmusicinstitute.org; Tel. 212–545–7536. Has an extensive Audio & Video Archive documenting past WMI concert events, a number of which have featured folkloric music and dance groups from the Caribbean and Latin America.

TEXAS

1294. UNIVERSITY OF TEXAS AT AUSTIN LIBRARIES – Benson Latin American Collection ((SRH) 1.108, Austin, TX 78713). Website: www.lib.utexas.edu/benson; Email: blac@lib.utexas. edu. One of the premiere collections of Caribbeana and Latin Americana in the United States along with the University of Florida and Schomburg Center.

Appendix I

List of Individuals and Ensembles by Idiom/Occupation

†*Indicates individuals not of African descent*

Banjo Players

Kali
Mark, Robertt

Bassists

Albicy, Jean-Marc
Bernard, Alex
Fanfant, Thierry
Henar, Vincent
Olicha

Bele/Belair

AM4
Belenou
Ti-Emile
Ti-Raoul

Biguine

Leardee, Ernest
Stellio, Alexandre

Cadence-lypso

Exile One
Henderson, Gordon

Chouval Bwa

Pakatak
Saint-Prix, Dede

Clarinetists

Godzom, Michel
Stellio, Alexandre

Dancers and Choreographers
See also **Folk Ensembles**

Destine, Jean-Leon
Elie, Arnold
Louinis, Louines
St. Lot, Paulette
Venet Danger, Gaudiosa
Williams, Lavinia

Drummers
See **Percussionists**

Flutists

Cilla, Max
Mona, Eugene
†Saieh, Issa El
Saint-Prix, Dede

Folk Ensembles
See also **Vocal Ensembles**

Ballets Folkloriques Martiniquais
Bonito Patua
Carabali Isuama
Caraibana
Cutumba
Emeraude

Zouk *(cont.)*

Naimro, Jean-Claude
Rapon, Jacky
Rotin, Jean-Michel
Rubinel, Ronald
Saint-Val, Tanya
Sartana
Saxe
Thamar, Ralph
Vaillot, Pascal
Virgal, Eric
Zouk Machine

Appendix II

List of Individuals
and Ensembles by Country

†*Indicates individuals
not of African descent*

Cuba

Bonito Patua
Carabali Isuama
Cutumba
Grupo Folklorico de
  Aficianados Caidije
Okay
Venet Danger, Consuelo
Venet Danger, Gaudiosa

Dominica

Exile One
Henderson, Gordon

France

Compagnie Creole, La
Creole Project
JND
Kreyol Syndikat
Legitimus, Gesip
†Meunier, Jean-Pierre
Rivel, Moune de
Salvador, Henri

French Guiana

Combette, Chris
Lefel, Edith
Lindor, Gaston

Mass, Josy
Wailing Roots
Wey Nov-Jonction

Guadeloupe

Aiglons, Les
Akiyo
Antoinette, Jean-Claude
Beco
Boisdur, Esnard
Caraibana
Carnot
Chomereau-Lamothe, Charly
Dao, Adelaide
†Debs, Georges
†Debs, Henri
Decimus, Georges
Decimus, Pierre-Edouard
Delos, Alain
Desvarieux, Jacob
Experience 7
Fanfant, Jean-Philippe
Fanfant, Thierry
Fostin, Jane
Foubap
Haliar, Paul-Emile
Ipomen
Jean-Marie, Alain
Kafe
Katel

Guadeloupe *(cont.)*
Konket, Guy
La Viny, Gerard
Lirvat, Al
Lockel, Gerard
Louisar, Curtis
Matheus, Mariann
Maurinier, Charles
Mavounzy, Robert
Meliano, Lewis
Nankin, Joel
Rotin, Jean-Michel
Saint-Cyrel, Felix
Saint-Eloi, Patrick
Saint-Val, Tanya
Sartana
Schwarz-Bart, Jacques
Ti Marcel
Vallot, Pascal
Valvert, Felix
Vamur, Claude
Van Leve
Velo
Vincent, Francky
Volt Face
Zouk Machine

Haiti
See also **United States**

7 Vedettes
Alexandre, Stephane "Stef"
Atis Endepandan
Ayizan
Azerot, Nestor
Bayard, Pierre "Pepe"
Bazile, Michel-Ange
Beaubrun, Daniel "Dadi"
Beaubrun, Marjorie
Beaubrun, Mimerose
Beaubrun, Theodore "Lolo"
Bigga Haitian
Bissainthe, Toto
Bossa Combo
Boukan Ginen
Boukman Eksperyans
Cadet, Anilus

Cameau, Anderson
Casimir, Lumane
Celestin, Louis
Chancy, Loubert
Charlemagne, Manno
Cimber, Alphonse
Colas, Roger
Coupe Cloue
Demesmin, Carole "Maroule"
Derose, Ansy
Dessalines, Antoine Charles
Difficiles
Dominique, Hans
Dorisme, Myriam
Dorismond, Andre
Dorismond Family
D.P. Express
Dupervil, Gerard
Durosier, Guy
Duval, Fritz "Toto"
Duviella, Serge
Elie, Justin
Emile, Dernst
Felix, Vladimir Jean
Foula
Francois, Eddy
Freres Dejean, Les
Gais Troubadours
G.M. Connection
Guillaume, Raoul
Gypsies de Petionville
Haiti Chante
Ibo Combo
Jaegerhuber, Werner
Jazz des Jeunes
Jean, Wyclef
Jean-Baptiste, Nemours
Jean Baptiste, Smith
Jean-Claude, Martha
Jean-Felix, Jimmy
Jeanty, Marco
Joseph, Ancy Dullon
Ju Baptiste, Maquel
Ju-Louis, Margarette
Juste, Farah
Kanpech

Haiti *(cont.)*

King Kino
Laguerre, Fedia
Lahens, Louis
Lalanne, Wagner
Lamothe, Charly
Larose, Dieudonne
Lataye
Ledan, Jean
Louis, Damas "Fanfan"
Louissant, Yvon
Magnum Band
Mambo Lucienne
Marcelin, Ernst Crepsac
Martino, Reynaldo
Martino, Roberto
Master Dji
Merceron, Gerald
Michel, Emeline
Miel
Milien, Rodrigue
Mini All Stars
Moise, Alfred
Moise, Thony
Molin, Robert
Morse, Richard
Number One
Obas, Beethova
Olicha
Orchestre Citadelle
Orchestre Saieh
Orchestre Septentrional
Orchestre Tropicana
Pascal, Alix "Tit"
Pasquet, Dadou
Paul, Fred
Pean, Pierre Michel
Philippe, Luc
Pirogue
Policard, Reginald
Pressoir, Michel
Pyroneau, Elysec
Ram
Rara Machine
Riske
Rodrigue, Johnny

Rodriguez, Georges
Rosenthal, Serge
†Saieh, Issa El
St Aude, Rene
Sakad
Sakaj
Sanba-Yo
Scorpio
Shleu Shleu
Seney, Evens
Seney, Gary
Shoubou
Sicot, Weber
Skah Shah
Skandal
Surin, William
Sweet Micky
Sylvain, Clifford
System Band
Thamad Band
Thifault, Gerard
Ti Manno
Ti Marcel
Ti Paris
Ti Pierre
Ti Plume
Ti Roro
Top Vice
Trouillot, Joe
Troupe Folklorique Nationale
T-Vice
Victor, Emmanuelle
Villevaleix, Leconte
Volcy, Mario de
Volel, Emile
Volo-Volo de Boston
Wawa
Zekle
Zinglin
Zou Zoul
Zshea

Martinique

Albicy, Jean-Marc
Alie, Mariejose
Alpha, Jenny

Martinique *(cont.)*

AM4
Antoine, Alfred
Bago
Bagoe, Michel
Baka, Gisele
Ba Lan
Ballets Folkloriques
  Martiniquais
Banguio, Maurice
Bel Alians
Belenou
Bernabe, Joby
Bernard, Alex
Bernard Brothers
Bernard, Jacky
Bernard, Nicol
Beroard, Jocelyne
Boislaville, Loulou
Brival, Roland
Cally, Sully
Canonge, Mario
Carmelite, Man
Charlery, Maurice
Chasseur, Tony
Cilla, Max
Coridun, Victor
Cultier, Marius
Dantin, Denis
Dezormo, Djo
Donatien, Fernand
Donatien, Franck
Don Miguel
Fal Frett
Feline, Regine
Fleriag, Celine
Flo et Douce 'in
Francisco
Gabriel-Soime, Leona
Galva, Lea
Guanaval
Godzom, Michel
Grocravla, Jojo
Guedon, Henri
Jehelman, Chyco
Jesophe, Krisyan

†Jurad, Simon
Kali
Kwak
Lagier, Jean Jose
Leardee, Ernest
Lisima, Jean-Michel
Louison, Bibi
Majumbe
Malavoi
Manga, Celia
Manga, Sekou
Marce
Marthely, Jean-Philippe
Metal Sound
Midonet, Gratien
Mona, Eugene
Montout, Lucien Fabien
Montredon, Jean-Claude
Naimro, Jean-Claude
Nardal, Paulette
Negri, Christian de
Pakatak
Palavire
Plastic System Band
Poglo
†Porry, Philippe
Ransay, Max
Rapon, Jacky
Rosine, Paulo
Rubinel, Ronald
Saint-Prix, Dede
Sardaby, Michel
Sasayesa
Sauss, La
Saxe
Seinin, Gertrude
Soime, Jean-Paul
Son Lawo
Stellio, Alexandre
Tanbou Bo Kannal
Taxikreol
Thamar, Ralph
Ti-Emile
Ti Moi
Ti-Raoul
Trebeau, Suzy

Martinique *(cont.)*

Ultra-Marine
Ursull, Joelle
Vadeleux, Guy
Varasse, Rosy
Virgal, Eric

St. Lucia

Auguste, Joyce
Francois, Luther
Hewanorra Voices
Mark, Robertt
Twop Chans

United States

Augustin, Frisner
Destine, Jean-Leon
Elie, Arnold
Louinis, Louines
Murray, David
Papa Jube
St. Lot, Paulette
Tabou Combo
Troupe Makandal, La
Vodu 155
Williams, Lavinia
Zin

Author Index

Subject Index

About the Author

JOHN GRAY is currently director of the Black Arts Research Center in Nyack, New York. His previous publications include *African Music* (1990); *Fire Music: A Bibliography of the New Jazz*, 1959–1990 (1991); *Blacks in Classical Music* (1988); *Blacks in Film and Television* (1991); *Black Theatre and Performance* (1990); and, *Ashe, Traditional Religion and Healing in Sub-Saharan Africa and the Diaspora* (1989), all published by Greenwood Press.